MEDIEVAL HISTORY AND CULTURE

Edited by
Francis G. Gentry
PROFESSOR OF GERMAN
PENNSYLVANIA STATE UNIVERSITY

A GARLAND SERIES

Topographies of Gender in Middle High German Arthurian Romance

Alexandra Sterling-Hellenbrand

GARLAND PUBLISHING, INC.
A MEMBER OF THE TAYLOR & FRANCIS GROUP
NEW YORK & LONDON/2001

Published in 2001 by
Garland Publishing, Inc.
A member of the Taylor & Francis Group
29 West 35th Street
New York, NY 10001

10 9 8 7 6 5 4 3 2 1

*Library of Congress Cataloging-in-Publication Data is available from
the Library of Congress.*

ISBN 0-415-93009-X

Printed on acid-free, 250 year-life paper
Manufactured in the United States of America

For Jack, Ryan, and Matthew

Contents

Acknowledgments

Adventures such as these are never solitary quests, and I have encountered many on my path to whom I owe thanks. I would like to take the opportunity here to mention just a few of those who have aided in the "becoming" of this text. I am greatly indebted to two academic mentors without whose advice and guidance and patience this project would not have come to fruition. My first thanks belong to my Ph.D. advisor, Dr. Francis G. Gentry. It was due to his forceful recruiting effort at the University of Wisconsin-Madison that I decided to become a medievalist in the first place. At Penn State, he patiently advised the dissertation that was the basis for this book, and he was instrumental in having the manuscript accepted into the Garland series on medieval history and culture. The successful completion of this manuscript is a tribute to his very capable guidance and could not have been accomplished without his (mostly) gentle prodding.

I can also scarcely express adequate thanks to Dr. Judith M. Davis, my colleague and mentor at Goshen College. During the summer of 2000, while recovering from hip replacement surgery, she graciously spent her time reading and rearranging and questioning my prose. She has been a source of inspiration and encouragement, both as a medievalist and a feminist; her wit and her insightful comments have been indispensible. Her editorial skills, added to those of the Garland staff, have helped shape the space and substance of this book in its current form.

Finally, I have to thank the three people who have displayed such grace and good will in sharing the writing and revising process with me. I could not have managed to finish this book without the support of my husband Jack, whose computer expertise and patience were absolutely invaluable from the time when this project was just the seed of an idea to its completion. My success would certainly not have been possible without him, especially his tireless creativity in finding ways to keep a preschooler and a toddler away from the computer during summer vacation. This book is dedicated to Jack and to our sons Ryan and Matthew, who make the topography of my life complete.

Shaping the Argument

> *Hence, within the inherited discourse of the meta-physics of substance, gender proves to be performative—that is, constituting the identity it is purported to be. In this sense, gender is always a doing, though not a doing by a subject who might be said to preexist the deed.*
>
> —Judith Butler[1]

> *Because of its capacity to transcend the 'here and now,' language bridges different zones within the reality of everyday life and integrates them into a meaningful whole. The transcendences have spatial, temporal and social dimensions.*
>
> —Peter L. Berger and Thomas Luckmann[2]

Over the course of the last five or six years, numerous books have dealt with the construction of identities in medieval culture: the construction of sexuality in the Middle Ages,[3] the construction of masculinity,[4] the construction of "mothering"[5] and queenship,[6] the construction of bodies,[7] the construction of medieval 'others'[8] as a means of courtly self-definition. These texts supplement an ever-growing corpus of work being done on the roles of women in the Middle Ages—work which fairly exploded on the scene in the mid-1980s and has enriched medieval studies at all levels ever since with compelling analyses that look at older texts through various lenses offered by modern theories. These works have benefited greatly from current discussions in gender theory as well as in queer theory. Certainly it is the case (as Cadden[9] and Laqueur[10] have shown) that medieval attitudes towards sexuality were not as rigid as we moderns might like to think. There was room for negotiation and "play," to a degree, though essentialist thought still mainly ruled the day—perhaps more applicable to women/female than to men/male. Crossing over (i.e. cross-dressing) was theoretically possible; noteworthy examples can be found in the mystical realm[11]) and there were also depictions of virile women (Gyburc, for example, in Wolfram's *Willehalm*[12]) and Amazons. This crossing over has a history of its own, however, that is coming to the forefront in more current discussions.

Particularly fruitful for recent research is the idea from Judith Butler and others that gender is performative: gender is relational, mobile, and negotiable. Furthermore, gender is not simply "always a doing," as Butler states, but it is also "a culturally specific process of becoming"[13] This process of becoming, which is the focus of a recent anthology of essays entitled *Becoming Male in the Middle Ages*, can be understood as part of a performative "trajectory" whose arc ceases to exist and "happen" as soon as "becoming" gets fixed into "being." In other words, the process (at least in terms of culturally specific norms) comes to an end as soon as we can say that something or someone **is**: male or female, for example, masculine or feminine.[14] The relationship between gender and sexuality has been blown open, in effect, since Butler, Cadden and Laqueur; sexuality and its categories are seen as "virtualities, bodies, and affects in motion that are always crossing lines, always becoming deterritorialized and reterritorialized."[15] Gender is negotiable and it is a series of possibilities (until the possibilities can no longer be tolerated, usually at the end of a given work, when they turn out not to be possible after all). These possibilities are offered to us as audience/as readers in the genre of romance, which has been the focus of gender discussions for quite some time now. Gaunt[16] compellingly argues, in fact, that gender discussions are constitutive of the romance genre—discussions of what it means to be male and what it means to be female, of what defines masculine and what defines feminine. These discussions are framed in romance in ways that epic could not accommodate them.

In this book , I intend to take a closer look at the way the construction of romance space participates in these discussions, in these on-going negotiations regarding gender construction—roles for men, roles for women—and in mapping possibilities for "becoming" male or female (masculine or feminine). I certainly do not want to generate a catalogue of characters or places; everyone can name the standard places that we find in romance: castle/court, forest, garden/*locus amoenus*. Certainly the places themselves are worthy of investigation—and they have been exhaustively investigated. These are the spaces and places in which people act and live; the process of delineating and illustrating them is what Derek Gregory terms the process of *spatialization* that occurs in the creation of geographical imagination.[17] Spatialization creates spaces which in turn allow for movement, movement allows for negotiation of gender roles. These negotiations inevitably involve power and they also invariably involve a process of 'othering'; this is part of Gregory's process of representation, which he describes as "the different ways in which the world is made present, re-presented, discursively constructed."[18] Sigrid Weigel's concept of gender topographies offers a framework in which we can combine Gregory's processes of spatialization and representation and apply them to a productive analysis of courtly literature. One way in which this framework is structured is by means of a dialectic between the self and the other, between one's "own" (*eigenem*) and one's "other" (*fremdem*).

The fiction of the romance offers many opportunities for us to observe this dialectic. The deliberate placement of men and women in spaces and the purposeful movement of these men and women through spaces create numerous encounters with various kinds of 'others.' These movements and these places in turn create various maps (and therefore models) of becoming: of becoming masculine, of becoming feminine, of becoming king, of becoming queen, of becoming knight, of becoming lady and even mother. For the modern feminist reader, it is always difficult to come to terms with what is at the conclusion of these romances— there is really no apparently serious threat to the patriarchal structure of courtly society, as least in its German manifestation. Romance has as one primary function, among others, to celebrate courtly culture and to perpetuate its ideals. One has only to think of the final tableaux in each of the romances, with couples newly reunited or newly married: Erec and Enite, Iwein and Laudine, Parzival and Condwiramurs. With the curious exception of *Tristan*, an unassailable order reigns at the conclusion of each narrative—at least this is what the poet (or the narrative) would have the audience believe.[19] Middle High German romances do have a tendency, in their adaptations of the French (particularly Chrétien), to emphasize this order. The fiction of the genre, the

gender, however, discussions inherent in the genre, and the topographical conventions of the genre enable and even inspire
unique re-writings and re-patternings of the romance world. The
end may not be changed by what comes before it; it is perhaps
compromised and questioned when placed against the relief of
the majority of the narrative. As Cohen puts it in *Becoming Male
in the Middle Ages,*

> . . . Being acquires its cultural meaning only as it ceases to be-
> come; it is also a process of finding a line of flight within that
> performative mapping, despite the fact that some determinative
> *telos* strives to freeze its meaning into place.[20]

The maps created by these patterns, and the gender negotiations
that they frame, are the subject of this book. Ultimately, I maintain, the becoming (as mapped in the romance topography) and
the being (as dictated by cultural norms) remain at odds—the tension between the two can never be fully resolved, as gender and
power relations must constantly be negotiated through the spaces
of the narrative. This is again where Weigel's idea of the dialectic
between the self and the 'other' comes into play, as poets strive to
negotiate experiences with a series of different 'others' in and
through various spaces. Since this cast of 'others' invariably included women (the 'other' that must be included and excluded simultaneously), and since these encounters were integral to the
process of becoming male or female, one can describe the spaces in
which these encounters occur as gender topographies. Ultimately,
the experiences of romance are enclosed within the space of a complete narrative (this is the essence of Wolfram's completion of
Chrétien's *Perceval* fragment). Gottfried's *Tristan* will remain an
exception, albeit a unique one.

   In the following chapters, I explore the configurations of
these maps and the negotiations that they display in each of the
major Middle High German Arthurian romances written around
the turn of the thirteenth century: Hartmann von Aue's *Erec* and
Iwein, Wolfram von Eschenbach's *Parzival* and Gottfried von
Strassburg's *Tristan.* The texts are taken in roughly chronological order and actually represent gender topographies of increasing complexity. One notices that, the more complex the topographies become, the more ultimately rigid the 'extra-textual' system
appears to be understood. I think, for example, that this is the
basic premise in *Parzival.* Does this mean that *Parzival* and its

poet are 'going against the grain' and the prevailing tendencies of the society? Perhaps. Wolfram's story, its people and its narrative, are largely determined by the "true" story of the search for the Grail. By contrast, it is apparent in Gottfried, whose story has a different history and background than the narratives of Hartmann or Wolfram, that other possibilities remain open. I believe, however, that these complex topographies solidify the notion of 'fiction'—they are not real, though they may put forth possibilities. They remain relegated to a realm outside 'real' experience, and are more clearly marked as such.

Certainly these texts have a socializing function, which lies at their core and does limit the options. What is fascinating, however, is the dialectic or the tension between old attitudes and new (perhaps more restrictive) attitudes that occurs in the romance genre and is supported by the topography as well as by the movement of the characters who inhabit these worlds. The negotiations implicitly question, and in many cases would seem to subvert, the socializing program. Wolfgang Iser's concept of *Leerstellen*[21] offers a model for showing how fiction interacts with the intended audience. The term *Leerstellen* has proved rather elusive in its definition, perhaps intentionally (at least according to Iser).[22] Usually translated as "blanks" or "gaps," *Leerstellen* are spaces within a text that appear to allow room for interpretation on the part of the reader. Gaps may become apparent in several ways, e.g. the contrast between "schematized views" and the reader's imagination.[23] They may also be syntactic in nature, generated by the juxtaposition of various text forms within the narrative. Since the text itself does not seem able to fill these spaces, the responsibility falls then upon the reader during the act of reading to interact with the text, by using his or her imagination to complete it.[24] The gaps in the text thereby provide the opportunity for the author or the text to engage the imagination of the reader and inspire the reader to construct his or her own text.[25] Certainly, Iser's theories present difficulties for the interpretation of medieval texts. Definitions of the *Leerstellen*, for example, remain as problematic and as indeterminate as the gaps themselves. In addition, Iser's theories of the implied reader derive specifically from his study of narrative strategies in eighteenth-, nineteenth-, and twentieth-century English novels. More recently, in his forays into what he terms literary anthropology, he has generalized further to talk about literature as an exercise in patterning and re-patterning human activity and thought: "a continual repatterning of the culturally conditioned shapes human beings have assumed."[26] Literature is a "panorama of what is possible"[27]—and, in the context of the following analysis, it is more specifically a panorama of possible negotiations of gender that romance offered its audiences of the twelfth and thirteenth centuries.

Gender was clearly an issue for the medieval audience. According to Iser, we can derive this from the focus of romance, because literature inevitably deals with the issues that concern the society that produces it:

> As a rule, literature addresses the problems inherent in the systems referred to [in it], so that we can construct whatever was concealed or ignored in the systems concerned or in the ideologies of the day, because their deficiencies form the focal point of the work. At the same time, the text must implicitly contain the basic framework of the respective systems, for these are what cause the problems that literature reacts to.[28]

Romance facilitates the patterning and repatterning of cultural models. The freedom of fiction allows for the play of ideas and imagination. Literature tests the boundaries of what is possible, even if the end result is the re-organization of those boundaries into a unified and stable (and perhaps in the poet's hope even immutable) structure. This process of testing and of play and of patterning and reorganizing is a distinguishing feature of romance, a feature that obviously differentiates it from the epic. In their unique repatternings of Arthurian romance, medieval German poets offer us a glimpse into the framework of their gender system, their perceptions of its deficiencies, and their range of possibilities for reconstruction.

Notes

1. Judith Butler, *Gender Trouble. Feminism and the Subversion of Identity* (Routledge: New York, 1990) 24–25.

2. Peter L. Berger and Thomas Luckmann, *The Social Construction of Reality. A Treatise in the Sociology of Knowledge* (New York: Doubleday, 1966) 39.

3. Karma Lochrie, Peggy McCracken, and James Schultz, ed., *Constructing Medieval Sexuality* (Minneapolis: University of Minnesota Press, 1997).

4. Clare A. Lees, ed., *Medieval Masculinities. Regarding Men in the Middle Ages* (Minneapolis: University of Minnesota Press, 1994).

5. John Carmi Parsons and Bonnie Wheeler, ed., *Medieval Mothering* (New York and London: Garland, 1996).

6. John Carmi Parsons, ed. *Medieval Queenship* (New York: St. Martin's, 1993 and 1998).

7. Sarah Kay and Miri Rubin, ed. *Framing Medieval Bodies* (Manchester and New York: Manchester UP, 1994).

8. Joan Young Gregg, *Devils, Women, and Jews. Reflections of the Other in Medieval Sermon Stories* (Albany: State University of New York Press, 1997); Michael Goodich, ed., *Other Middle Ages. Witnesses at the Margins of Medieval Society* (Philadelphia: University of Pennsylvania Press, 1998); Jeffrey Jerome Cohen, *Of Giants. Sex, Monsters, and the Middle Ages* (Minneapolis: University of Minnesota Press, 1999).

9. Joan Cadden, *The Meanings of Sex Difference in the Middle Ages: Medicine, Science, and Culture* (Cambridge: Cambridge UP, 1993).

10. Thomas Laqueur, *Making Sex. Body and Gender from the Greeks to Freud* (Cambridge: Harvard UP, 1990).

11. Caroline Walker Bynum, *Jesus as Mother. Studies in the Spirituality of the High Middle Ages* (Berkeley: University of California Press, 1982).

12. Wolfram's work is, as one might expect, loosely based on Aliscans.

13. Jeffrey Jerome Cohen and Bonnie Wheeler, ed., *Becoming Male in the Middle Ages* (New York: Garland Publishing, 2000), xi.

14. I wish to distinguish here between cultural/social and philosophical/spiritual processes. The thirteenth-century understood human beings as existing in a constant state of becoming; for Christians, the body and the soul were always changing (though the essence of the soul did not change). Cultural norms were responsible for determining and enforcing the restrictions on becoming male and female.

15. Cohen and Wheeler, xi.

16. Simon Gaunt, *Gender and Genre in Medieval French Literature*

(Cambridge: Cambridge UP, 1995).

17. Derek Gregory, *Geograpical Imaginations* (Blackwell: Cambridge MA and Oxford UK, 1994).

18. Gregory, 104.

19. It is significant that Tristan, at least in Gottfried's version of the poem, is technically a fragment—though from later versions of the story it is clear how the narrative reaches its conclusion.

20. Jeffrey Jerome Cohen, "Gowther Among the Dogs: Becoming Inhuman c. 1400," *Becoming Male in the Middle Ages* (New York, 2000), 238–239.

21. See Wolfgang Iser, "Die Wirklichkeit der Fiktion. Elemente eines funktionsgeschichtlichen Textmodells der Literatur," in *Rezeptionsästhetik,* ed. Rainer Warning (Munich, 1975) 277–321.

22. For an overview of major theoretical problems, see Robert C. Holub, *Reception Theory. A Critical Introduction* (London: Methuen, 1984) especially 92–101.

23. See Wolfgang Iser, *The Implied Reader. Patterns of Communication in Prose Fiction from Bunyan to Beckett* (Baltimore: Johns Hopkins UP, 1974) particularly 38–39.

24. Wolfgang Iser, "Die Appellstruktur der Texte," in *Rezeptionsästhetik,* ed. Rainer Warning (München: Wilhelm Fink, 1975) 228–252.

25. See Iser's final chapter in *The Implied Reader,* entitled "The Reading Process: A Phenomenological Approach." (274–294) Iser views the reader/text interaction as essential to the creation of the literary work, which exists between two poles: the artistic (the text created by the author) and the aesthetic (the text created by the realization of the reader): "From this polarity it follows that the literary work cannot be completely identical with the text, or with the realization of the text, but in fact must lie halfway between the two." (274)

26. Wolfgang Iser, "Do I Write for an Audience?" *PMLA* 115.3 (May 2000): 314.

27. Iser, "Do I Write for an Audience?" 314.

28. Iser, "Do I Write for an Audience?" 312.

CHAPTER 1

Cultural Topography and Arthurian Romance

dô dahte ich mir vil ange,
wie man zer welte solte leben
—Walther von der Vogelweide[1]

Genres are not neutral descriptive categories; they in-
stitute a reality and inscribe a subject.
—Zakia Pathak[2]

Gender shapes bodies as they shape space and are in
turn shaped by its arrangements
—Ivan Illich[3]

INTRODUCTION

In the latter half of the twelfth century, the Arthurian romance made its entrance onto the stage of medieval vernacular literature and found an eager audience in German courtly culture. The works of Chrétien de Troyes formed the basis around which the genre flourished, quickly (at least by medieval standards) finding their way into German adaptations through Hartmann von Aue and Wolfram von Eschenbach and Gottfried von Strassburg, among others. Intended for a secular and noble audience, these Arthurian romances celebrate the feudal court and its way of life, offering listeners an appropriate measure of both *delectatio* and *utilitas* in the idealized Arthurian mirror of their own society. Within the parameters that the genre of romance allowed them, poet and audience interacted in the medieval equivalent of "virtual reality,"[4] which aimed to facilitate these twin goals of pleasure and usefulness. Following Gaunt's argument that issues of gender are fundamental in any discussion of genre, this book will examine the interaction of gender and romance in the four Middle High German Arthurian romances of the late twelfth and early thirteenth centuries, an interaction that is literally structured and thematically supported by means of spatial arrangements that we can call (with Sigrid Weigel) gender topographies. French feminist Luce Irigaray envisions gender quite literally as a space that can accommodate sexual difference, a third sphere that enables the two genders (conventionally interpreted as male and female) to meet on new ground.[5] If we consider the Arthurian romance in the context of Irigaray's suggestion, romance can be interpreted as an imagined 'real' place where the third space can be explored.

Interpreted in this way, as a figurative meeting place, the romance presented medieval poets with an innovative means of expression at the end of the twelfth century to explore, as Walther von der Vogelweide succinctly expressed it, "wie man zer welte solte leben."[6] The way in which one ought to live in the world was by becoming appropriately man or woman: by becoming appropriately gendered. The topography of gender in romance charts the possibilities for becoming (and, by contrast, also for being) "woman" and "man", thus participating in and reshaping in secular form the discourses on gender that had escalated over the course of the twelfth century. Historian Jo Ann McNamara has described a "masculine identity crisis" (the "*Herrenfrage*") precipitated by disturbances in the gender system of the eleventh and twelfth centuries.[7] The gender system began to destabilize after the First Lateran Council with its injunction against clerical marriage, for "if celibacy redefined masculinity, it also redefined femininity."[8] According to McNamara, celibate men gained public power during the early twelfth century, but they also became essentially ungendered, losing their unequivocally male identity: "If a person does not act like a man, is he a man?"[9] Eventually, masculine identity reasserted itself through a more rigid demarcation of gender boundaries and roles.[10] Before examining the role of romance topography in the construction of gendered identity, and in the demarcation of the boundaries for that identity, I will review briefly various aspects of the concept of "topography" as they pertain to cultural and literary analysis.

CULTURAL TOPOGRAPHY

The study of topography, which deals specifically with the description of localities and their relative positions, belongs primarily to the realm of geography. Indeed, place is one of the "most fundamental concepts"[11] of the science of geography, which aims to investigate the physical, social, cultural, and economic boundaries that separate (and simultaneously differentiate) one place from another. This study of localities acquires broader cultural dimensions when one considers culture as a process in which people are actively engaged, constantly producing what they perceive to be realities.[12] These realities inevitably involve spaces which structure society and which help individuals to "make sense of surroundings that are otherwise chaotic and random, and to define and locate themselves with respect to those surroundings."[13] People make sense of their surroundings, then, by creating and constructing geographies.[14] These geographies are a type of cultural representation in that they provide society with an image of itself, thereby reinforcing the societal structures created to make sense of otherwise random surroundings.

If we understand place and space as forms of cultural representation, then it becomes clear that these constructs are of interest not only to geographers but also to scholars in a wide range of fields. Spatial metaphors have proven particularly adaptable in recent literary and cultural studies. Mitchell's anthology *Landscape and Power* addresses the question of how landscape functions as a cultural practice, attempting to explore landscape not simply as a genre of the visual arts but as a medium of exchange between the human and the natural. Mitchell defines landscape as "a material 'means' (to borrow Aristotle's terminology) like language or paint, embedded in a tradition of cultural signification and communication, a body of symbolic forms capable of being invoked and reshaped to express meanings and values."[15] Aitken and Zonn focus their attention more specifically on cinematic space and the geography of film. Kirby combines an analysis of literature and culture in her evaluation of the usefulness of a concept of flexible space for postmodern cultural theory and a critique thereof.[16] She focuses primarily on the shifting and restructuring of boundaries that characterize the postmodern world, occasioning a crisis of identity. While Kirby's definition of subjective space is specifically tailored to this postmodern crisis, her definition has at least two applications to medieval narrative space: 1) the idea of a space as a place for reaction and response and 2) the concept of the manipulation of space as a means of (re)structuring society. In literary narrative itself, spaces and relationships are manipulated by the narrator to offer the audience a certain structure, a certain arrangement of relationships (between social levels, between genders). Clearly, narratives play a key role in orienting individuals with respect to their cultural milieu, "locating" and providing appropriate models for readers to emulate. The influence of the author's voice (through a hand or a pen or a voice) can be felt literally from the beginning of a text, for the act of narrating a work for an audience establishes a relatively exclusive spatial relationship from the start. The notion of the existence of an "I/we" inherently creates space, since it implies a complementary "you/they," a *here* as opposed to a *there*.[17] The space of the literary narrative expands to locate an internal textual reality in which the narrator manipulates certain spaces and relationships to offer the audience a particular structure, thus advocating a particular arrangement of these relationships in the world of the text. The "map" of the world provided by the narrator thus reflects a certain accepted view of that world, a certain relationship or balance between ideal and real that is posited as more favorable than another. Other arrangements (we could also understand them as maps) are implicitly or explicitly discouraged.[18] In this way, the space of the literary narrative and the world it offers serve as a place that allows the poet a means for creative response to his surroundings, perhaps even an opportunity to (re)structure society, in theory if not in practice.

The on-going search for self-definition evolves through the process of cognitive mapping. Frederic Jameson introduced the term into postmodern discourse, describing the "mental map of the social and global totality"[19] that all individuals carry with them in various forms. Ideology bridges the gap that individuals inevitably experience between perception and reality, in that ideology "attempts to span or coordinate, to map, by means of conscious and unconscious representations."[20] Thus, one can understand the concept of cognitive mapping on a basic level, divested of Jameson's own ideological bias, as the representation of the world or a landscape in which a mind, in the form of a writing subject, finds itself. Barnes and Duncan direct their attention to the more concrete representation of actual landscapes through writing. They point out that landscape itself may be analyzed as text because "it too is a social and cultural production."[21] Landscapes and their spaces are forms of cultural practice;[22] they can be 'read' as texts [23] that one can see "as constitutive of reality rather than mimicking it, as cultural practices of signification rather than as referential duplications."[24] In this way, the world constructed within the text serves as an indication of "who" the poet thinks he is, "who" the society he describes thinks it is or wishes to be.[25]

ROMANCE SPACE

The creative act of "writing a world"[26] certainly describes the work of the poets who were composing medieval romance at the turn of the thirteenth century. Not surprisingly, the world of romance acquires a uniquely imaginary shape,[27] its fantastic nature revealing the creativity of the poets at work.[28] A distinct element of what we would tend to call fantasy is one particular characteristic of medieval geographical writing and cartography that finds its way into the literature is its distinct element of what we would tend to call fantasy.[29] This fantasy becomes most evident in medieval accounts concerning India, a region which seems to have held special fascination for the inhabitants of the medieval Christian west. "Associated in their minds with fantastic wealth, natural wonder and magic,"[30] India was conceptualized rather broadly by medieval audiences. Wherever its actual geographical position might have been, it had found a unique place in the medieval imagination as part of the Alexander legends told since Antiquity and remained, according to Simek, "ein Reich mit stark fabelhaften Zügen, das in den Schilderungen wie kein anderes Land durch eine Mischung aus Fakten und Legenden charakterisiert wurde."[31] This fantastic place was the conjectured residence of the fabulously wealthy Prester John. The references to this eastern Christian monarch first appeared in the work of Otto of Freising around 1145, spurring an interest in the search for his realms that endured for at least a century. Simek attributes the popularity and credibility of a counterfeit letter, allegedly sent by Prester John to the Byzantine emperor Manuel I around 1160, to the fact that it confirmed all the information about India that the medieval world knew from contemporary travel literature and, above all, from the various encyclopedias.[32] Wolfram draws upon the popularity of the myth at the end of his *Parzival*, when he gives his version of Prester John's genealogy:

> Repanse de schoye mohte dô
> alrêst ir verte wesen vrô.
> diu gebar sît in Indyân

ein sun, der hiez Jôhan.
priester Jôhan man den hiez:
iemmer sît man dâ die künege liez
bî dem namn belîben. (822,21–27)

[Then for the first time Repanse de Schoye was able to be glad
of her journey. Later, in India, she gave birth to a son, whose
name was John. People called him Prester John. Ever since, people have given that name to the kings there.][33]

Certainly, the literature produced at this time reflect the significance and the cultural ramifications of the medieval world's expanding geographical margins as they were interpreted by the
poets of the late twelfth century. The Crusades, for example,
brought forth an outpouring of literary responses.[34] As poets re-
sponded to the challenges offered by the changing world around
them,[35] they presented their audiences with images that can be observed, in the words of Sigrid Weigel, "eher als *Denk*bilder denn
als *Ab*bilder ...als verräumlichtes Sinnbild einer Kultur, als para-
digmatischer Ort von Zivilisationsarbeit und Kristallisationspunkt
einer als Fortschritt konzipierten Geschichte."[36] Poets left their
present and future audiences with metaphorical and discursive imprints that would survive through the persistence of perceived images ("*Denk*bilder"), in contrast to actual images ("*Ab*bilder").
The perceived image carries an added dimension, functioning on
the conceptual as well as on the concrete level as locus for the
process of civilization ("Zivilisationsarbeit") that enables a culture
to define itself. For the culture intended to receive them, these images symbolize a perceived reality rather than actual reality (inas-
much as "actual reality" may ever be determined).

This contrast between perceived images and actual images can
be observed in the spaces depicted in romance. Instead of directing
the reader to "real" places,[37] however, the landscape of romance
appears to consist predominately of the *topoi* that characterize
Curtius' ideal landscape, most prominent among them the forest
and the *locus amoenus*.[38] Both of these spaces, the forest and the
locus amoenus, have been the particular focus of previous discussions of twelfth-century Arthurian topography. According to Vermette, romance geography reflects the medieval concept of "uni-
versal symbolism" in which nature, "the *anima mundi* or soul of
the world," offers a concrete manifestation of the universe in har-
moniously balanced physical form. The Arthurian Round Table,

for example, offers a space that can include human beings into this balanced order, its circle representing the perfect cosmos, as did medieval circular maps with Jerusalem at the center.[39] As a manifestation of nature, the forest plays an important role in the romance narrative, combining with other geographical space to serve as a backdrop for the experimental "space" of the romance itself.[40] It is not by accident that the forest provides the locus for the knight's passage to and through the "other world where chaos, disharmony, and injustice reign."[41] According to Saunders, the romance forest functions as a "limen, offering to the hero the means of embodying chivalry and of fulfilling his role as knight, justifying, indeed, the life of the court."[42] Whereas Vermette and Saunders concentrate on the role of the physical forest landscape in Arthurian romance,[43] Schmid-Cadalbert presents a narrower focus in his discussion of "der wilde Wald" and the concept of "*wilt*" in Middle High German. Exploring what he calls the "Doppelnatur" of literary wilderness and its real counterpart, Schmid-Cadalbert draws connections between the historical appropriation of forest land for economic use in the twelfth century and the symbolic meanings ascribed to the wilderness in the literature. He attributes the proliferation of forest motifs around 1200 to the decrease of actual forest land in Europe, commenting that the threatening wildness of the forest had to diminish, "um in der Literatur als symbolischer Raum für Flucht-, Weltflucht-und Selbstfindungsräume verfügbar zu werden."[44] There are other places that organize the spaces of the romance landscape as well. The court, in any of its manifestations, stands most obviously in contrast to the 'wildness' of the forest; there are the courts of Arthur, Lac (Erec's father), Laudine, there is the Grail castle Munsalvaesche. There are also 'intermediate' forests like Soltane, which depict inhabited and domesticated land somewhere between the court (of Waleis, in the case of Herzeloyde) and the wider wilderness; perhaps one can include the gateway fountain of *Iwein*. There is the ultmate cocoon of civilized courtliness as manifested in the Cave of Lovers in *Tristan*. And there are the lands of the east as depicted in the first two books of Wolfram von Eschenbach's *Parzival*.

GENDER TOPOGRAPHIES

The discussion of cultural topography has established the depiction of space, whether visual (as in Mitchell's landscape) or written (as literary narrative) as a process of signification. The brief discussion of romance space has also established that, as part of 'writing the romance world,' this space is variously inscribed and organized. I wish now to consider how this process of signification takes place in the spaces of romance. Derek Gregory has described four categories in the process of what he calls the geographic imagination. The category of *articulation* is the first of what he terms "the most important considerations in the conduct of any critical project." Articulation requires "an identification of the modalities thorugh which time and space are bound into the constituation of social life." While the final category of four (*authorization*) raises questions about "the privilege of position, and about authorship and authority, representation and rights," it is the two middle categories that are most useful for the purposes of the following analysis: the process of *spatialization* and the process of *representation*. According to Gregory, space is coded in physical and social terms. The term spatialization refers "to the opening and occupation of different sites of human action and to the differences and integrations that are socially inscribed through the production of place, space and landscape." Associated with the process of spatialization, and indeed perhaps preceeding it as a crucial preparatory step, is the process of representation. Representation literally shows us "the different ways in which the world is made present, re-presented, discursively constructed." Integral to the process of representation is a process of "othering" (which is seen as a necessary or at least inevitable aspect of representation). The process of "othering" is one that is "never neutral" and inevitably "works through grids of power."[46] Spatialization can be understood then as a form of articulation that facilitates and structures representation.

The process of "othering" inevitably involves power, the power to define an "other" in the process of attempting to define a "self." Power is also invariably connected with gender; indeed, Gregory's power grids are structured through gender roles and relationships. The construction of gender roles is central to the dynamic between spatialization (where and how social life takes place) and representation (the way in which the world is presented and discursively constructed). The "sites of human action" that Gregory mentions are (in literature) the discursive constructs that structure the literary world. In a sense, we can indeed say that the process of the formation of identities is "nothing less than a

process of spatialization."[47] Identity is also a process of negotiation in a "space of play," where it can be constantly "revised in relation to external reality and, more crucially, to other possible
identities."[48] Romance describes a process of courtly self-definition, of becoming, of forming the identities of the men and the
women in the audience. This process can be seen to occur in distinct places within an equally distinct form of literary space. The
question to pursue at this juncture is not simply whether the spaces
of romance are gendered but how they function as a mechanism
for the inscription of gender roles, as a representational framework
that maps this inscription for the audience. The inhabitants of
these spaces, the agents at Gregory's "sites of human action", do
not often remain stationary. Indeed, their placement and their
movement from those places support Iser's panorama of possiblities. German feminist Sigrid Weigel offers insight into the way in
which the interactions of topography and gender may be explored.
In a provocative reading of Sophocles' *Antigone*, Weigel coins the
term "gender topographies" ("Topographien der Geschlechter") to
describe schematically the constellation of Creon and Antigone,
the former firmly ensconced within the city walls as the representative of its law and order, the latter forced into action outside of
those ordered walls and branded a threat by the people within.[49]
For Weigel, the tragedy of *Antigone* describes "eine mythische
Urszene"[50] emblematic of the different places occupied by women
and men in the history of western civilization. She goes on to describe these places as a pattern of gender topographies that have
left their marks on history, shaping later perceptions of feminity
and masculinity in literature:

> Diese unterschiedlichen *Orte* der Geschlechter in der
> abendländischen Kulturgeschichte haben auch in der Schrift ihre
> Spuren hinterlassen: in der Metaphorik, in Denkmustern,
> Diskursfiguren und in spezifischen Praktiken der Bedeu-
> tungskonstitution. Die <<Topographien der Geschlechter>>
> verzeichnen diese Spuren im Blick auf exemplarische Konstella-
> tionen von <Weiblichkeit> und <Männlichkeit> in der Liter-
> atur.[51]

The actual places become absorbed into metaphors (*Metaphorik*),
forms of discourse (*Diskursfiguren*), and patterns of thought
(*Denkmuster*). This process of cultural absorption tends to dis-

tance or abstract these places from "actual" geographical location; simultaneously, the depicted places establish and reinforce cultural models or precedents, which in turn leave distinct traces (*Spuren*) in literature as texts attempt to illustrate exemplary models of male and female roles for their respective audiences. In literature, these traces of "places" continue to map these models for us. They emerge in various patterns and representations that form and re-form over time. These patterns are themselves internalized or reinforced by the encouragement of particular attitudes and behaviors at particular times. The topographical outlines become the framework of experiments in rearranging and renegotiating the world in text and image.

In its negotiations, courtly romance offers a particularly vivid example of the dialectic that Weigel describes between "own" (*eigenem*) and "other" (*fremdem*).[56] The twelfth and thirteenth centuries are a period of time when one can arguably see the tension between new and old patterns. Courtly literature aims to resolve the tension but cannot quite achieve such a resolution. The tension inherent in this dialectic remains and the topography supports the tension in its places (garden, forest, court, *locus amoenus*, castle). Weigel's dialectic can also be illustrated in the dynamics of several kinds of oppositional relationships, which have spaces and places as integral components: self/other (*eigen/fremd*), inside/outside, freedom/imprisonment or enclosure, cultured court/uncultured nature.[53] Ultimately, the dialectic results from a fundamental contradiction at the basis of medieval thought, namely that woman must both be included in and yet excluded from the dominant (male) culture. The topographical arrangements in the literature, both actual and perceived, provide at least one of the means by which the authors (deliberately or not, consciously or not) represent these tensions for the contemporary and subsequent audiences. Women and their places are constitutive of otherness and therefore integral to the process of othering that Gregory describes as an crucial aspect of representation.

Before we turn our attention to the processes of spatialization and representation in the Arthurian romances of Hartmann von Aue, it will be useful to examine further the general role that the genre of romance played in structuring these processes. We will look at the relationship between romance reality and ideology through the lenses of Iser's reader-response theory as well as current feminist theories on gender. These theories enable modern readers to understand more clearly the possibilities for experimentation available through the fiction of romance, through the creation of gendered spaces. The versatile metaphor of topography played an important part in allowing poet and audience, at least in the context of the romance narrative, to give form and shape to some of these possibilities.

THE REALITY OF COURTLY ROMANCE

Performed in a social setting, the courtly romance functioned as a vehicle for the dissemination of cultural values, presented by the predominately male poets in their works and directed towards the courtly society for which the poets wrote. The discourse of romance was particularly suited to take up the discussion of gender in the context of secular literature and for a courtly audience. Simon Gaunt has recently offered a compelling analysis of the relationship between gender and genre in medieval French literature. In this context, Gaunt maintains that individual genres represent different voices and methods of dealing with issues presented by changing (or the possibility of changing) gender roles in the larger society. Following Jameson and others, Gaunt asserts that genre is a reflection of ideology. Since ideology is interested in constructing gender roles that will support itself, issues of gender are fundamental in any discussion of genre. Indeed, genres "represent constructed symbolic resolutions to social tensions and contradictions and thereby inscribe ideologies"; therefore, one must understand how gender is constructed and represented in those ideologies in order to understand how those ideologies function.[54] Gaunt distinguishes between epic (*chanson de geste*) and romance, for example, by recognizing that they are written for the same courtly audience; however, they suggest "different imaginary resolutions to cultural and social tensions."[55] Gender is a key factor in these resolutions. Whereas, according to Gaunt, the epic hero's identity is constructed in relation to other men, romance "constructs masculinity in relation to femininity, developing a strong sense of alterity."[56] In providing poets with the means to construct and deconstruct these relationships, romance provided a powerful mechanism of socialization.

Of course, the world of Arthurian romance, populated by knights and fair maidens who live alongside giants and dwarves and other remarkable creatures in a place where happy endings are the rule rather than the exception, seems to belie any connection to the historical or social conditions of the late twelfth and early thirteenth centuries.[57] Much recent research has been done on the "usefulness" of Arthurian romance (and its "Märchenwelt") and its, in terms of its function as a vehicle for the socialization of its audience.[58] This function certainly did not escape the medieval contemporaries of Chrétien, Wolfram, and Gottfried. In his moral treatise *Der wälsche Gast*, written around 1215, the cleric Thomasin von Zerklære emphasizes the prescriptive values illustrated by the main actors in romance, casting the Arthurian characters as exempla for his readers.[59] Turning his attention to instruction of the youth following the prologue, Thomasin states his intention to reveal the useful things that young people should glean from his work:

> nu wil ich sagen waz diu kint
> suln vernemen unde lesen
> und waz in mac nütze wesen.[60]

[Now I will tell you what the children should hear and read and what might be useful to them.]

In the lines that follow, he praises as models figures from both classical (Penelope and Oenone, for example, as well as the great king Karl [Charlemagne] and Alexander) and more modern Arthurian works (Enite and Blanscheflor, Erec and Iwein). Thomasin does not, of course, recommend following the example of the hapless Keie:

> si suln hœren von Ênît,
> daz si die volgen âne nît.
> si suln ouch Pênelopê
> der vrouwen volgen und Oenonê,
> Galjênâ und Blanscheflôr,
> . . . unde Sôrdamôr.
> sint si niht all küneginne,
> si mügen ez sîn an schœnem sinne.
>   Juncherren suln von Gâwein
> hœren, Clîes, Êrec, Îwein,
> und suln rihten sîn jugent
> gar nâch Gâweins reiner tugent.
> volgt Artûs dem künege hêr,
> der treit iu vor vil guote lêr,

und habt ouch in iwerm muot
künic Karln den helt guot.
lât niht verderben iuwer jugent:
Alexanders tugent,
an gevuoc volgt ir Tristande,
Seigrimos, Kâlogrîande.
wartâ, wartâ, wie si drungen,
die rîter von der tavelrunden,
einr vürn ander ze vrümkeit.
kint, lât iuch niht an trâkeit
und volget vrumer liute lêre,
des komt ir ze grôzer êre.
irn sult hern Key volgen niht
von dem mir vil unwirde geschiht:
der tuot mit allenthalben nôt.[62]

[They should hear of Enite, that they gladly follow her example. They should also follow the example of lady Penelope and Oenone, Galjena and Blanscheflor...and Sordamor. Even if they are not all queens, they could be because of their fine manner.

Young men should hear of Gawein, Cliges, Erec, Iwein and should model their youthful efforts on Gawein's pure virtue. If you follow Arthur, the noble king, he will bring you much good instruction. And also remember king Karl [Charlemagne] the good hero. Do not let your youth be corrupted: think about Alexander's virtue, do not hesitate to follow Tristan, Seigrimos, Kalogrenant. Oh, how they fought, the knights of the Round Table, one against the other for renown. Children, do not succumb to laziness and follow the teaching of good people, in this way you will come to great honor. You should not follow the example of Sir Key, of whom I have been told much that is not worthy: I feel sorry for him.]

By interpreting and judging his present according to the Arthurian ideal, Thomasin gives the courtly romance a new meaning in *Der wälsche Gast*.[63] Thomasin recommends the figures of Parzival and Gawein as acceptable role models, thereby creating a context in *Der wälsche Gast* that allows secular fiction to become an acceptable vehicle for moral teaching.[64] In this way, Thomasin indicates that he believes the romance exceptionally well-suited for the education and socialization of noble women and men, superior even to other didactic literature of the time.[65] *Der wälsche Gast* shows that the process of Arthurian reception took a significant step toward encouraging the internalization of these literary figures and scenes, an acceptance of them into the world and value system of the audience. The romance world can clearly privilege certain behaviors and actions while discouraging others.

THE EXPERIMENT OF FICTION

To what extent would the medieval audience have understood the romance world as any kind of fiction and how would that fiction have related to any aspect of medieval reality? These questions direct our attention once more toward the relationship between fiction and reality, for it is in the interaction of these two apparent opposites that the process of socialization occurs. Auerbach compares the courtly romance unfavorably to the earlier *chanson de geste* because the former lacks political and social reality.[66] In contrast to Auerbach, Jaeger explains Middle High German romances primarily as instructive manuals influenced by French courtly ideals and motivated by the desire of the Germans to imitate them; the German poets were looking for "the required enlightenment, instruction and guidance in courtly ways" and found it in the guise of courtly romance.[68] Jaeger goes so far as to assert that romance was produced according to the need for education and instruction of the lay population. It was Erich Köhler, however, who first proposed a dialectical relationship between the ideal and reality, as the two poles that determine the dynamics of romance. Köhler's main premise is that (French) courtly poetry deals with feudal reality by consciously offering a contrast to it. Arthurian romance represented "der großartige Versuch des höfischen Rittertums, die mit Beginn der zweiten feudalen Epoche gestellte Sinnfrage zugunsten des Individuums und zugleich ein letztes Mal von der ständischen Gemeinschaftswelt als dem übergeordneten Prinzip her zu beantworten."[69] While Köhler drew his conclusions and examples almost exclusively from the literature itself, ultimately creating a circular argument, he inspired the socio-historical methods that have shaped much of the research today.[70]

Admittedly, the terms "ideal" and "reality" carry certain connotations for modern theorists that did not necessarily apply in the Middle Ages. And the question of their relevance to medieval literature, particularly courtly literature, has remained the subject of lively debate. Jauss' essay "Alterität und Modernität der mittelalterlichen Literatur"[71] inaugurated a flood of essays puzzling over the medieval understanding of "fiction" in the late 1970's and early 1980's. Gumbrecht points out that there are indeed two forms of fictionality that come into being in the course of the twelfth century: the "Poesie des Unsichtbaren" of allegory promoted by the Chartres school, and the vernacular courtly literature.[72] Those critics who have preferred to interpret romance according to the former have focussed on medieval aesthetics and exegetical interpretations. Accordingly, they view romance through an exegetical lens against the backdrop of developments in twelfth-century Christian spirituality.[73] Historian R.W. Southern interpreted the quest, the primary activity of the Arthurian world, as a spiritual experience. The quest offered a solitary knight, representing the individual soul, the opportunity to undertake a secular journey toward self-knowledge comparable to the personal spirituality advocated in the writings of Anselm and Bernard.[74] In *The Rise of Romance*, Vinaver also notes that the narrative strategy of romance similarly invites the reader to share in the journey of the quest for meaning.[75]

Vinaver goes on to comment on the function of romance as concerned, not with human realities, but with problems, their elaboration and their solution.[76] In other words, romance provided a vehicle for an experiment in expression, an experiment that we might perhaps classify as "fiction." D. H. Green has recently discussed the phenomenon of thirteenth-century romance as an emergent understanding of fiction and the nature of fictional truth as opposed to historical truth; the medieval German authors intentionally differentiated among *res factae* as opposed to *res fictae*.[77] These poets perfected the art of representing fictional truth, despite (or perhaps because of) German literary backwardness in the late twelfth century. This backwardness "did not prevent German authors from seizing the opportunity which the discovery of fiction afforded them, but it does mean that, more emphatically than Chrétien, they found it necessary to point out the nature of fictional truth in the hope of training their audiences to it."[78] Green points out several examples (such as the inability of the narrator in *Erec* to describe the dress of Mabonagrin's lady because he was not there) that indicate Hartmann is trying to emphasize for his audience the impossibility of seeing what he describes, because it is not "real" on that level. This does not, of course, discount the possibility of a higher truth in the fiction; it merely underscores the importance of the written form as a legitimation of this truth.[79] Walter Haug offers a slightly different view of this development of fiction, placing the idea of fiction in the context of a gradual "demystification of the world" that begins in the Middle Ages. As the first in a series of changes in a consciousness of "fictionality," the courtly novel offers "a conscious structural experiment,"[81] based fundamentally upon "a new recognition of the 'true' fiction."[82] This fiction does not, however, aim towards a concrete solution of the problems it described and elaborated. On the contrary, it is characterized by reflection upon the conditions of its own existence, of the existence of its ideals as the process of "Entzauberung" continues.[83] Haug goes so far as to coin the term "das Mittelalterlich-Fiktionale" to describe the phenomenon of reflection as it occurs in the romance literature, placing the emphasis on the experimental possibilities that the genre allows: "Das Mittelalterlich-Fiktionale, wie es sich im arthurischen Roman konkretisiert, beruht gerade nicht auf der Idee des Wahrscheinlichen, *diese neue Fiktionalität kommt vielmehr über das freie Spiel mit dem Unwahrscheinlichen zu sich selbst.*"[84] This literary experiment in "fictional truth" thus enables poets to impress their messages upon their even more effectively than through means of a more sober didactic style. The interplay ("free play") of the probable and the improbable ("wahrscheinlich" and "unwahrscheinlich") creates a useful dynamic for the fiction of medieval romance, in which the authors purposefully manipulate elements of truth and probability in their narratives. It is the improbable that highlights the "true" sense behind the fiction.

At this point, it is useful to refer once again to Iser's reader-response theory. These texts, understood as "a process of demonstration"[85] that revolves around Haug's interplay between the probable and the improbable, invite a relationship between text and audience ("ein Mitteilungsverhältnis") wherein the text communicates something about reality to that audience.[86] Two aspects of this communicative relationship will prove useful for our analysis of romance. The first is the idea that the text contains a specific and selected code from the pool of all possible codes or combinations thereof.[87] These codes contribute to the privileging of certain standards for behavior, resulting in the formation (or at least the reaffirmation) of a homogeneous social group.[88] The second implies (although Iser seems to attribute a certain autonomy to texts and rarely speaks of authors as such) that the hand of the author is actively involved in this process of selection.[89] A medieval poet thus contributes to the socialization process mentioned above by encoding certain behavior patterns in his text and by subsequently offering this code through the text to the audience. That the poet expected his audience to receive and accept these codes is illustrated in part by the poet's interactions with and admonitions to his listeners. As Thomasin demonstrates in *Der wälsche Gast*, the mechanism of this encoding involves the illustration of certain values and behaviors through exemplary models. Romance clearly provided these models, by describing them and by demonstrating the processes through which they became exemplary. Romance provides the fictional space to explore various processes of becoming and to reflect further on them.

THE GENDER QUESTION

To say that models generally played an important role in medieval culture is to understate their significance. The twelfth century, however, seems to have been a particularly fruitful time for the formation of groups according to desirable models.[90] Thomasin's reliance on courtly romance for models suggests that secular literature was capable of effectively performing a similar function for its audience, emphasizing membership in one particular group, namely the nobility. Courtly romance does not function exclusively as an advocate of the aristocracy, nor does it represent the only voice speaking in the late twelfth and early thirteenth centuries; however, the genre offered poets a new forum in which they could deal with issues of immediate concern for their noble audience, especially since the male and female characters whom we know through the courtly romance are portrayed and constructed in a social context. The context remains exclusive, of course, and limited to the nobility, a pre-condition of courtly literature. On the one hand, these issues treated ideals that were perceived as important for any member of the group, such as ideals of rulership, courtliness (*hôher muot*), loyalty (*triuwe*), honor (*êre*), love (*minne*). On the other hand, Roberta Krueger points out that, while the romance audience may have been united as a group by class, this same group was nonetheless divided by gender.[91]

In order to function, courtly society required a delicate and well-structured gender balance that enabled it to function. The potentially catastrophic effects of imbalance in gender roles are illustrated by the following scene from Book XIII of Wolfram's *Parzival* (636,15–641,30), in which Gawan heals the rift Clinschor's magic has created among the members of the court at the *Schastel marveile.*[92] Imprisoned within the castle, the women and men suffer from an inability to communicate with one another in the language of standard courtly interactions; their confinement has become all the more painful because of their isolation from one another.[93] In this way, Clinschor's castration, itself a violent and disfiguring injury, has manifested itself in the situation of the castle's inhabitants. In reacquainting the women and men with one another, Gawan supplies the long awaited remedy for the dysfunctional illness that has afflicted the court. At last able to function and interact as courtly society dictates they should, they can once again perform *together* the appropriate rituals of dancing, eating, and speaking.[94]

Gawan's story has recently come to be regarded by *Parzival* critics not simply as a mere digression from the more serious business of Parzival's quest for the Grail, but as an essential part of Wolfram's message in the work. Indeed, both Gawan and Parzival function as healers. The wounds suffered by Clinschor and Anfortas, originating in both cases from a sexual transgression, produce cataclysmic rifts that threaten the gender balance of their respective worlds. The opening of another such rift, caused by Laudine's ultimatum, sends Hartmann's Iwein rushing madly off into the forest. As these scenes demonstrate, the question of gender relations in proper balance offers a key to our understanding of the dynamics and the function of German courtly romance.

In order to listen with a twentieth-century ear to the discussions about gender that take place in the courtly romances, we will need to orient ourselves with respect to two sets of theories about gender in the section that follows: the theories available in the late twelfth century that might have made their way through the fabric of the German Arthurian narratives to the medieval audience and the theories current in the late twentieth century that influence modern readers. Gender and theories of gender have gained increasing prominence over the past decade in feminist and cultural studies and, in the process, they have left an indelible mark on medieval studies as well. Indeed, they offer medievalists at least one solution for a chronic hermeneutic dilemma, namely the question of how to access medieval texts from a position in the twentieth century and imbue them with relevant meaning.[95] Interests in feminism and women's issues have provided a sort of hermeneutic link between the texts and their present-day interpreters, illuminating and expanding the horizons of research in all disciplines that touch the Middle Ages.[96] This hermeneutic link will serve, it is hoped, to resolve the potential conflicts between the issue of historicity (which necessarily presents itself in the study of older texts) and the feminist approach that lies at the basis of this author's investigation. These twin issues of historicity and feminist perspective need not be mutually exclusive, as more conservative medievalists continue to believe.

The history of feminist approaches to medieval literature has followed the same general plot one can trace in other disciplines. Feminist scholars first concentrated on discovering women characters and writers and/or resurrecting those who had been previously neglected by androcentric history. A next step involved an unveiling of the patriarchal structures that acted upon and influenced these women as well as the ways in which these women coped with and within them. In the development of its most recent chapter, the story has experienced what Elaine Showalter has called "one of the most striking changes in the humanities in the 1980s... the rise of gender."[97] Since "male and female genders always exist in relation to each other, never in splendid isolation,"[98] the primary focus at this stage has shifted from sex and biology to the construction of social and sexual roles in the larger cultural context. Of course, the shift to a focus on gender has produced a certain degree of critical discomfort; it has unsettled and destabilized traditional feminist criticism centered around women's issues. In Showalter's words, "talking about gender means talking about men *and* women."[99] This new development seems to have occasioned a certain "uneasiness at the most sophisticated levels,"[100] particularly among scholars who fear the new focus will detract from the political commitment of feminism, neglect issues of race and class, or represent a "pallid assimilation of feminist criticism into the mainstream (or male stream)."[101]

Although its focus does remain somewhat blurred by the ambivalence of some critics, gender can and does continue to function as "a primary interpretive map"[102] for those who participate in a culture as well as for those who purport to analyze it. This map can facilitate the study of a multitude of cultures, past as well as present, literary as well as historical. In her 1986 essay entitled "Gender: A Useful Category of Historical Analysis," historian Joan Scott develops a series of criteria for a productive application of the category 'gender' to the analysis of historical situations and contexts— in other words, for reading this map.[103] After a general overview of the three main approaches to the analysis of gender,[104] Scott proposes a flexible two-fold definition, whereby gender is recognized as "a constitutive element of social relationships based on perceived differences between the sexes and a primary way of signifying relationships of power."[105] Many theorists have tried to describe the relationship between the biological (sexual difference) and the social (gender). Julia Kristeva comes close to Scott when she describes her concept of sexual difference in the essay "Women's Time":

> Sexual difference— which is at once biological, physiological, and relative to reproduction— is translated by and translates a difference in the relationship of subjects to the symbolic contract which *is* the social contract: a difference, then, in the relationship to power, language, and meaning.[106]

The resulting power differential becomes the foundation of the social contract, so to speak, rooted in (biological) sexual difference and manifested through language. Kristeva's association of sexual difference, language, and power permits an understanding of the sexual (or the feminine) in terms of the social.[107] Scott's definition of gender expands this understanding in terms useful for historical (and literary) analysis. As an element of social relationships based on sex differences, gender involves four aspects according to Scott: a) cultural symbols with multiple representations,[108] b) normative interpretations of these symbols that limit their possibilities,[109] c) critical review of the interpretations, and d) subjective identity.[110] All of these factors interact and operate with one another, never in isolation. The second component of Scott's definition of gender proposes gender as a "primary field within which or by means of which power is articulated,"[111] an assertion that she proceeds to illustrate in a discussion of the relationship between gender and power in the hierarchy of the political arena.

Scott's article was written in response to the movement among historians in the mid-1980's to use feminist criticism as a tool for historical analysis. Gerda Lerner, whose ambitious attempt to trace the origins of patriarchy in *The Creation of Patriarchy* is a product of this movement, has defined history as the "process by which human beings record, interpret, and reinterpret the past in order to hand it down to future generations."[112] This process has been made possible by the ability of interpreters to manipulate the symbols through which they attempted to represent their stories. Although Lerner does not explicitly mention gender in connection with these symbols, it becomes clear from Scott's analysis that gender does indeed play a major role in the formation and the interpretation of these symbols.[113] Indeed, as Judith Lorber argues, gender has actually grown into an institution itself, having developed into the major organizing principle behind human social relations.[114] But this institution can be broken down into the three major aspects of Scott's definition (social relationships, sex differences, and power), which one can examine through a historical lens. In this way, these aspects offer an analytical blueprint for scholars in any discipline who seek to investigate historically gendered and gendered historical phenomena. The literature and history of the early modern period has proven extremely fruitful for other research in this area .[115]

GENDER, ROMANCE, AND THE ISSUE OF SPACE

The lens has steadily moved further back along the historical timeline, however, to produce much exciting research during the last decade. Joan Cadden made a significant contribution to the discussion by addressing the topic of the relationship between sex differences and gender in the Middle Ages in *The Meaning of Sex Differences in the Middle Ages*,[116] offering the most complete treatment of the issues to date. From the outset, Cadden takes issue with Laqueur's[117] blanket attribution of the Aristotelian one-sex model to all thought about sex before the eighteenth century. In the eleventh through the fourteenth centuries, as Cadden observes, "the elaboration of male and female reproductive roles provided a firm, if not solid, base for defining male and female natures."[118] This insight reveals nothing new. Yet, Cadden goes on to explain that the medieval gender system does not seem to have been as rigidly *dualistic* as the prospect of strict definitions according to reproductive roles would imply. Medieval medicine could, for example, admit the possibility of middle terms, and a certain degree of flexibility did remain in the application of masculine and feminine attributes to both men and women where they were deemed appropriate.[119]

Evidence from medieval theological and scientific discourse(s) indicates that gender relations provided a focal point for discussion in each area, as Cadden convincingly shows.[120] These discussions suggest that the definition of gender (the discourse perhaps) was in the process of becoming more clearly delineated over the

course of the twelfth and thirteenth centuries. The roles and behavior acceptable for women, and for men, became classified and
demarcated more precisely, particularly in the areas of family and
marriage.[121] Marriage was intimately connected with women's sexuality, having been since Eve the only acceptable expression of
women's sexual nature, a quality perceived as a constant threat to
the order that men worked so hard to maintain.[122] Like the institution of marriage, the concept of family had also been changing
over the course of the High Middle Ages,[123] particularly during the
twelfth century.[124] These changes bring us back to McNamara's
Herrenfrage, that reasserted a "masculinist ideology" and effectively eliminated the so-called *Frauenfrage*, the question of
women's increasingly powerful roles particularly among the religious, before 1120.[125] Eventually, masculine identity reasserted itself through a more rigid demarcation of the gender boundaries
and roles— in short, of the spaces in which the genders could act
and relate.[126]

The process of structuring such arrangements does not support strict definition, however, and it demands frequent reevaluation and re-construction. In this way, it enables the modern critic
to find the 'play' in an undeniably dualistic patriarchal medieval
system that fundamentally defined women as "Other" and yet, as
Cadden and others have demonstrated, paradoxically contained elements of variation.[127] Historian Jacques Le Goff describes this
meeting space of the social and the sexual as a cultural object, one
which he does not explicitly identify but which could certainly be
represented by the romance: "Biological man met social man in a
space that was a cultural object, defined in different ways in different societies, cultures, and eras, and shaped in part by ideologies
and values."[128] Through the space he creates for his work and by
means of the topography that structures his world, the romance
poet plays a vital role in shaping these ideologies and values. This
is one of the ways that they can be communicated in an under-
standable form to the audience, so that the audience can visualize
the map and follow the markers to the correct destination. A genre
such as romance can never be neutral with respect to the ideology
of those who produce it; genres by their very nature must institute
a reality and inscribe a subject.[129] To paraphrase Iser, romance
gives the poet a chance to reformulate the formulated as well as the
unformulated[130] in a medium that offers the opportunity for the
possible restructuring of boundaries. For lack of concrete evidence,
one cannot prove that the medieval audience's boundaries were in-

deed redrawn through their experience of the courtly romance; nevertheless, these boundaries certainly could be stretched, expanded, and explored, especially with respect to gender.[131] In other words, while 'being' may ultimately be fixed by cultural and social norms, the spatialization of romance offers creative and imaginative spaces for 'becoming.'

This space for 'play' is built into the genre of Arthurian romance, of course. It is, in fact, one of the reasons that the 'matter of Britain' gained international popularity over the course of the Middle Ages and that it remains so popular today. The malleable fiction of the romance also allows the poet a certain flexibility in dealing with the margins, as Terkla has convincingly argued in his study of visual and narrative spaces in medieval literature and art.[136] As we will see in our analysis of the literature, for instance, women may often be said literally to occupy marginal *positions* with respect to the established societal norms, neither wholly inside nor outside these norms, but inhabiting a boundary area between. Romance thus offers possibilities of empowerment not available through the patriarchal medieval Church, which necessarily defined women as marginal to its symbolic order. Romance also offers various opportunities to create and to encounter the "other," in a process of self-definition not only (predominately) for the male hero but also (perhaps more importantly) for the audience. As Gaunt convincingly argues, a defining characteristic of romance is the construction of masculinity and femininity in relation to one another. A sense of self is necessary for becoming masculine or feminine, and fundamental to any sense of self is a sense of otherness. In romance, the topographies of gender illustrate how spaces are constitutive of such otherness.

The questions that form the basis of the following chapters are: how does the "spatialization" of romance manifest itself as a topography of gender and how does this topography support (or oppose) the process of "becoming" masculine or feminine? We will ask these questions of Hartmann von Aue's *Erec* and *Iwein* (chapter 2) and Wolfram von Eschenbach's *Parzival* (chapter 3) and Gottfried von Strassburg's *Tristan* (chapter 4). As we will see, gender topographies become the mechanism for inscribing gender in romance; indeed, "gender shapes bodies as they shape space and are in turn shaped by its arrangements."[132] By offering and discussing various arrangements, the genre of romance offers the opportunity for a multivalent exploration of social and individual identity.

Notes

1. "Then I thought very intently about how one should live in the world." Walther von der Vogelweide, *Gedichte*, ed. Karl Lachmann (Berlin: Walter de Gruyter, 1965) 8,9–10.

2. Zakia Pathak, "A Pedagogy for Postcolonial Feminists," in *Feminists Theorize the Political*, ed. Judith Butler and Joan W. Scott (New York: Routledge, 1992), 432.

3. Ivan Illich, *Gender* (Berkeley, 1982) 118.

4. Wolfgang Iser, *PMLA*, (May 2000), 311

5. Luce Irigaray, "Sexual Difference," in *An Ethics of Sexual Difference*, trans. Carolyn Burke and Gillian C. Gill. (Ithaca: Cornell UP, 1993) 5–19.

6. Walther von der Vogelweide, *Gedichte*, 8,9–10.

7. Jo Ann McNamara, "The *Herrenfrage*. The Restructuring of the Gender System, 1050-1150," in *Medieval Masculinities. Regarding Men in the Middle Ages*, ed. Clare A. Lees (Minneapolis: University of Minnesota Press, 1994) 3.

8. McNamara, "*Herrenfrage*," 22. The gradual process of power redistribution through the family is described in Jo Ann McNamara and Suzanne Wemple. "The Power of Women through the Family in Medieval Europe: 500-1100." *Women and Power in the Middle Ages*. Ed. Mary Erler and Maryanne Kowalewski. (Athens: University of Georgia Press, 1988) 83–101. According to McNamara and Wemple, part of this re-definition of femininity had to do with women's loss of political (and public) power. As patriarchal family structures became more rigid and relocated women in a more private sphere, women's political influence declined.

9. McNamara, "*Herrenfrage*," 5

10. According to McNamara, this revisionary and reactionary trend continues as one of the effects of increasing urbanization and restrictions on the activities of women through the thirteenth and fourteenth centuries. Jo Ann McNamara, "City Air Makes Men Free and Women Bound," in *Text and Territory. Geographical Imagination in the European Middle Ages*. ed. Sylvia Tomasch and Sealy Gilles (Philadelphia: University of Pennsylvania Press, 1998) 143–159.

11. Gillian Rose, *Feminism and Geography. The Limits of Geographical Knowledge* (Minneapolis: University of Minnesota Press, 1993) 41.

12. For discussion of geography defined in terms of the cultural process, see Kay Anderson and Fay Gale, ed. *Inventing Places. Studies in Cultural Geography* (Melbourne: Longman Cheshire, 1992).

13. Stuart C. Aitken and Leo E. Zonn, "*Re*-Presenting the Place Pastiche," in *Place, Power, Situation, and Spectacle. A Geography of Film*, ed.

Stuart C. Aitken and Leo E. Zonn (London: Rowman and Littlefield, 1994), 6. See also the entire collection of essays *Text and Territory*, edited by Sealy Gilles and Sylvia Tomasch.

14. Anderson and Gale, p. 2.

15. W.J.T. Mitchell, "Imperial Landscape," in *Landscape and Power*, ed. W.J.T. Mitchell (Chicago: University of Chicago Press, 1994), 14.

16. Kathleen Mary Kirby, "Indifferent Boundaries: Exploring the Space of the Subject," Ph.D. diss., University of Wisconsin-Milwaukee, 1992, 29–33, 61.

17. Harvey Birenbaum, *Myth and Mind* (Lantham, MD: University Press of America, 1988) 56.

18. The representations offered by medieval romance poets captured the imaginations of their audience, if one take into account the number of manuscript copies made of any given work. According to this standard, *Parzival* and *Iwein* can be considered among the most popular German works of the early 13th century. Additional reception of the works were 'publicly' received by contemporary authors (Thomasin's *Der wälsche Gast* and Gottfried's *Tristan*, for example). There were not only literary but also artistic "copies" made, as can be seen in the Iwein-frescos at Schloss Rodenegg. For an extensive discussion of these visual representations, see James A. Rushing, Jr. *Images of Adventure. Ywain in the Visual Arts* (Philadelphia: University of Pennsylvania Press, 1995).

19. Frederic Jameson, "Cognitive Mapping," in *Marxism and the Interpretation of Culture*, ed. Cary Nelson and Lawrence Grossberg (Urbana: Univesity of Illinois, 1988), 353.

20. Jameson, 353.

21. Trevor J. Barnes and James S. Duncan, *Writing Worlds. Discourse, Text and Metaphor in the Representation of Landscape* (New York: Routledge, 1992), 6. According to the authors, landscape meets the four criteria for text established by Ricoeur: concretization when in written form, extension beyond author's intent, subjection to continual reinterpretation, implication for wide audience. (6) Conversely, texts may also function as landscapes.

22. In his introduction to *Landscape and Power*, Mitchell deals with the question of how landscape works as cultural practice. Mitchell's concept of landscape can be understood metaphorically, "as space, as environment, as that space within which 'we' (figured as 'the figures' in the landscape) find— or lose— ourselves." (2) In his article "Imperial Landscape," which appears in the same volume, Mitchell also discusses the conditions of the metaphorical landscape, "embedded in a tradition of cultural signification communication, a body of symbolic forms capable of being invoked and reshaped to express meanings and values. (14)

23. Daphne Spain even posits the existence of a "morphic language," a language expressed through form and placement that becomes one of the means by which society can be interpreted by its members. This language of spatial relations exists, in turn, only because of social processes that require certain spatial arrangements and thereby reinforce them. Daphne Spain. *Gendered Spaces.* (Chapel Hill: University of North Carloina Press, 1992), 17.

24. Barnes and Duncan, 5. This understanding of text derives from the authors' "postmodern" perspective. Of course, texts constitute discourses, and discourses subsequently gain authority as metaphors through the authority of the written word. Simultaneously a result of past and a participant in future discourse, the text offers an intersection of space and social process in which gender "becomes" and then comes ultimately into being.

25. Barnes and Duncan, 8. It is perhaps appropriate at this point to make a disclaimer about the almost exclusive use of the masculine pronoun when referring to the "poet" here and throughout the book. The identification of the poet as male simply reflects a medieval reality in which the majority of the poets were male. And this is certainly the case in the present discussion of Hartmann, Wolfram, and Gottfried. The interesting dynamic arises, of course, out of the inevitable interaction of the male poets and female audience members (or patrons).

26. Wolfgang Iser addresses the concept of construction in his essay "The Play of the Text," in *Languages of the Unsayable*, ed. Sanford Budick and Wolfgang Iser (New York: Columbia UP, 1989) 325–340. According to Iser, the author uses the existing world to create a text "made up of a world that is yet to be identified and is adumbrated in such a way as to invite picturing and eventual interpretation by the reader." (327)

27. For examination of literary explorations of various landscapes and worlds (both "real" and "imaginary") in other medieval genres, see Scott D. Westrem's anthology *Discovering New Worlds: Essays on Medieval Exploration and Imagination* (New York, London: Garland, 1991). At least two other studies have dealt with the shape and space of romance on a purely structural level. Karin Boklund discusses the versatility of a "topological" model for courtly romance in her article "On the Spatial and Cultural Characteristics of Courtly Romance," *Semiotica* 20 (1977): 1–37. Boklund focuses primarily on the boundaries between courtly and non-courtly space, internal and external cultural space. In *The Shape of the Round Table. Structures of Middle High German Arthurian Romance* (Toronto: University of Toronto Press, 1983), James A. Schultz defines six functions that determine the structure of Arthurian romance: the natural world, society, the other, the individual, the mediator/narrator, and the recipient/audience. The "causal and ideological" space in which romance

exists is created primarily by the intersection of society and the natural world, as the hero tries to navigate the boundary between the two. (49–52) One must not ignore another space, however, namely that defined by the boundaries of the narrative itself, "the space in which M [the mediator/narrator] draws material from the world of actions, transforms it into narrative, and presents it for the delight and edification of R [the recipient/audience]." (53) Schultz's detailed structural analysis unfortunately does not attempt a broader literary/historical interpretation of the structures he defines.

28. German scholar Helmut de Boor characterizes the places of Arthurian romance as a fantastical "nowhere" ("Nirgendslande") in *Die höfische Literatur: Vorbereitung, Blüte, Ausklang: 1170-1250. Geschichte der deutschen Literatur*, vol. 2 (Munich: C. H. Beck, 1964), 159. The geography of romance is not entirely unreal, however. Mention of real place-names—especially but not exclusively in French romance—support the illusion of "virtual" reality and certainly contribute to the verisimilitude of the work.

29. Phillips, 190.

30. Kimble, 128.

31. Rudolf Simek, *Erde und Kosmos im Mittelalter. Das Weltbild vor Kolumbus* (Munich: C. H. Beck, 1992), 80.

32. Simek, 91. The existence of Prester John could be attributed to reports of Nestorian Christians who lived in the Far East. (Kimble, 129) The purpose of the letter, probably written by a western European cleric, remains a matter of conjecture. Simek speculates: "In dieser Situation war es das Ziel des Verfassers, dem Römisch-Deutschen Kaiser ebenso wie dem Papst und der Kirche überhaupt das Idealbild einer theokratischen Herrschaft vorzuhalten, eine Utopie gegen das Europa seiner Zeit." (Simek, 91) The author may also have desired to create the impression of a powerful Christian ally in the East to encourage the hopes of the Europeans against the Islamic threat, thus laying the moral groundwork for another crusade. Though these two purposes failed, according to Simek, the letter was an unqualified literary success and widely translated.

33.

34. All English translations of Wolfram's *Parzival* are from *Wolfram von Eschenbach. Parzival*, trans. Helen M. Mustard and Charles Passage (New York: Vintage Books, 1961). In the counterfeit letter, Prester John describes the river Indus as it flows through his land of milk and honey: "In one of the provinces flows a river called the Indus which, issuing from Paradise, extends its windings by various channels through all the province; and in are found emeralds, sapphires, carbuncles, topazes...and many other precious stones." (From E. Dennison Ross, *Travel and Trav-*

ellers in the Middle Ages. ed. A.P Newton, 174; cited in Kimble, 130) These are terms that resonate in *Parzival*, in Wolfam's descriptions of Secundille's realm. (519,13–17).

35. It was the cataclysmic failure of the second Crusade that inspired the German cleric Konrad to write his *Rolandslied* around 1170, incorporating the events of the first and second Crusades into his interpretation of the French source. For an anthology of Middle High German crusade literature, see F.-W. Wetzlaff-Eggebert, *Kreuzzugsdichtung des Mittelalters* (Berlin: Walter de Gruyter, 1960).

36. Poets effected these changes by contributing to the "enlarging of the field of vision beyond the confines of highly localized interests," according to Southern. R.W. Southern, *The Making of the Middle Ages* (New Haven: Yale UP, 1953), here 221.

37. Sigrid Weigel, *Topographien der Geschlechter. Kulturgeschichtliche Studien zur Literatur* (Hamburg, 1990), 156.

38. See Geoffrey Ashe, "Topography and Local Legends," in *The Arthurian Encyclopedia*, ed. Norris Lacy (New York: Garland, 1986) 554–559. The romance map does not figure in the topography here, for its places do not seem to correspond to concretely identifiable geographic sites; on the contrary, as the author of this entry comments, "it is remarkable how little it has stamped itself on the landscape." Furthermore, most actual Arthurian sites are "in places that the romances never mention, often obscure and out of the way." (557)

39. See Ernst Robert Curtius, *European Literature and the Latin Middle Ages*, trans. Willard R. Trask (New York: Harper & Row, 1953) especially 183–202. The two are connected, of course. See also Schmid-Cadalbert, "Der wilde Wald. Zur Darstellung und Funktion eines Raumes in der mittelhochdeutschen Literatur," in *Gotes und der werlde hulde*, ed. Rüdiger Schnell (Bern: Francke, 1989) 24–47. He points out that the *locus amoenus* in romance often lies on the far side of the forest (33) and that, most importantly, the forest functions as a "Raumschwelle zwischen diesseitiger Welt und jenseitigem Ort." (35)

40. Rosemary Vermette, "Terrae Incantatae: The Symbolic Geography of Twelfth-Century Arthurian Romance," in *Geography and Literature. A Meeting of the Disciplines*, ed. William E. Mallory and Paul Simpson-Housley (Syracuse: Syracuse University Press, 1987) 145–161. According to Vermette, Arthurian romance of the twelfth century "reflects the Augustinian tradition that maintains that the world is the exterior sign of the Word of God, the divine principle. The world, therefore, is God speaking to man." (146–147)

41. Vermette, 157.

42. Vermette, 151. For Vermette, wilderness represents here an 'uncon-

scious' in a sense, not simply nature but also a state of mind that human beings have the power to change and thereby "contribute to the beneficial processes of cosmic fulfillment." (155) The concepts of order and chaos and their connection with romance space will be discussed later.

43. Corinne J. Saunders, *The Forest of Medieval Romance. Avernus, Broceliande, Arden* (Cambridge: D.S. Brewer, 1993) 80. In her third chapter, entitled "The Forest of Courtly Romance: The Twelfth Century," Saunders describes the forest as "a place of transformation, it offers both exile and idyll, pain and delight, the ideal yet the impossible escape." (94) Saunders focuses primarily on the examples of Yvain and the lovers Tristan and Iseut. While Yvain experiences madness and uncivilized nature in the forest, he is not abandoned to the wildness. (70) Tristan and Iseut experience the forest as a blissful yet fleeting escape from Mark's court.

44. Admittedly their focus is French.

45. Schmid-Cadalbert, 31. See also Jacques Ribard, "Espace romanesque et symbolisme dans la littérature arthurienne du XIIe siécle," *Espaces romanesques,* ed. Michel Crouzet (Université de Picardie, Centres d'Études du Roman et du Romanesque, Paris: Presses Universitaires de France, 1982) 73–82. Ribard understands the forest as a point at which the romance heroes abandon the familiar shores of civilization, with all of its limitations but also with its security, returning to an original human state: "C'est le lieu où l'on reprend, où l'on retrouve, sa dimension originelle d'*homme sauvage.*" (77) Ribard also discusses rivers and the sea as obstacles that, like the forest, constitute these spaces and enable passage through and to another world, the Other World ("dans un autre monde, dans l'Autre Monde," 79). He prefers to take an allegorical Christian view of the places and their function: "...pour renaítre à une autre Vie. Il faut, à l'école des alchemistes, transmuter le plomb de nos vies lourdement terrestres en l'or affiné d'une perfection intérieure." (80-81) Thus, romance space is more spiritual than real.

46. Derek Gregory, *Geographical Imaginations* (Blackwell: Cambridge MA and Oxford UK, 1994) 103–105. Gregory's categories also provide the organizational structure of Tomasch and Gilles' *Text and Territory.*

47. Michael Uebel, "On Becoming-Male," in *Becoming Male in the Middle Ages,* ed. Jeffrey Jerome Cohen and Bonnie Wheeler (New York: Garland, 2000), 368.

48. Uebel, 378.

49. Weigel uses the term "Verwilderte," (11) emphasizing the juxtaposition of the two places in which Creon and Antigone act and speak: the city and the wilderness. Weigel further explores the city/wilderness relationship with reference to foundation myths and depictions of cities in chapter 2. (149–179)

50. Weigel, 11.

51. Weigel, 11–12. For a similarly compelling analysis of women in-scribed paradoxically both as uncolonized wilderness and as innocent na-ture in the literature of the Enlightenment, see also Weigel's essay "Die nahe Fremde—das Territorium des 'Weiblichen.' Zum Verhältnis von 'Wilden' und 'Frauen' im Diskurs der Aufklärung," in *Die andere Welt. Studien zum Exotismus*, ed. Thomas Koebner and Gerhart Pickerkodt (Frankfurt: Athenäum, 1987) 171–199.

52. Weigel, *Topographien der Geschlechter* 121.

53. One should note that these oppositions are seldom exclusively pos-itive or negative. For the romance hero, for example, the 'uncultured na-ture' of the forest is a place to acquire a 'true' understanding of cultural or societal interaction. In that sense, it is more 'cultured' than the Arthurian court that the hero must leave.

54. Simon Gaunt, *Gender and Genre in medieval French literature.* (Cambridge: Cambridge UP 1995), 16.

55. Gaunt, 73.

56. Gaunt, 75. In German literature, this is clear in examples such as *Herzog Ernst* or the *Nibelungenlied*. Although *Herzog Ernst* displays enormous geographic variation, it does not gender this topography in any way. At least, since it is clear from the poet's depiction of the queen Adel-heid that she does have to act within fairly distinct boundaries, the poet does not make the nature of these boundaries an issue; in this sense, the representation of gender is rather neutral. As a hybrid of older epic and newer courtly traditions, the *Nibelungenlied* does confront gender issues. While it addresses (among other issues) questions of women, authority, and property (Frakes), it actively promotes traditional boundaries that are strictly gendered. See Jerold C. Frakes, *Brides and Doom. Gender, Prop-erty, and Power in Medieval German Women's Epic* (Philadelphia: Uni-versity of Pennsylvania Press, 1994).

57. This discrepancy brings Erich Auerbach to the conclusion that Chré-tien's *Yvain*, at least in comparison to the epic *chanson de geste*, represents "nicht dichterisch gestaltete Wirklichkeit, sondern ein Abweichen ins Märchen." See Auerbach's *Mimesis. Dargestellte Wirklichkeit in der abendländischen Literatur* (Bern: Francke, 1946) 134.

Other critics have likewise commented on the apparent unreality of the Arthurian world. In the second volume of his *Geschichte der deutschen Literatur von den Anfängen bis zur Gegenwart entitled Die hö-fische Literatur. Vorbereitung, Blüte, Ausklang. 1170-1250* (Munich: C.H. Beck, 1953), for instance, Helmut de Boor terms the Arthurian world "eine unwirkliche Märchenwelt." (65) Karl Bertau continues to em-phasize the fantasy theme in the 1970's, describing it as a "Phantasie- und

Wunschwelt" in *Deutsche Literatur im europäischen Mittelalter* (Munich: C. H. Beck, 1972), 95. For an earlier evaluation see also Vogt's *Geschichte der mittelhochdeutschen Literatur* (Berlin: Walter de Gruyter, 1922), 214. Although Auerbach evaluates romance unfavorably on the basis of its fairytale-like qualities, de Boor and Bertau do not. In this respect, they follow Gustav Ehrismann, who maintains that the courtly romances do not simply represent "bloßes Spiel der Phantasie zur Unterhaltung einer verfeinerten Gesellschaft." *Geschichte der deutschen Literatur bis zum Ausgang des Mittelalters. Zweiter Teil. Die mittelhochdeutsche Literatur. II. Blütezeit. Erste Hälfte* (Munich: C. H. Beck, 1927), 139. On the contrary, says Ehrismann, in these works "spielen mögliche und unmögliche Geschehnisse durcheinander"; the interplay of possible and impossible occurrences reinforces the interplay of a social awareness based in reality and the message of the ideal based on moral values. (Ehrismann, 140)

58. See, for example, Petra Kellermann-Haaf's *Frau und Politik im Mittelalter* (Göppingen: Kümmerle, 1986); Ursula Liebertz-Grün's "On the Socialization of German Noblewomen 1150-1450," *Monatshefte* 82 (1990): 17–37; Roberta Krueger, *Women Readers and the Ideology of Gender in Old French Verse Romance* (Cambridge: Cambridge UP, 1993).

59. Gründkorn discusses Thomasin in *Die Fiktionalität des höfischen Romans um 1200.* (Berlin: Erich Schmidt, 1994). Thomasin's reception of Arthurian romance shows his audience as a developing "textual community," according to Stock's definitions in *Implications of Literacy. Written Language and Models of Interpretation in the 11th and 12th Centuries* (Princeton: Princeton UP, 1983). Thomasin allows us a glimpse into the process of how medieval society interpreted these texts, which Texts distill diverse experiences and transmit them back into the social system: "As experience became richer, deeper, and more complex, it also demanded a different shape. Interpretive models evolved from texts, whether disseminated by verbal or written means, were increasingly called upon to provide explanations for behavioral patterns." (Stock, 455)

60. Thomasin, *Der wälsche Gast*, ed. Heinrich Rückert (Berlin: Walter de Gruyter, 1965) 1026–1028. All English translations from Thomasin are mine unless otherwise noted.

61. *Der wälsche Gast*, 1033–1061.

62. See Walter Haug, *Literaturtheorie im deutschen Mittelalter. Von den Anfängen bis zum Ende des 13. Jahrhunderts. Eine Einführung* (Darmstadt: Wissenschaftliche Buchgesellschaft, 1985). Haug devotes an entire chapter to Thomasin and the problem of fiction and truth. ("Fiktionalität zwischen Lüge und Wahrheit: Thomasin von Zerklaere und die Integumentum-Lehre," 222–235)

63. Haug sees here an application of the *Integumentum* principle from

Chartres. (*Literaturtheorie*, 232)

64. Liebertz-Grün does not mention Thomasin in her article "On the Socialization of German Noblewomen 1150-1450," but she comes to the same conclusion regarding the function of courtly literature in general.

65. *Mimesis*, 127.

66. C. Stephen Jaeger, *The Origins of Courtliness. Civilizing Trends and the Formation of Courtly Ideals 939–1210* (Philadelphia: University of Pennsylvania Press, 1985), 175 and 234. The book's premise is that courtesy/courtliness originates as "an instrument of the urge to civilizing" (9) not as an outgrowth of the process, as Norbert Elias would have it in his *Process of Civilization.*

67. Jaeger, 234.

68. Erich Köhler, *Ideal und Wirklichkeit in der höfischen Epik* (Tübingen: Max Niemeyer, 1956; 2d ed. 1970), 239.

69. Ursula Peters accuses Köhler of falling victim to circular reasoning in his attempts to derive the historical circumstances of romance from the literature itself. Ursula Peters, *Frauendienst. Untersuchungen zu Ulrich von Lichtenstein und zum Wirklichkeitsgehalt der Minnedichtung*, Ph.D. diss. Köln, 1970, 36. Using Hartmann's *Iwein* as an example, Ragotzky and Weinmeyer also demonstrate that Köhler's are specifically tailored to French courtly society. In addition, although Köhler wishes to establish the poles of ideal and reality as the permanent opposition that determines the structure of the romance ("Doppelwegmodell"), this does not necessarily hold, at least in *Iwein*. See Hedda Ragotzky and Barbara Weinmayer, "Höfischer Roman und soziale Identitätsbildung. Zur soziologischen Deutung des Doppelwegs im *Iwein* Hartmanns von Aue," in *Deutsche Literatur im Mittelalter: Kontakte und Perspektiven. Hugo Kuhn zum Gedenken*, ed. C. Cormeau (Stuttgart: Metzler, 1979), 249.

70. Hans Robert Jauß, "Alterität und Modernität der mittelalterlichen Literatur," *Alterität und Modernität der mittelalterlichen Literatur. Gesammelte Aufsätze 1956–1977* (Munich: Wilhelm Fink, 1977) 9–49.

71. Hans Ulrich Gumbrecht, "Wie fiktional war der höfische Roman?" in *Funktionen des Fiktiven*, ed. Dieter Henrich and Wolfgang Iser (Munich: Wilhelm Fink, 1983), 433.

72. The religious interpretation generally characterizes the scholarship until the 1950s. It has gradually been supplanted by the socio-historical approach introduced by Köhler as well as other modern theoretical methods.

73. This is the essence of Southern's account of the development from epic to romance in *The Making of the Middle Ages*. Southern's analysis lends *aventiure* more significance than de Boor's description of it as "zweckentkleidete Tat." (de Boor, 65)

74. Meaning is revealed in the contrast between MHG *sin* and *meine*, OF *sen* and *matière*. In this context, Vinaver points out the similarities between exegesis and the narrative strategy employed in the romance, which represents the first appearance of such a method in the secular sphere. Eugene Vinaver, *The Rise of Romance* (Oxford: Oxford University Press, 1971), 16–17.

75. Vinaver, 31. In fact, it was "the poetry that assumed in the reader both the ability and the desire to think of an event in terms of what one's mind could build upon it, or descry behind it." (23)

76. D. H. Green, *Medieval Listening and Reading. The Primary Reception of German Literature 800-1300* (Cambridge: Cambridge UP, 1994). See particularly chapter 9.

77. Green, 256.

78. Green, 257. For a general discussion of literary fiction as a development of the twelfth century renaissance, see Per Nykrog, "The Rise of Literary Fiction," *Renaissance and Renewal in the Twelfth Century*, ed. Robert L. Benson and Giles Constable (Cambridge: Harvard UP, 1982) 593–612.

79. Walter Haug, "Wandlungen des Fiktionalitätsbewusstseins vom hohen zum späten Mittelalter," in *Entzauberung der Welt. Deutsche Literatur 1200-1500*, ed. James F. Poag and Thomas C. Fox (Tübingen, 1989) 1–18. Haug refers to romance as "ein bewusstes strukturelles Experiment." (8)

80. John M. Clifton-Everest, "Fingierte *warheit*," *Von Aufbruch und Utopie. Perspektiven einer neuen Gesellschaftsgeschichte des Mittelalters. Für und mit Ferdinand Seibt aus Anlass seines 65. Geburtstages*, ed. Bea Lundt und Helma Reimöller (Köln: Weimar, Wien: Böhlau, 1992), 203: "Erkenntnis der 'wahren' Fiktion." Though his treatment of the topic is by no means as comprehensive as Green's, Clifton-Everest also concerns himself with the self-conscious nature of literary fiction in the classical period of Middle High German literature, focusing primarily on *Iwein*, *Parzival*, and *Tristan*.

81. Haug comments on the situation as it develops in the later Middle Ages: "Die fortschreitende Entzauberung der Welt drängte in der Literatur zu einer härteren Auseinandersetzung zwischen der sinnlos werdenden oder gewordenen Wirklichkeit und den sinngebenden Strukturen der fiktionalen Entwürfe." ("Wandlungen des Fiktionalitätsbewußtseins vom hohen zum späten Mittelalter," 8)

82. emphasis mine; Haug, *Literaturtheorie*, 106. The authors manipulate elements of truth and probability in an experiment, whereby the improbable is what highlights the "true" sense behind the fiction.

83. Roland Barthes describes text this way in his essay "From Work to

Text," in *Debating Texts. Readings in 20th Century Literary Theory and Method*, ed. Rick Rylance (Toronto: University of Toronto Press, 1987), 118. With its emphasis on the text as discourse, this definition can encompass texts transmitted both orally and in written form, expanding the applications of Iser's theory to medieval texts.

84. The reality of texts is always one that is constituted by the texts; as a result, textual reality is inevitably a reaction to reality 'outside': "**Die Wirklichkeit der Texte ist** immer erst eine von ihnen konstituierte und **damit Reaktion auf Wirklichkeit.**" (Iser, "Die Appellstruktur der Texte," 232; emphasis mine) Iser reiterates this concept of textual reality in his most recent essay, emphasizing that "as a rule, literature addresses the problems inherent in the systems referred to [in it]" ("Do I Write for an Audience?").

85. "Das heißt, fiktionale Rede *selektiert* aus den verschiedensten Konventionsbeständen, die sich in der historischen Lebenswelt vorfinden. **Sie stellt diese so zueinander, als ob sie zusammengehörten.**" (Iser, "Die Wirklichkeit der Fiktion," 287; emphasis mine)

86. As described by Michel Foucault in "The Means of Correct Training," in *The Foucault Reader*, ed. Paul Rabinow (New York: Pantheon, 1984), 196. In this case, our homogeneous social group is the late twelfth-century nobility. Foucault is concerned in this essay with the effects of an oppressive normalizing gaze that differentiates and judges its objects. (197) Foucault's argument cannot apply strictly to courtly romance, for one would then have to consider romance as a type of disciplinary apparatus or a technique of surveillance. While I believe that such an assessment would be too extreme, it is certainly the case that the poet does exhibit a distinct normalizing gaze by which he in turn unmistakably directs the gaze of the audience.

87. Iser reasons: "Denn ein fiktionaler Text bildet nicht die in der Lebenswelt herrschenden Normen- und Orientierungssysteme ab, vielmehr selektiert er nur aus ihren Beständen und erweist sich durch die Anordnung gewählter Elemente gegenüber solchen Systemen als kontingent." (Iser, "Die Wirklichkeit der Fiktion," 294)

88. Caroline Bynum has observed the strong concern for conformity among religious groups in the twelfth century in *Jesus As Mother. Studies in the Spirituality of the Middle Ages* (Berkeley: University of California Press, 1982) 105.

89. See Roberta Krueger, *Women Readers and the Ideology of Gender in Old French Verse Romance* (Cambridge: Cambridge UP, 1993), 26.

90. Bindschedler has suggested the medical metaphor for Gawan, arguing that he serves as doctor for the courtly soul, which he proves in his actions at the *Schastel marveile* as well as in his relationship with Orgeluse,

as we shall see in chapter 3. See Maria B. Bindschedler, "Der Ritter Gawan als Arzt oder Medizin und Höflichkeit," *Schweizer Monatshefte für Politik, Wirtschaft, Kultur* 69 (1984): 729–743.

91. Curiously, Wolfram does not mention whether this inability extends to communication between members of the same group, i.e. among men or among women. Queen Arnive and her daughters speak with one another, and they also speak with Gawan. The court is suffering because the two genders cannot interact:

> si wârn ein ander unbekant,
> unt beslôz se doch ein porte,
> daz si ze gegenworte
> nie kômen, frouwen noch die man.
> dô schuof mîn hêr Gâwân
> daz diz volc ein ander sach;
> dar an in liebes vil geschach. (637, 20–26)

[They were unknown to each other, though a single gate closed them in, and had never exchanged a word with each other, the ladies and the men. My lord Gawan gave the word that this company should meet, and they were very pleased.]

Wolfram von Eschenbach, *Parzival,* ed. Karl Lachmann. (Berlin: Walter de Gruyter, 1965) 637, 20–26. All further references to Parzival will appear in the text.

92. Joachim Bumke focuses on the rehabilitative effect Gawan has on the isolated and divided court at the *Schastel marveile.* See Joachim Bumke, "Geschlechterbeziehungen in den Gawanbüchern von Wolframs *Parzival,*" *Amsterdame Beiträge zur älteren Germanistik,* vol. 38–39 (1994): 105–121.

93. E. Jane Burns, for instance, gives an example of the kind of criticism medievalists should not practice. See E. Jane Burns, *Bodytalk. When Women Speak in Old French Literature* (Philadelphia: University of Pennsylvania Press, 1993). Burns critiques poststructuralist readings of medieval texts that are looking for 'the feminine' or female subjectivity because they tend (like the medieval theologians) "to efface the specificity of women as speaking subjects behind the creation of a mythic and silenced woman." (14) And such an approach will not take the investigator very far.

94. Notable among the fields in which feminist approaches have been successfully employed are theology, history, and literature. Feminist scholarship in the field of literature continues to flourish on many fronts.

95. Elaine Showalter, "Introduction: The Rise of Gender," in *Speaking of Gender* (New York: Routledge, 1989), 1.

96. Elizabeth Fox-Genovese, *Feminism Without Illusions. A Critique of Individualism* (University of North Carolina Press: Chapel Hill, 1991) 120.

97. Showalter, 2; emphasis mine.

98. See Alan Frantzen, "When Women Aren't Enough," *Speculum* 68 (1993), 452.

99. Showalter, 10. See also Mary Poovey's review of Showalter's anthology, "Recent Studies of Gender," *Modern Philology* 88 (1991): 415–420. Poovey expresses her reservations about the "new age of gender" in which "feminists— both women and men— must now discover how to reconceptualize the politics of oppression. (420) As Alan Frantzen wryly puts it: "We can see that the debate about 'gender' is another sign of the fear that, once more, 'women' will be left out." (Frantzen, 453)

100. Fox-Genovese, 162.

101. Joan W. Scott, "Gender: A Useful Category of Historical Analysis," *American Historical Review* 91 (1986): 1053–1075. Scott's goal is to provide a working theory and/or definition for understanding how an analysis of gender "provides a way to decode meaning and to understand the complex connections among various forms of human interaction." (1070)

102. Scott broadly divides the theories to date (the article appeared in 1986) into three major categories: 1) attempts to explain and determine the origin of patriarchy, 2) combinations of feminist critique and Marxist analysis, and 3) interpretations according to various schools of psychoanalysis. (1057–1058)

103. Scott, 1067. With respect to the construction of identity and the task of historians, Scott continues: "Historians need instead to reexamine the ways in which gendered identities are substantively constructed and relate their findings to a range of activities, social organizations, and historically specific cultural representations." (1068)

104. Julia Kristeva, "Women's Time," *Feminist Theory: A Critique of Ideology*, ed. Nannerl O. Keohane, Michelle Z. Rosaldo, and Barbara Gelpi (Chicago: University of Chicago Press, 1982), 39. Kristeva goes on to maintain that language marginalizes women by placing the power of symbolic meaning in the hands of men. (41) One can thus view this conceptualization of meaning as spatial and connect it with Irigaray's spatial understanding of gender in her *Ethics of Sexual Difference*, where she asserts that "the feminine is experienced as space, but often with connotations of the abyss and night . . ." (Irigaray, 7)

105. Anthropologists and historians have also noted this connection between the sexual and the social. See, for example, Sherry B. Ortner and

Harriet Whitehead's "Accounting for Sexual Meanings," the introductory essay in the anthology *Sexual Meanings: The Cultural Construction of Gender and Sexuality,* ed. Ortner and Whitehead (Cambridge: Cambridge UP, 1981). Ortner and Whitehead view the sexual, which they term the erotic, and the social as inextricably intertwined: "The erotic and the social are too deeply mutually implicated [in the area of sexual meanings] to be passed off as entirely different dimensions." (24) See also Danielle Jaquart and Claude Thomasset, *Sexuality and Medicine in the Middle Ages,* trans. Matthew Arnold. (Oxford: Polity Press, 1988). Jacquart and Thomasset emphasize the importance given to control of the erotic experience in discourses about sexuality in the Middle Ages. As they say, "sexual activity was linked to fear in the medieval West... The most dangerous moment was when man encountered woman . . ." (5–6)

106. Scott mentions in this context myths of purification or pollution, for example, or the representation of woman by the figures of Eve and Mary in western Christian tradition. (Scott, 1067)

107. Limitations are imposed by religious or political doctrines, for example. (Scott,1067)

108. Although Scott warns against what she observes as the universalizing tendency of psychoanalysis, she does admit its usefulness in an examination of "the ways in which gendered identities are substantively constructed." (1068) She cites recent biographical studies as successful examples of this aspect of gender analysis. (1069)

109. Scott, 1069. Here, Scott seems very close to Catherine MacKinnon. MacKinnon describes her *Feminist Theory of the State* (Cambridge, London: Harvard UP, 1989) as a study of "gender as a form of power and power in its gendered forms."(xi) For MacKinnon, gender inequality creates a social hierarchy of men over women and this is based on a sexual inequality, perpetuated by the men who benefit from it: "sexuality is a construct of male power: defined by men, forced on women, and constitutive of the meaning of gender." (128)

110. Gerda Lerner, *The Creation of Patriarchy* (New York: Oxford UP, 1986) 200. The second volume was published under the title *The Creation of Feminist Consciousness* (New York: Oxford UP, 1993).

111. Referring to the German approach to "historische Frauenforschung," Gisela Bock proposes the combination of a feminist analysis of history with a historical discussion of gender similar to Scott's approach. See Gisela Bock, "Geschichte, Frauengeschichte, Geschlechtergeschichte," *Geschichte und Gesellschaft* 14 (1988): 364–391. Bock advocates the study of history from both male and female perspectives, since an apparently neutral approach is not satisfactory: "Geschichte ist nicht nur Geschichte männlicher, sondern ebenso auch

weiblicher Erfahrung. Sie sollte nicht nur in männlicher oder scheinbar geschlechtsneutraler Perspektive studiert werden, sondern auch in weiblicher und geschlechtergeschichtlicher Perspektive." (390) Thus one utilizes the full range of perspectives necessary for adequate interpretation.

112. See Judith Lorber, *Paradoxes of Gender* (New Haven: Yale UP, 1994).

113. In *Women, Production and Patriarchy in Late Medieval Cities* (Chicago: University of Chicago Press, 1986), Martha Howell examines the changing economic situation in the late Middle Ages, in which the intersection of gender and economic structures eventually resulted in women's departure from the market. See also the work of Natalie Zemon Davis in *Society and Culture in Early Modern France. Eight Essays* (Stanford: Stanford UP, 1975); Merry Wiesner *Working Women in Renaissance Germany.* (New Brunswick, N.J.: Rutgers University Press, 1986) and *Women and Gender in Early Modern Europe.* (Cambridge: Cambridge UP, 1993); Heide Wunder, *"Er ist die Sonn', sie ist der Mond." Frauen in der frühen Neuzeit.* (Munich: Wilhelm Fink, 1992); Lynne Tatlock, ed. *The Graph of Sex and the German Text: Gendered Culture in Early Modern Germany 1500–1700* (Amsterdam: Rodopi, 1994)

114. Joan Cadden, *Meanings of Sex Difference in the Middle Ages. Medicine, Science, and Culture* (Cambridge: Cambridge UP, 1993).

115. Thomas Laqueur, *Making Sex. Body and Gender from the Greeks to Freud* (Cambridge: Harvard UP, 1990). Laqueur was one of the first who attempted to illustrate the historical process of the construction of sex, not simply gender.

116. Cadden, 167.

117. Cadden, 202. Examples would include figures such as the Amazon and 'mother' abbots. See Bynum's *Jesus as Mother* for a detailed discussion of the latter.

118. The study of sexuality and medicine done by Jacquart and Thomasset provides an excellent companion to Cadden's book.

119. For a detailed discussion of medieval marriage practices and theories, see James Brundage, *Law, Sex, and Christian Society in Medieval Europe* (Chicago: University of Chicago Press, 1987). Peter Brown also deals with sexuality, marriage, and virginity as religious issues that resonate throughout the Middle Ages from their beginning in late Antiquity in *The Body and Society. Men, Women, and Sexual Renunciation in Early Christianity* (New York: Columbia UP, 1988).

120. According to Jacquart and Thomasset, a primary motivation for the discussions of sexuality in the Middle Ages was the desire to control sexuality and the erotic experience. (4) The Middle Ages were a dangerous time, and this danger was represented most intimately by sexual activity

and passion and woman: "The most dangerous moment was when man encountered woman: so many moralists had warned him of the dangers he was running! Woman was the creature of discontinuous time; she was a threat during menstruation, often out of bounds during pregnancy and the nursing period and prohibited on holy days." (5–6)

121. Historian David Herlihy did extensive research in the area of the medieval family and its structure. See in particular his article "The Making of the Medieval Family: Symmetry, Structure, and Sentiment," *Journal of Family History* (1983): 116–131, as well as his book *Medieval Households* (Cambridge: Harvard UP, 1985).

122. The following studies offer an overview of the topic: Philippe Ariès, "Die unauflösliche Ehe," in *Die Masken des Begehrens und die Metamorphosen der Sinnlichkeit. Zur Geschichte der Sexualität im Abendland*, ed. Philippe Ariès und André Bejin (Frankfurt: Fischer, 1984 [orig. 1982]) 176–196; Christopher Brooke, *The Medieval Idea of Marriage*. (Oxford: Oxford UP, 1989); Georges Duby, *The Knight, the Lady, and the Priest The Making of Modern Marriage in Medieval France* (New York: Pantheon, 1983) as well as *Medieval Marriage. Two Models From Twelfth-Century France*, trans. Elborg Forster (Baltimore: Johns Hopkins UP, 1978) and most recently *Love and Marriage in the Middle Ages*, trans. Jane Dunnett (Chicago: University of Chicago Press, 1994); Jack Goody, *The Development of Family and Marriage in Europe* (New York: Cambridge UP, 1983); David Herlihy, "The Medieval Marriage Market," *Medieval and Renaissance Studies VI*, 1976; Michael Müller, *Die Lehre des hl. Augustinus von der Paradiesehe und ihre Auswirkung in der Sexualethik des 12. und 13. Jahrhunderts bis Thomas von Aquin. Eine moralgeschichtliche Untersuchung* (Regensburg: F. Pustet, 1954); Michael M. Sheehan, "Choice of Marriage Partner in the Middle Ages: Development and Mode of Application of a Theory of Marriage," *Studies in Medieval and Renaissance* N.S. 1 (1978): 1–33.

123. McNamara, *"Herrenfrage"* 20.

124. Thus, McNamara uses Hildegard of Bingen as well as the monastery at Fontevrault as examples of women's authority recognized. (14) Penny Schine Gold also discusses these changes in terms of visual images in *The Lady and the Virgin* (Chicago: University of Chicago Press, 1985). See also Claudia Opitz, "Vom Familienzwist zum sozialen Konflikt. Über adelige Eheschließungspraktiken im Hoch- und Spätmittelalter," in *Weiblichkeit in geschichtlicher Perspektive*, ed. Ursula A. J. Becher and Jörn Rüsen (Frankfurt: Suhrkamp, 1988) 116–159. Opitz discusses the creation of new spaces and the elimination of others, concentrating on "welche Auswirkungen dies auf die Struktur und Gestaltung der Gesellschaft insgesamt hatte" (141) specifically in the area of marriage

practices.

125. Thus, the modern critic need not succumb to the temptation of merely repeating the platitudes about misogyny in the Middle Ages. For representative discussions of the topic, see the following: Katherine Rogers, *The Troublesome Helpmate. A History of Misogyny in Literature* (Seattle: University of Washington Press, 1966); Andrée Kahn Blumstein *Misogyny and Idealization in the Courtly Romance* (Bouvier: Bonn, 1977); R. Howard Bloch, *Medieval Misogyny and the Invention of Romantic Love* (Chicago: The University of Chicago Press, 1991).

126. Jacques Le Goff, *The Medieval Imagination* (Chicago: University of Chicago Press, 1988), 85.

127. Pathak, 432.

128. In the final chapter of *The Implied Reader*, Iser comments that "literature gives us the chance to formulate the unformulated." (294)

129. These boundaries are, however, ultimately restricted, especially for female characters.

130. See Daniel Paul Terkla, *The Centrality of the Peripheral: Illuminating Borders and the Topography of Space in Medieval Narrative and Art, 1066–1400*, (Ph.D. diss., University of Southern California, 1992). Terkla's work will be discussed further in the next chapter.

131. Illich, 118.

CHAPTER 2

The Topography
of Hartmann von Aue
Negotiating Spaces and Power
in *Erec* and *Iwein*

> *Space is fundamental in any exercise of power.*
> —Michel Foucault[1]

> *Hartman der Ouwære*
> *âhî, wie der diu mære*
> *beide ûzen unde innen*
> *mit worten und mit sinnen*
> *durchverwet und durchzieret!*
> *wie er mit rede figieret*
> *der âventiure meine!*
> *wie lûter und wie reine*
> *sîniu cristallînen wortelîn*
> *beidiu sint und iemer müesen sîn!*
> —Gottfried von Straßburg[2]

De Boor characterizes the place of Arthurian romance as a fantastical "Nirgendslande" compared with the geographical reality of the epic, which seem to make a conscientious effort to remain within the confines of actual places. In contrast to the epic, romance inspires its audience to allow their "Phantasie" to roam freely over an imaginary landscape. In terms of gender topographies, one could say that romance (as fiction) can be much more creative with the processes of othering that figure so prominently for Weigel and Gregory. Through various depictions of the other and of encounters with the other, romance can be creative as it depicts not only processes of 'othering' but also the concommitant processes of 'becoming.'[3]

It is Chrétien de Troyes, of course, who first brings the Arthurian material into the realm of fiction. Unlike Geoffrey of Monmouth or Wace, he does not attempt to maintain that his narratives represent "actual history." Instead, Chrétien displays a narrative persona consciously aware of the fiction he is creating.[4] Hartmann von Aue, as the author of the first Arthurian romance in German, introduces the genre of romance and its fiction to his patrons, adapting the material for them.[5] Such adaptability is, in fact, one of the reasons that the 'matter of Britain' gained international popularity over the course of the Middle Ages[6] and that it remains so popular today. Then, as now, the fiction of the romance allowed the poet to modify the stories for his audience. In addition, within the parameters of the romance's characteristic *Doppelwegstruktur*, the fiction allowed the poet great freedom to deal with various kinds of spaces, and with those who inhabit or move in those spaces, as well as with the margins of those areas.[7]

In fact, the relationship between the peripheral and the central remains a defining characteristic of the romance, if not *the* defining characteristic of the genre.[8] The process of *aventiure*, which structures this movement between the center and the margins, provides a background for experiences to occur away from the court, experiences that cannot be accommodated by courtly society and that might otherwise threaten the stability of the court.[9] Through the travels of the "chosen" hero,[10] the margins of fictional geography "become the central loci of signification" in the romance, creating tension between the conventional center (namely the Arthurian court) and the geographically peripheral "centers of attention."[11] The Arthurian romance relies "heavily on the knight errant moving along the road away from the court and seemingly accidentally meeting people and creatures whom he might never meet if he stayed at Arthur's court, the conventional center."[12] To a certain degree, then, the romance could be understood as a text that actually lacks a center. More precisely, since the hero's meetings are contrived by the poet/author, the romance presents a text that is immediately involved in re-presenting the world as the audience might expect to see it. Through the hero, the text renegotiates or rearranges the relationships between the center and the periphery.

Terkla's comprehensive study of the centers and the peripheries of medieval art and literature does not view these spaces specifically through a gendered lens. Terkla does discuss the role of Meleagant's sister as an opposing figure in the Lancelot-Guinevere constellation of Chrétien's *Chevalier de la Charette*. The introduction of Meleagant's sister functions to problematize the centrality of adultery in the courtly love topos, juxtaposing the private world of adultery with the public geography of the chivalric romance "to show that the two are fundamentally incompatible and, indeed, potentially destructive."[13] Thus, although Terkla does not specifically address the idea, his discussion implies the gendering of the spaces of and between the center and the periphery. Focusing a gendered lens on these spaces and particularly on the figures who move through them does prove revealing, however.

Certainly, the journey has long been recognized as a fundamental structural principle of romance. Ott sees the structural principles of the courtly novel as "Ortsveränderung ,"[14] which is the most basic definition of travel. Since travel has not only a destination but also a point of departure, it must also be defined as movement between two places; it cannot take place "im leeren Raum."[15] And it is in the romance that movement becomes meaningful, where this movement can also accommodate gender differences. In this respect, romance differs from lyric. Ingrid Kasten has examined the motif of travel in medieval lyric as opposed to narrative, noting the following distinction in the two genres:

> Bedeutsam ist in diesem Zusammenhang, daß in der Lyrik von Reisen nur im Blick auf Männer die Rede ist. Frauen spielen beim Abschied zwar oft eine zentrale Rolle, aber sie selbst haben nicht teil an der Mobilität des Mannes, sondern werden allenfalls symbolisch mit auf die Reise genommen. Ihre Reiseerfahrungen erfüllen sich daher in dem Schmerz der Trennung oder in der Sehnsucht nach einem in der Ferne weilenden Mann.[16]

The fate of the women in lyric is inactivity. They watch and wait while their men travel, journeying along with them only in spirit.

This is not the case in romance. The reason for this difference has to do with the fact that the topography of the romance is constructed within a less rigid framework than that of the epic. In a comparison of Gawan and Parzival, Lilo Szlavek offers a way of looking at this difference with respect to what may be termed "determinate" and "indeterminate" geography. While Gawan's travels keep him within the ordered confines of courtly society, as he journeys from castle to castle, Parzival's path to the Grail "ist aber nicht geographisch zu ermitteln."[17] Gawan's path leads him toward well-defined localities that have a distinct shape and place;

Parzival's path leads him through geographically indeterminate spaces: through forests and wilderness that are not part of ordered society and that cannot be described specifically. The vaguely defined spaces in which Parzival finds himself, however, connect him to women in the work who move relatively freely within as well as to and from such places: Herzeloyde, Sigune, and Cundrie. Hartmann's Lunete and Enite also share this indeterminacy of location at various points in their poems as well. It appears that the placement of women in the geographically indeterminate spaces of romance alleviates the need for the women to assume inappropriate gender roles. From these spaces, women can move with, speak with and offer direction to the men who need their help; yet these women and their actions do not threaten to pull apart the fabric of the social order. The 'other' can be encountered and at the same time safely (if only imaginatively) contained. In this way, the romance can embrace and support Iser's "panorama of possibilities," offering an array of Foucauldian *heterotopias*. *Heterotopias*, defined as "those singular spaces to be found in some given spaces whose functions are different or even opposite of others,"[18] become a range of simultaneous and subverting spaces that create a sense of multiple possibilities existing together and resonating with one another. In this context, Hartmann's romances open new territory for exploration, concentrating on gender roles and the landscapes they occupy. In this chapter, I will examine the three most prominent landscapes Hartmann depicts (the forest, the court, and the *locus amoenus*) and the roles of the men and women who move in and through them. *Erec*'s Enite, for example, does participate integrally in the mobility that her partner demonstrates; indeed, the journey that Erec and Enite undertake together makes up the major portion of the work. By contrast, *Iwein*'s Laudine remains in her own realm while Iwein journeys with his lion companion to find his way back to her. The women in *Erec* and *Iwein* exhibit considerable authority in the social and physical spaces that they occupy, and they thereby (to borrow Derek Gregory's term) draw attention to the poet's process of spatialization. Through their speech and actions, Hartmann's women play an important role in and (perhaps more importantly through) various spaces in the works.[19] In this way, for the most part indirectly, they also encourage the audience to consider the ways in which the spatial arrangements participate in the process of representation (Gregory) with respect to the construction of gender. In the passage from *Tristan* cited at the beginning of this chapter, Gottfried praises Hartmann for his verbal artistry, his unique ability to capture in his work the meaning of *aventiure,* which shines through the decorative ("durchverwet und durchzieret") words of his poetry as clear as crystal. As Gottfried says, this clarity functions to communicate the figurative as well as the literal sense of the *aventiure* unequivocally to Hartmann's audience. Hartmann's artfully constructed plots also reflect and subsidize this clarity through their well-structured composition. Hartmann's narrative also supports "der âventiure meine" in both *Erec* and *Iwein* through the delineation of appropriate spaces for both male and female characters in each text. Upon closer analysis, however, Hartmann's use of space(s) allows for the possibility of ambiguities that belie the clarity of the presentation that Gottfried deems so worthy of praise.

EREC: "WAN BÎ DEN LIUTEN IST SÔ GUOT"

Plot Synopsis: Erec, son of King Lac, has joined Arthur on the hunt for the White Stag. He is accosted by an insolent dwarf who insults the honor of Queen Guinevere. Erec continues on his pursuit of the stag and comes to a town where he seeks shelter for the night. He stays with an impoverished knight (there is a status difference between German and French) who has a beautiful daughter, Enite. Erec enters the tournament at Tulmein and wins Enite as his prize. He takes her first to Arthur's court, where they are wed, and then to his father's court at Karnant. King Lac abdicates in favor of his son and new wife, in order to honor his son's new status and success as a knight. Erec, however, does not understand how to act as king. He and Enite would rather while away the day in their bedchamber. Enite hears some of the court gossip about their behavior but does not tell Erec; he overhears her lamenting their misfortune and, in his shame, forces her to leave the court with him—to travel until they have regained their reputations. Enite is forbidden to speak on pain of death.

The couple embarks on a series of adventures, which can be divided into two groups of three adventures each. The first adventures test Enite's resolve to keep silent or speak in the face of danger to herself and her husband (the robbers, Count Galoein, ? and the fight with the dwarf Guivreiz). The couple recuperate from the fight with Guivreiz at Arthur's court. Then they set out again on a second series of adventures that focus on Erec's ability to 'hear' the cries of those in need (the giants, Count Oringles,

and a second encounter with Guivreiz). These adventures culminate in Erec's apparent death in the forest and his subsequent
rescue of Enite from the unwanted attentions of Duke Oringles
of Limors. The climax of the narrative is the episode of the *Joie
de la court* in which Erec confronts the grim Mabonagrin in the
garden of Brandigan. Erec defeats Mabonagrin, thereby bringing
an end to twelve long years of grief and despair in that realm.
Erec and Enite then return in triumph to Karnant and take up
their crowns again. They live happily ever after and receive their
heavenly rewards upon their deaths.

Placed near the conclusion of *Erec*, the *Joie de la court*
episode depicts a space that illustrates these possibilities most
clearly. Because of a rash promise that he made to his lady,
Mabonagrin has withdrawn to the garden of Brandigan at her request. The quintessential *locus amoenus*, this tree-filled garden
("boumgarte") is a place of stunning beauty; the flowers fill the
air with their scent, the birds sing sweetly, and the fruit trees are
in bloom:

> swer ouch zuo dem selben zil
> von geschihte in kam,
> der vant dâ swes im gezam
> von wünneclîcher ahte,
> boume maneger slahte,
> die einhalp obez bâren
> und andersît wâren
> mit wünneclîcher blüete:
> ouch vreute im daz gemüete
> der vogele süezer dôz.
> ouch enstuont dâ diu erde niht blôz
> gegen einer hande breit,
> diu enwære mit bluomen bespreit,
> die missevar wâren
> und süezen smac bâren.[20]

[Whoever chanced to go in there discovered all sorts of delights to
please him: many kinds of trees that bore fruit on one side and were
filled with lovely blossoms on the other, beautiful songs of birds that
made his heart rejoice, and sweet-smelling flowers of manifold col-
ors that covered the earth until not a hand's breadth of it was bare.]

The wonders of this place compel all who enter to forget all cares and all sorrows, overwhelmed by the beauty of the garden's sights and sounds:

> hie was der wâz alsô guot
> von dem obeze und von der bluot
> und der vogele widerstrît
> den si uopten zaller zît
> und selh diu ougenweide,
> swer mit herzeleide
> wære bevangen,
> kæme er dar in gegangen,
> er müeste ir dâ vergezzen. (8730–8738)

[The odor of the fruit and the blooms, the contesting voices of the birds on every side, and the sight itself were all so charming that anybody who entered with a heavy heart would soon forget his troubles.]

In his study of medieval landscapes, Derek Pearsall considers the garden in *Erec* the best example of a medieval garden landscape.[21] Indeed, this *locus amoenus* lacks only a spring to meet Curtius' criteria.[22] Brandigan's beauty is, however, enhanced by another very important addition to the *topos*, namely a woman. After glimpsing the splendid tent, "rîch und wol getân," ("beautiful and splendid," 8903) Erec catches sight of

> ein wîp, als im sîn herze jach,
> daz er bî sînen zîten
> âne vrouwen Ênîten
> nie dehein schœner hete gesehen.
> wan der muoste man eht jehen
> daz ir wünneclîcher lîp
> geprîset wære über elliu wîp
> diu dô wâren oder noch sint. (8927–8934)

[the most beautiful woman that [he] had ever seen—except for Enite, who was more lovely, it must be admitted, than any other woman of that time or this.]

The poet goes on to describe this woman with the same care and perhaps excessive attention to detail as he devoted to his portrayal

of the garden and the tent (to which Hartmann devotes more than
twenty lines of description in 8903–8925); in other words, the lady
is 'just' another object of beauty that is found in this magical and
exceptional place. The comparison of the lady and Enite's beauty
later reveals a double meaning, for the woman in the garden is actually related to Enite as a cousin (and their faults are similarly
related).

Pearsall notes that the landscape often functions to provide a
form of natural imagery that supports a rhetoric of love; however,
the landscape frequently illustrates an inverse rather than a direct
relationship with the love depicted in its environs: "in other words,
the delights of the landscape do not always correspond to the legitimate delights of love."[23] And this is indeed the case in the garden of *Joie de la court*. Hartmann has indicated from the first mention of this adventure that something is amiss here. For twelve long
years, the events that recur in this garden have caused much suffering, leaving eighty grieving widows and a despairing lord to
lament their misfortune. Clearly, this place cannot represent a paradise. Two physical features of the garden reinforce its threatening
quality. First, it seems to be magically surrounded by something intangible: neither wall nor trench, neither moat nor hedge can be
seen or felt around it. The narrator vouches for this:

> ich sage iu daz dar umbe
> weder mûre noch grabe engie
> noch in dehein zûn umbevie,
> weder wazzer noch hac,
> noch iht daz man begrîfen mac. (8704–8707)

[I tell you that there was neither a wall nor a moat around it, nor
was it enclosed by hedge, fence, water, or anything tangible except a trail.]

In fact, there is only one narrow hidden path that leads into the
garden that only few know of. Hartmann, the poet, later reveals
what literally envelops the garden: a cloud so thick that no one can
penetrate it except by finding the narrow path. (8745–8753) Sec-
ondly, the beauty of the tree-filled garden also contrasts sharply
with the oaken posts that those entering with Erec find soon after-
wards, displaying the heads of Mabonagrin's vanquished foes.

Defeating Mabonagrin, Erec frees not only the knight but also
his lady, both of whom have remained hitherto isolated in the gar-

den. The new Erec, having learned his own lessons and having now successfully faced his final challenge,[24] cannot understand why Mabonagrin would have consented to remain in the garden in the first place; as Erec says "wan bî den liuten ist sô guot." ("for it is very nice to be with other people," 9438). All members of society have a duty and an obligation to serve the others around them, especially if they hold a position of power and authority. The garden, a place of beauty and pleasure, is incapable of serving the greater social good and therefore it must be negated, at least symbolically done away with and absorbed somehow into acceptable courtly space.

And it is no coincidence that this is a place of potential female agency. For Karen Pratt, Hartmann's depiction of the lush garden of Brandigan represents one manifestation of the distinct male bias that Hartmann adds to his source. Pratt unfavorably compares Hartmann's *Erec* with Chrétien's original; through a narrative strategy that "smacks of . . . phallogocentrism."[25] Hartmann transforms Chrétien's "multi-layered, polysemic romance . . . into an ideologically less ambiguous work, in which the harmonizing narratorial voice leaves little scope for dissent or questioning."[26] Chrétien allows Maboagrain's *amie* to tell her version of their story in her own voice and therefore one can interpret this garden as a place of female agency, according to Pratt. In this way, Chrétien portrays "the complexities of relations between the sexes" more clearly than Hartmann,[27] where the story is told exclusively by Mabonagrin. I maintain, however, that the German poet does not completely eradicate the complexity either. In Hartmann, too, Mabonagrin's lady is the one responsible for his retreat from the courtly world. Unwilling to face the prospect of losing him, she elicits a fateful promise from him. She asks that they remain in the garden together, since "wir haben hie besezzen/daz ander paradîse." ("we are sitting [in] a second garden of Eden," 9541–9542) And she continues:

> hie wil ich inne
> mich nieten iuwer minne.
> diz ist diu gâbe der ich bite:
> hie beherte ich wol mite
> deich iuwer müge belîben
> âne angest vor andern wîben:
> daz ir hie inne mit mir sît,
> wir zwei . . . (9550–9557)

[This is where I want to enjoy your love. The gift I ask of you is
one which will ensure that I remain yours and have no need to
be afraid of other women. It is that you stay in the park with me,
just the two of us together . . .]

She literally rules this space, having created it through her request
in the first place, and she essentially keeps Mabonagrin prisoner
within it.[28] This arrangement has a devastating effect on the society around the garden, symbolized by the heads on the posts that
encircle it, and such an affront to courtly order cannot be allowed
to continue. For this reason, the narrative effectively works to
eliminate this space of the lush garden of Brandigan in favor of a
more appropriate social space, gendered male and represented by
Erec and Mabonagrin. Hartmann uses the stagnated relationship
between Mabonagrin and his lady in the garden, a relationship
that threatens the social order, as a means to underscore the instability of the erotic attraction that initially endangered Erec and
Enite.[29] By privileging the married state of Erec and Enite over the
passionate lawlessness of Mabonagrin and his lady in the garden,
Hartmann seems to advocate the conjugal relationship, among
other things, as a way to limit and contain female space. The conjugal relationship simultaneously limits and permits female space.
It is the only space in which the Middle Ages would consistently
sanction any kind of "equality" between partners, upheld in legal
and theological circles.[30]
    Clearly space is thematically important in *Erec*. The "liberation"
of garden of Brandigan represents a culminating negotiation, as it
were, that sets all to rights and reintegrates previously isolated and
censured members of society. This is the point at which, upon de-
parting from the garden as a foursome, Erec and Enite as well as
Mabonagrin and his lady enter into a state/space of societal 'being'—
their trajectory of becoming is nearing the end that (at least for Erec
and Enite) it finally reaches at Karnant. The narrative allows the garden to disappear, having established the limits female space in the garden's dramatic representation of otherness. That space was home to
man's 'other,' sexually and symbolically, and the place exemplified
the danger that man might fall prey to her whims as Mabonagrin did.
Yet, in *Erec*, Hartmann also allows the opportunity for the negotiation of other spaces even as his narrative ultimately limits them. The
space of the garden of Brandigan is clearly marked as female space
because of the presence and agency of Mabonagrin's lady, though this
space finally proves inappropriate. Several other alternatives are of-

fered, however, which entail negotiation. Hartmann creates spaces
both for men and for women, keeping them separate but also allowing for the possibility that they may intersect. In this way, other negotiations are allowed in the two other major areas of *Erec*'s topography: the castle at Karnant and the forest.

The life that Erec and Enite lead at Karnant would seem to
support Hartmann's limitation of the female role in the conjugal
relationship. Technically, they have been together since the tournament at Tulmein, at which Erec defeated Iders for the spar-
rowhawk prize. They were also wed at Arthur's court afterward.
At Karnant, however, they are on their own; thus, the castle at
Karnant frames the story of Erec and Enite as a couple. It is there
that they begin and end their life together, carrying out the atten-
dant responsibilities of rulership with varying degrees of success.
At first, the couple clearly seem unable to fulfill their social obligations at court. Though they have been given the throne by Erec's
father, the inexperienced couple does not know how to earn or
maintain that authority, instead falling victim to the sin of *verligen*
(which is a Middle High German translation of sloth). Though it
obviously can happen only because both members of the couple
like one another's company, this is consistently seen by Hartmann
to be <u>Erec's</u> sin. Hartmann describes the situation using masculine
subject pronouns almost exclusively:

> Êrec wente sînen lîp
> grôzes gemaches durch sîn wîp.
> die minnete er sô sêre
> daz er aller êre
> durch si einen verphlac,
> unz daz er sich sô gar verlac
> daz niemen dehein ahte
> ûf in gehaben mahte. (2966–2973, emphasis
> mine)

[Erec turned to a life of ease because of his wife, whom *he* loved
with such passion that, to be with her, *he* gave up all striving for
honor and became indolent to the point where no one could respect him.]

Erec enjoys great contentment ("gemache") on account of his wife
("durch sin wîp"), fleeing his people for more pleasurable diver-
sions in the bedchamber ("mit sînem wîbe er dô vlôch/ze bette von

den liuten," 2949–2950).[31] Hartmann seems to imply that, as the active party in this relationship and the one who does the *minnen*,[32] Erec should know better than Enite what consequences would ensue as a result of this neglectful behavior, namely that he would lose his honor at court ("daz niemen dehein ahte/ûf in gehaben mahte" 2972–2973). Enite's role is a passive one here: she is the object her husband loves immoderately,[33] the woman whose presence causes the seduction of man's reason and better judgment.[34] Hartmann has constructed Enite at this point in the relationship as an Eve-figure, as a negative and potentially destructive element of Erec's consciousness, medieval Christian man's ultimate 'other .'[35] This is the exact opposite of the socially desirable relationship, of course. The courtly ideal of marriage (at least in Middle High German literature) promoted an "equal" partnership, a relationship which could incorporate the passion of *minne* and in which each partner fulfilled her or his role appropriately. Hartmann even comments that Enite realizes her guilt in the matter of Erec's disgrace and their apparently failed partnership,[36] though she does not bring the problem to his attention because she fears to lose him. (3007–3012) At this juncture, Enite foreshadows the life of her nameless cousin in the garden of Brandigan, though her cousin certainly does not share Enite's initial passivity.

The analogy to the garden leads one to characterize this episode at Karnant as a similar illustration of inappropriate female space, or at least an inappropriate use of space on the part of the female. In this sense, it is significant that in their fight, Erec and Mabonagrin must all but physically destroy Brandigan. The garden is a threat to society in that it excludes society completely; its beauty is an affront to the social order, a façade that hides abominable behavior. The passage at 9162–9166 shows the audience this destruction, describing how the grass is trampled and the fact that the garden ends up looking like it might in the middle of winter. The eroticism of spring—essential to the ambiance of *minne*—has been vanquished.

The danger of the garden and the initially inappropriate use of space at Karnant are corrected and balanced by parallel spaces that illustrate an appropriate existing balance or a process of negotiating it. This becomes clear in a comparison of the court at Karnant with that of Arthur. The Arthurian court is a place where appropriate spaces are clearly marked for men and for women. With the court at Karnant, Arthur's court frames the action of the couple's story. The Arthurian court represents a fixed point in the narrative,

literally a place to "check back in" and show the progress of the
process of becoming; it is a place that gives form and purpose to
the negotiations for power and space that occur in the forest. The
Arthurian court provides the poet with the opportunity to show
how they are working, how the negotiations are progressing, to
structure them. It provides both Erec and Enite with the opportunity to put the "private" negotiations that occur in the forest into
practice in the social setting of the court.

This is illustrated, for example, by the interactions that occur
between the queen Ginover and Enite. When Erec first brings his
bride to the court after the tournament at Tulmein, Enite is still
dressed in the tattered clothes she was wearing when he met her.[37]
Ginover takes Enite aside to her private quarters, "in ir heimlîche."
(1533) There, she personally oversees Enite's toilette, ensuring that
she is properly attired for the wedding. (1538–1578) For a second
time, as Erec and Enite find respite at Arthur's court from their
first set of adventures, the queen again cares for Enite in Ginover's
own private quarters:

> Ginovêr diu künegîn
> tete süezen willen schîn,
> dô ir vrouwe Ênîte kam.
> in ir phlege si si nam
> und vuorte si von danne
> besunder von ir manne
> in ir heimlîche.
> dâ wart vil wîplîche
> von in beiden geklaget,
> vil gevrâget und gesaget
> von ungewonter arbeit
> die vrouwe Ênîte erleit.
> sô kumberlîcher sache
> ergazte si mit gemache
> diu vil edel künegîn
> die wîle und daz mohte sîn. (5100–5115)

[The queen Ginover showed her goodness when Enite came to
her. She took her and led her away from her husband to her private chambers. In the manner of women, they sympathized together, and much was asked and told of the unaccustomed hard-
ship that Enite had suffered. For all this misery, the queen com-
pensated her through comfort as long as she could.]

In this separate and private place ("heimlîche"), Ginover can offer Enite the comfort and support that the younger woman is denied in her husband's company.[38] They speak in the way of women ("vil wiplîche"), they enter into dialogue ("[dâ wart...] vil gevrâget und gesaget") within a comforting setting (implied by the words "mit gemache") that offers Enite a welcome respite "von ungewonter arbeit." The privacy or separateness of the conversation is emphasized also by the fact that the poet, while he allows the audience to know the general topic of conversation, gives no further details as to its specific substance. In this passage, the grammar again reinforces this privacy/exlcusion of the audience in the use of passive constructions in lines 5107–5108 (*geklaget, gevrâget, gesaget*), that appear after the women retire to Ginover's "heimlîche." In a sense, Enite performs Ginover's role for her cousin at the conclusion of the *Joie de la court* episode, reestablishing the prescribed separation from Mabonagrin by reasserting the bond between women.

> manec wehselmære
> sageten si dô beide
> von liebe und ouch von leide
> und gesselleten sich dâ mite
> nâch wîplîchem site.
> von lande und von ir mâgen
> begunden si do vrâgen
> und sich mit rede engesten
> und sageten swaz si westen. (9707–9715)

[The two exchanged many words of happiness and unhappiness and sealed their friendship as women do. They asked one another about their families and countries and became closer through their words and told everything they knew.]

In this way, "nâch wîplîchem site," both women demonstrate their newfound understanding of proper space. They then rejoin their men and leave the garden, entering once again into the larger society to take their places there.

In the new Karnant, the spaces have been realigned and the boundaries readjusted. The previous hardships are appropriately transformed now: "ze gemache unde zêren/und ze wünne manecvalt." ("comfort, honor, and manifold slendor", 10113–10114) The new realignment subordinates Enite, however, in the space occupied by the couple at the conclusion. The moderation that has returned to the marriage relationship is Erec's, who knows now to fulfill Enite's wishes "niht sam er ê phlac/ dô er sich durch si ver-lac." ("not as it was formerly when he became indolent becaue of her," 10122–10123) The crown also belongs to him; Enite does not receive her own crown in their coronation ceremony, unlike her French counterpart.[39] The first Karnant represents inappropri-ate female space; the new Karnant has become appropriate male space.

The courts of Erec and Arthur, as well as the garden of Brandi-gan, are stationary fixed points in the narrative that also function to reinforce (or even to "fix") the boundaries and the roles that are renegotiated and realigned in the third major space of the narra-tive: the forest. In this first German Arthurian romance, the nego-tiations are fairly well-defined and surprisingly well-balanced. As Hartmann demonstrates, Enite's incomplete understanding of her own role plays no small part in precipitating the crisis that leads to their departure from Karnant. She laments her husband's misfor-tune as any woman would ("si begunde dise swære/harte wî-plîchen tragen," 3009–3010), and yet she remains silent until one day Erec hears her lamenting when she thinks he is asleep. Sharon Farmer refers to Orderic Vitalis, noting that wives were praised when they used their charms to influence their husbands, particu-larly in a spiritual way.[40] Unfortunately, Enite does not seem ma-ture enough to realize her obligation to act more spiritually, and thus she cannot take advantage of space that is allotted her in order to show Erec where he belongs.[41] In this way, both Erec and Enite reveal an improper understanding both of female and of male space, which renders them unable to recognize suitable and necessary boundaries.

While critics have generally agreed that Erec's task is to dis-cover for himself the correct relationship needed between court and king, Enite's role has not been so clear. Much of *Erec*'s critical history has been characterized by attempts to ascertain the respec-tive guilt or innocence of the protagonists, to determine how much blame should be attributed to Erec and how much to Enite. Many scholars, following Hugo Kuhn's assessment of the purity of Enite's character, have faulted Erec for a variety of reasons.[42] Ranawake believes that it is ". . .not Erec's *minne*, but his sloth, *verligen*, constitutes the actual guilt that he has to atone for before he can return to his royal position."[43] Erec's marriage simply ag-gravates a pre-existing condition, an inherent tendency toward sloth. Thus, Ranawake effectively relieves Enite of any responsibility in the matter.[44] For Fisher, Erec does not suffer from any innate failing; however, he is guilty of making Enite suffer, an offense for which he must atone.[45] Refuting Cramer,[46] Fisher maintains that, even though Enite may live in poverty before Erec finds her, it is clear from her beauty that she is worthy of nobility.[47] It is Erec who treats her beneath her station. Fisher offers a passive image of Enite,[48] as does Pratt. According to Pratt, Hartmann encourages a passive view of women and discourages any debate on gender issues in that he focuses most of his attention on Erec's activities and his rehabilitation. The woman plays a subordinate role as part of an ideal couple "in which the male should be supported and aided in his royal duties and knightly pursuits by the love of a good woman."[49]

There are critics, however, who maintain a certain equality of the relationship between Erec and Enite, illustrated by the fact that both of them have to learn; this is why they undergo the central journey(s) of *Erec* together. According to Hrubý, Hartmann maintains Enite's innocence and attempts to explain Erec's uncourtly behavior: "Daran läßt sich Hartmanns entschiedene Absicht erkennen, die Abenteuerfahrt nicht bloß als Erecs, sondern auch als Enitens Prüfungsfahrt darzustellen."[50] Because Hartmann insists that Erec is testing Enite as a wife not as his lady (as would be expected in a case of "Troubadorminne"), Hrubý believes that Hartmann wishes to depict "ein reales Eheverhältnis"[51] in the late twelfth century. On the question of Enite's guilt, Wapnewski points out that two standard adventure-types are depicted here: the trial of the knight and the 'Treueprobe ,' the one applicable to Erec and the latter to Enite.[52] A central problem for Wapnewski is that Hartmann does not make readily apparent the reason why Enite must undergo a trial of her loyalty. After all, Erec is the one who seems to feel the need to test her, not the narrator. But then Wapnewski continues:

> Nicht weil sie schuldig ist, muß sie auf Leidensfahrt. Wohl aber haben diese Dichter, das alte Treuprobenmotiv unwillig mitschleppend, ihm einen neuen Sinn verliehen: Ereks und Enites Liebe war nicht 'wirklich ,' nicht errungen, sondern rasch erworben, nicht verdient, sondern schnell gewährt, hatte keine steigernde und läuternde Kraft, war nicht in *arebeit* zum eigenen Besitz geworden, begrenzte sich in ichhaftem Selbstgenuß—nunmehr muß sie sich 'erproben.' "[53]

Once again, Wapnewski emphasizes the self-less social ideal of love that Hartmann seems to advocate in his work. The sensual erotic love of the newly married couple cannot be maintained in the society in which they must live. Tax concurs, seeing the problem with the couple as one of *concupiscentia*, "indem die Einstellung des Paares gegenüber der ehelichen Liebe so verkehrt (*inordinata*) war, hatten beide sich der *concupiscentia*, damit aber der Gewalt des Teufels ergeben."[54] For Willson, Erec and Enite have lost their *geselleschaft*, their loss indicated by their anti-courtly behavior, in other words their "distance" from one another and from society in general. Willson connects this to their alienation from the "brotherhood of man".[55] According to Gentry, both Erec and Enite have to learn their proper roles and responsibilities and earn their places as rulers. They both have parallel series of adventures, in which "Erec is educated to show his qualities of compassion and justice, and Enite is educated to evidence the virtues of loyalty and steadfastness."[56] McConeghy does not necessarily see both partners educated to assume their places as rulers. Rather, Hartmann focuses on the interdependence of marriage, makes it "the key to the relationship and underscores it with Erec's physical intervention to save Enite's life from Oringles and then Enite's verbal intervention to save Erec's life in the battle with Guivreiz."[57] At the conclusion, both Erec and Enite return to their rightful places: he as leader with public honor, she as good wife.

The space in which these 'rightful' places and their boundaries can be best negotiated, the space where Erec and Enite "become" [rulers], is in the forest. The greater part of the narrative follows Erec and Enite as they undergo their adventures in this geographically indeterminate and often menacing place, isolated from the rest of courtly society. The indeterminacy is indicated by the fact that Erec and Enite, in typical *aventiure*-fashion, do not seek a path through this wilderness. The path finds them, as it were. After they leave Arthur's court for their second series of adventures, for instance, Hartmann tells us that the direction of their travels does not matter:

> nû reit der ritter Êrec
> als in bewîste der wec,
> er enweste selbe war:
> sîn muot stuont niuwan dar
> dâ er âventiure vunde. (5288–5292)

[Now the knight Erec rode where the path directed him, he did

not know himself where. He only wanted to go to a place where
he could find *aventiure*.]

The relative "inaccuracy" of medieval landscape depictions in
courtly literature has been well documented. Gruenter says of both
Erec and *Parzival* that the depiction of distances is just as incon-
sistent as in medieval painting: objects that are supposed to be far
away appear near and vice versa.[58] The indeterminacy, the literal
and figurative lack of perspective,[59] contribute also to the depiction of the forest as an unfriendly and menacing place. The wilderness symbolizes a place of peril, "wo sich das Tugendsystem zu
entfalten und zu bewähren hat, das mit dem Handlungsträger
demonstriert werden soll."[60]

Hartmann communicates its danger through the (albeit few)
adjectives he chooses to describe his forest:

> nâch âventiure wâne
> reit der guote kneht Êrec.
> nû wîste si der wec
> in einen *kreftigen* walt:
> den hâten mit gewalt
> drîe roubære. (3111–3116)[61]

[Emphasis mine. The brave knight Erec rode directionless, seek-
ing adventure. The path led him into a thick forest. Three thieves
brutally controlled it.]

The "kreftic" is also reinforced here through mention of the
robbers who hold this forest in their power and who soon make
their appearance. The forest is also "wilt," as described in the
scene in which Erec leaves Enite to investigate a woman's cry for
help:

> des endes huop sich Êrec
> durch rûhen walt âne wec
> unerbûwen strâze,
> wan daz er die mâze
> bî des wîbes stimme nam,
> unz daz er rehte dar kam
> dâ si von klage michel leit
> in dem *wilden* walde erleit. (5312–5319)

[Emphasis mine. Erec rode in the direction [of the woman's voice] through a thick and pathless forest and unmarked routes and he oriented himself only by the woman's voice until he came to the place where she had suffered great sorrow in the wild forest.]

According to Schmid-Cadalbert, this is the only passage where a "raumqualifizierendes *wilt*" [62] appears in *Erec*. The wildness of this space is also conveyed by the uncultivated path ("unerbûwen strâze") that Erec and Enite travel here. The isolation of this space resonates with the cries of those unfortunates who find themselves in its midst, like the woman in the above passage or like Enite in her lament for her (as she believes) dead husband:

> ir wuof gap alselhen schal
> daz ir der walt widerhal.
> nû enhalf ir niemen mêre
> klagen ir herzesêre
> niuwan der widergelt
> den ir den walt ûz an daz velt
> mit gelîchem galme bôt. (5746–5752)

[Her cry was so loud that the forest echoed. But, other than the echo that the forest and fields threw back at her, no one helped her lament her heart's wound.]

The wood echoes with Enite's cries, further isolating her by reminding her (and the audience) of the absence of other human voices and of the human civilization that could offer her comfort. [63]

For both Erec and Enite, the forest represents a place of maturation, a place of becoming: Erec learns to put his prowess to use serving others (becoming a knight), and Enite learns to speak and assert herself at appropriate moments (becoming a queen). The "soziale Programmatik" [64] in Hartmann's *Erec* deals with the growth and development of those who must eventually assume the responsibilities of leadership—and this includes the queen as well as the king. In view of Hartmann's equal treatment of both major characters here (and, although equal must necessarily be understood in the context of the twelfth century, the degree of equality depicted here is still impressive) it seems particularly noteworthy that Hartmann portrays Enite's development first.

When they first set out, Erec forbids Enite to speak on pain of death. When they ride away from Karnant, Hartmann says that Erec:

> . . . gebôt sînem wîbe
> niuwan bî dem lîbe,
> der schœnen vrouwen Êniten,
> daz si muoste vür rîten,
> und verbôt ir dâ zestunt
> daz ze sprechenne ir munt
> zer reise iht ûf kæme . . . (3094–3100)

In this way, Erec attempts to punish Enite for what she has done to him. This creates a dilemma for her when she notices the band of robbers riding towards them as they travel through the forest. Erec is wearing his armor and cannot see very well; consequently, if she does not speak out and warn him, he will remain unaware of the danger until it is too late. Confronting the very real possibility of losing her life if she disobeys Erec's command, she is forced to think of Erec instead of herself and finally speaks out of love for him, as well as out of a sense of "triuwe" and obligation; after all, his life has greater value than hers. (3149 ff.) When the robbers return in greater number, Enite must make another similar decision and does, after another soul-searching monologue. (3353–3377) Her "disobedience" naturally angers Erec, but Hartmann leaves no doubt that she has chosen the right course of action. Fortune and God also support her (3460–3467) and keep her from harm. The question of whether to speak or not arises yet again when Enite receives a proposal of marriage from count Galoein, but she eventually does confess this to Erec. (3995 ff.) Erec is upset, to say the least; however, if Enite had not spoken, they both would have lost their lives, for the count had threatened to attack the inn where they were spending the night if Enite refused him. (4122)

The culmination of Enite's learning process occurs shortly after this incident with the count. Erec does battle with giants who have been abusing a knight and his lady—this marks the beginning of his development, as he seeks for the first time not to gain honor but to help others in need. But he faints from the wounds that he receives from his opponents, causing Enite to believe that he is dead. In an incredible monologue of over three hundred lines (5743–6110), she pours out her grief and fear alone in the woods. Angry with God for having taken Erec and left her, she offers herself in his place. She calls to the wild animals to come and relieve her of her misery, and when they fail to respond to her plea, she decides to take her own life. The honor and wealth she possesses as a great lady in the eyes of the world can mean nothing to her if God has left her to suffer such anguish. (6031–6041) The world calls her a queen and showers her with good fortune, but God has taken Erec from her and she no longer wishes to live. One has to remember the complete image here, though: Erec lies on the ground at her feet, Enite takes up *his* sword. In this picture, Erec is still present, and the tools of patriarchy are still the only ones available (i.e. his sword and a phallic symbol) to Enite as she determines to end her life. And, of course, she is prevented from doing this by another male voice, namely that of Oringles. Interestingly, though not surprisingly, death is also represented as a male actor in this play. Enite literally woos him, despite the fact that it is against custom:

> vil lieber Tôt, nû meine ich dich.
> von dîner liebe kumt daz ich
> alsô verkêre den site
> daz ich wîp mannes bite.
> nâch dîner minne ist mir sô nôt.
> nû geruoche mîn, vil reiner Tôt.
> ouwê wie wol ich arme
> gezim an dînem arme!
> dû bist vil wol ze mir gehît.
> wan nimestû mich enzît? (5886–5895)

[Dear Death, I mean you. It comes from my love for you that I act against custom and, as a woman, woo a man. I demand your love. Take me dearest Death. Oh, how I long for your embrace. I am a fitting bride for you, why don't you come for me now?]

Providence intervenes in the person of count Oringles just as Enite seizes Erec's sword and prepares to use it. The count appears just in time to stop her and escort her along with Erec's "corpse" to his castle. There Enite suffers still further, for the count beats her when she refuses to marry him but once more her voice saves her and Erec, for her laments rouse him from his faint and he rushes to her aid.

The incident at Oringles' castle marks the turning point for both Erec and Enite. They have faced the prospect of losing everything, they have returned from the brink of death, and they now have to start over together—on foot, no less, for they no longer have a horse. Hartmann calls them at this point "disen ellenden," (6699) the exiles who must go in search of their home. Enite, who has proven herself since the journey began, has at last earned the title of queen, and Hartmann specifically calls her "künegin" in line 6732 for the first time.[65] She has shown herself worthy of her rank and of Erec; now he must prove himself worthy of his title. His final test comes, of course, at the *Joie de la court*, where Enite plays a role only through her absence and her silence. Neither her presence nor her voice is required in this context, though each is certainly appropriate in others.[66] One of the purposes of the narrative was to make Enite and the audience aware of the distinction. According to McConeghy, the scene at the 'new' Karnant shows that

> the husband's traditional dominance over his wife, demanding obedience and silence, is abandoned in favor of an equal part-nership in the private sphere, where the woman's voice con-tributes as much to the health and survival of the marriage as does her husband's physical might and prestige.[67]

This "equal partnership" may not be equal in every space, but it can successfully negotiate a balance that enables it to survive in a world where the boundaries have been distinctly marked. In seek-ing this balance, Erec and Enite find their ways into appropriate 'being' at court and "bî den liuten," where the poet hopes they can continue to live in honor and in the hope of eventually receiving their heavenly reward

> und sô daz im got gebete
> mit veterlîchem lône
> nâch der werlde krône,
> im und sînem wîbe,
> mit dem êwigen lîbe. (10125–10129)

[so that God with fatherly praise gave him and his wife, after the worldly crown, that of eternal life]

Order is restored. Enite's being is once again fixed as she is incor-porated into Erec's identity as his wife ("sînem wîbe"). In this re-gard, the journey of Erec and Enite does not reflect the equality and reciprocity of sexual desire that Baldwin attributes to ro-mance. [68] Inequality remains, as illustrated by the repudiation both

of the garden and of the 'inappropriate' relationship it fosters.
However, one cannot 'be' without 'having become.' The fascinating aspect of Hartmann's topography in *Erec* is that both Erec and
Enite have their own opportunities to negotiate their paths of becoming over the course of the narrative, and they actively do so.

IWEIN: A WOMAN'S PLACE IS HER CASTLE

> Plot synopsis: King Arthur is celebrating yet another lavish Pen-
> tecost feast. After the king and queen have retired to bed, five
> knights (Iwein among them) listen Kalogrenant's tale of his ad-
> ventures at in the forest of Breziljan. Hearing of the extraordi-
> nary fountain, Iwein decides that he cannot resist seeing this
> wonder for himself—nor can he resist the challenge of the un-
> known knight. He goes to the spring and does battle with the
> knight, pursuing the knight to his castle after mortally wounding
> him. Unwittingly trapped between the gates of the portcullis,
> Iwein is rescued and hidden by the maid Lunete from capture.
> Smitten by love for Laudine, the widow of the slain knight
> Ascalon, Iwein eventually reveals himself with the help of
> Lunete, and Laudine agrees to marry him, for he can keep her
> lands safe. At the insistence of Gawein, who urges him to avoid
> Erec's fate, Iwein asks Laudine's leave to absent himself from her
> court to pursue the knightly life. She allows him to leave on the
> condition that he return in one year.
>   Iwein does not keep his promise, and Lunete appears to de-
> nounce him before Arthur's court and return Laudine's ring to
> him. In shock, Iwein is overcome, and he rushes off into the for-
> est. He eventually finds his way back to civilization and begins
> his career anew as the Knight with the Lion, after saving a lion
> from battle with a serpent (or dragon). Together, the master and
> the lion have several adventures; Iwein's main task is to save
> Lunete from a death sentence imposed by Laudine as punish-
> ment for Iwein's negligent behavior. Finally, Iwein returns to the
> fountain and issues a challenge to Laudine, who has in the mean-
> time promised to marry the Knight with the Lion as the only
> knight who can protect her domain. She agrees to take Iwein
> back after he reveals himself to be none other than that same
> Knight with the Lion.

Hartmann carefully outlines the spaces in *Erec*, encouraging the negotiation of gender roles that ultimately follow those outlines closely. Any ambiguities are effectively removed by the end of the narrative: Enite's assertive speech is relegated to the 'private' sphere of the forest or the bedchamber, the subversive garden has been destroyed, Mabonagrin and his lady are reintegrated into courtly society. *Iwein*, Hartmann's second (and last) Arthurian romance, offers a marked contrast to the structured boundaries of *Erec*. Written around 1205, *Iwein*'s narrative expands the horizon of possible spaces and trajectories through them. This extended panorama of possibilities has particularly intriguing results for the female characters in *Iwein*, which are more numerous than in *Erec*.[69] At first glance, this expansion seems rather pardoxical; in contrast to *Erec*, *Iwein* does not tell the story of a couple's progress. Erec and Enite, however one wishes to deal with the problem of blame or guilt, do move together through the forest from the Arthurian court and back again as they grow into their respective roles. Although Laudine does not accompany Iwein on his adventures, Laudine's role is no less central than that of Enite. In fact, Laudine's court replaces the Arthurian court as a point of reference for Iwein during the second half of the work. The fact that Iwein returns to this place and remains there, outside of the Arthurian realm, combines with other signals to send a more ambivalent message at the conclusion of *Iwein* than Erec's simple affirmation of the social good: "bî den liuten ist sô guot." Hartmann seems to present an optimistic vision of the future at the end of *Iwein*, after Iwein and Laudine have been reunited through the persistent efforts of Lunete:

> swâ man unde wîp
> habent guot und lîp,
> schœne sinne unde jugent,
> âne ander untugent,
> werdent diu gesellen
> ein ander behalten,
> lât diu got alten,
> diu gewinnent manege süeze zît. (8139–8147)

[When man and woman have health, wealth, beauty, wit, youth, and no bad traits; and when these companions cherish each other; and when God lets them grow old; they win a great deal of happiness.[70]]

The narrator betrays a hint of uncertainty in these last lines, however, ending the above passage with the comment: "daz was hie allez wænlîch sît." ("presumably this was all found here in the future," 8148[71]) This "wænlîch" ("presumably"), which is repeated in line 8189 ("ez was guot leben wænlîch hie") and echoed in the "ouch wæn ich" of 8157, communicates a sense of doubt on the part of the narrator. While he thinks that life was probably good following the events of the story just related, he nonetheless implies that he is not certain. The reunion itself also seems questionable, in light of the fact that Laudine's promise to marry the knight with the lion was once again made and kept under duress; her oath literally traps her. This ambivalence underlies the narrative as a whole, supported by the spaces in which Hartmann's characters must negotiate their places and their roles. More so than in *Erec*, the threat of impropriety or of inappropriate boundaries is expressed in images of constriction or of imprisonment. An examination of the spaces that *Erec* and *Iwein* share—the Arthurian court and the forest—shows that Hartmann changes their function slightly, thus altering their message.

The Arthurian court is portrayed as almost a caricature in the opening scene of *Iwein*. As a caricature, it becomes a kind of anti-courtly 'other.' Arthur, depicted here not as a powerful ruler but a tired host, retires with his queen after a Whitsun celebration, leaving six of his knights (Iwein, Keii, Gawein, Dodines, Segremors, and Kalogrenant) to discuss their adventures. The caricature becomes most apparent in the story that Kalogrenant tells of his unfortunate journey to a fountain, an undertaking that becomes a withering commentary on the traditionally Arthurian concept of *aventiure*, offered most bluntly in the form of a seemingly naive query made by the wild man: "âventiure? waz ist daz?" ("Adventure? What is that?" 527) The weakness of the court is further emphasized in another major incident later in the romance that has, in turn, drastic implications for several others. Seeking to pacify an irate guest, Arthur makes a rash promise, only to discover that the visitor intends to abscond with the queen.[72] Keii and Kalogrenant, among others, attempt to recover Ginover in Gawein's absence, but they do not succeed. Consequently, when Gawein returns to the court, he immediately sets out to rescue the queen. (4716 ff.) Unfortunately, this action deprives the rest of the kingdom of their champion's services, leaving those in need to suffer. One of these is Lunete, who unjustly awaits execution for her part in arranging Laudine's mismatched marriage with Iwein, who proved himself an irresponsible defender of the land. When Iwein comes upon her in the chapel, he asks her why Gawein, "der ie nâch vrouwen willen schein/ie ranc und noch tuot," (who has always done whatever is requested by the ladies... who has always striven to please them?" 4280–4281) has not come to her rescue. She replies that he was not available, having gone to free the queen. (4285–4302) Another who suffers because of the court's incompetence is the lord besieged by the giant Harpin. Since this lord's wife is Gawein's sister, he should have been able to depend upon Gawein's aid in his dilemma, but Gawein had to go after Arthur's queen. (4730–4739) It is left to Iwein to remedy both situations, which he eventually does.

These episodes illustrate the impotence of the Arthurian court; in his depiction of this court in *Iwein*, Hartmann implies that it cannot perform the same exemplary/model function that it does in *Erec*: not for men or women, not for rulers or knights. It does not function to establish boundaries, as one does not find the same sense of separate male/female spaces as in *Erec*. In fact, the topography of *Iwein* takes the familiar spaces (Arthurian court, other court, garden, forest), rearranges them, and alters the spatial relationships of people to and through those spaces. If anything, the court seems more male-centered in *Iwein*. Hartmann also does not configure *Iwein*'s forest as a space for women here, at least not in the way that it becomes a place of growth for Enite. Women like Lunete and the daughter of the Count of the Black Thorn ride through a rather benign wilderness, remaining curiously unharmed and unchanged. There are also the two young women who ride through the country looking for a knight to defend the younger daughter of the Count of the Black Thorn in the quarrel with her sister. (5625 ff.) Their experiences show that such travel is not, however, without its dangers. The younger daughter herself searches for the knight with the lion until she falls ill. (5761–5770) The kinsman who cares for her sends his own daughter to continue her search along cold and dark paths (5780 ff.), finally meeting with Iwein and success. The female characters do move through the forest, but it nonetheless remains predominately a male domain. Two types of men encounter and "engage" the forest: the Arthurian knights, whose comprehension of it seems limited to a flawed understanding of *aventiure*; and Iwein, the only character in the work who experiences the forest as a limen, as a place of becoming such as we encountered in *Erec*.

This forest represents a much more powerful force than that of *Erec*. On his adventure to the spring, the intrepid Kalogrenant initially reacts with terror to the strange forest creature, whom he encounters in a lonely clearing that echoes with the frightening sounds of fighting animals:

> dan schiet ich unde reit vil vruo
> ze walde von gevilde.
> dâ râmet ich der wilde
> und vant nâch mitten morgen
> in dem walde verborgen
> ein breitez geriute
> âne die liute.
> da gesach ich mir vil leide
> ein swære ougenweide,
> aller der tiere hande
> die man mir ie genande,
> vehten unde ringen
> mit eislîchen dingen. (396–408)

[Very early in the morning I departed and rode from the open country back into the forest. I hurried toward the wilderness and in the late morning found a clearing which showed no signes of human habitation. There, to my distress, I saw something frightful: a savage battle of all the kinds of animals of which I had ever heard.]

Shocked by the sounds, Kalogrenant regrets the fact that he has come this way, praying that God will help him out of this plight and fearing that he will not be able to defend himself. (412–416) His fear is compounded as he encounters the wild man, who presents Kalogrenant with an extraordinary picture, a being constructed from all manner of animal parts. (425–470) It is the wild man, however, who directs Kalogrenant to the spring. The power of nature is demonstrated by the spring's capacity for destruction. Once again, Kalogrenant fears for his life after he pours the water on the stone, unleashing a storm the like of which he has never experienced. The light of the sun is extinguished ("do erlasch diu sunne diu ê schein," 638), the birdsong ceases ("und zergienc der vogelsanc," 639), and the clouds converge from the four ends of the earth, bringing such fearsome thunder and lightening with them that Kalogrenant seeks refuge on the ground:

> diu wolken begunden
> in den selben stunden
> von vier enden ûf gân:

> der liehte tac wart getân
> daz ich die linden kûme gesach.
> grôz ungnâde da geschâch.
> vil schiere dô gesach ich
> in allen enden umbe mich
> wol tûsent tûsent blicke:
> dar nâch sluoc alsô dicke
> ein alsô kreftiger donerslac
> daz ich ûf der erde gelac. (641–652)

[Clouds gathered from every direction, and the clear day became so dark that I could barely make out ht elinden. Very soon I saw all around me a thousand thousand flashes of lightning, followed by as many thunderclaps of such violence that I fell to the ground.]

Hail and rain pelt the earth ("sich huop ein hagel unde ein regen," 653), the trees appear to have been burned to the ground, and all living things vanish:

> was iender boum dâ sô grôz
> daz er bestuont, der wart blôz
> und loubes alsô lære
> als er verbrennet wære.
> swaz lebete in dem walde,
> ez entrünne danne balde,
> daz was dâ zehant tôt. (659–665)

[those trees large enough to withstand [the storm] were as stripped of leaves as if they had been burned. all living things that didn't flee quickly died at once.]

The storm, however, passes "in kurzer wîle" (671) and the clearing around the spring becomes more beautiful than before in line 687, "daz ander paradîse."[73] While the devastation caused by the storm is temporary, the threat nonetheless remains constant. On four separate occasions throughout the work, various knights come upon it and unleash the same destruction. The first three times, Kalogrenant, Iwein, and Arthur (in succession) pour the water on the stone on a quest for *aventiure*, a concept that has been challenged by the seemingly naïve question of the wild man. Iwein makes the final visit to the fountain, unleashing the

storm and thereby announcing his presence to an unsuspecting
Laudine who does not yet know his true identity as the Knight
of the Lion. This time his decision to go to the spring is legitimate and correct, for his life remains incomplete without
Laudine:

> in dûhte, ob in ze kurzer stunt
> sîn vrouwe niht enlôste
> mit ir selber trôste,
> sô müesez schiere sîn sîn tôt. (7786–7789)

[He felt as if he would soon die if she did not save him at once
with help that only she could give]

Iwein's action here has direction and purpose, as he wishes to facilitate his reconciliation with Laudine and thus reassert his rightful position at her side.

But, as mentioned above, Iwein also experiences the forest as
a limen, a place through which he passes on his way toward becoming a better knight. He reaches this threshold forest following
his denunciation by Lunete before Arthur's court. The humiliation
causes Iwein to lose control of himself completely, succumbing to
madness. Hartmann describes a terrifying scene, in which Iwein
leaves the company in stunned silence and then divests himself of
all trappings of civilized courtly society:

> dô wart sîn riuwe alsô grôz
> daz im in daz hirne schôz
> ein zorn unde ein tobesuht,
> er brach sîne site und sîne zuht
> und zarte abe sîn gewant,
> daz er wart blôz sam ein hant.
> sus lief er über gevilde
> nacket nâch der wilde. (3231–3238)

[His sorrow then became so great that rage and madness seized
his brain. He forgot all decency, tore off his clothes until he was
as bare as one's hand, and ran naked across the fields toward the
wilderness.]

Now the forest takes on "a new and deeper meaning,"[74] not destructive but productive, not chaotic but controlled. Hartmann

conveys this new meaning through the experiences of his protagonist in this place. While making clear that this forest is wild ("wilde," 3238), Hartmann emphasizes what Iwein does here and how he survives:

> er schôz prîslichen wol:
> ouch gie der walt wildes vol:
> swâ daz gestuont an sîn zil
> des schôz er ûz der mâze vil. (3271–3274)

[He was a fine marksman, and the forest was filled with game. He shot a great deal of what came within range of his bow.]

This passage indicates that the forest is a place of plenty for Iwein; "wildes" (3272) underscores the wildness of the place, but refers in this context to the game that provides Iwein with his sustenance. Characteristically, Iwein's life is described in negative terms, as Hartmann tells his audience what trappings of civilization are missing:

> ouch muose erz selbe vâhen,
> âne bracken ergâhen.
> sone heter kezzel noch smalz,
> weder pfeffer noch salz:
> sîn salse was diu hungers nôt,
> diuz im briet unde sôt
> daz ez ein süeziu spîse was,
> und wol vor hunger genas. (3275–3282)[75]

[But he had to chase [the game] down himself without the aid of hounds. He had neither kettle nor lard, neither pepper nor salt: his sauce was the pangs of hunger, which broiled and stewed the meat to make it tasty and satisfy his appetite.]

Hartmann continues to use the same technique of *negatio* to describe Iwein's appearance as the passage, completely transforming Iwein into the ultimate 'other' of the civilized courtly knight. It matters not how many women Iwein had known nor how many spears he had broken in combat nor how courtly and wise he had once been. (3350–3353) Now, Iwein roams the forest as bereft of his senses as he is of his clothing: "er lief nû nacket beider/der sinne und der cleider." (3359–3360) In his present state, he has no memory of his previous life, no awareness of his previous self or of previous deeds. In his present state, he (and the audience with him) would not recognize

> ob er mit manheit ie begie
> deheinen lobelîchen prîs,
> wart er ie hövesch unde wîs,
> wart er ie edel unde rîch,
> dem ist er nu vil ungelîch. (3354–3358)

[no one would have quessed to look at him that he had ever bravely won great fame, been clever and courtly, noble and rich.]

Hartmann's audience would have understood the understatement of the poet's word choice here ("ungelîch"), for Iwein's transformation is so complete that it extends even to the color of his skin; his skin is now so black from dirt, that he resembles a Moor. (3345–3349) At this point, he has become 'other.'

This state of 'otherness' is, of course, only temporary, a phase that will inevitably lead to the development ("becoming") of an improved 'self .' After all vestiges of civilization have been stripped from him, Iwein begins to find his way back: learning to hunt and then to cook and then to share bread and water with the hermit. (3261 ff.) As a wild man in the forest, Iwein may indeed represent madness and uncivilized nature; however, for Saunders, the hermit's care of Iwein indicates that Iwein is never totally abandoned by fate and his destiny.[76] This 'care' is further illustrated by the fact that Iwein is eventually healed by the countess of Narison, who, with two of her ladies, comes upon the sleeping knight in a miserable, unsightly, and extremely uncourtly condition "bi der lantstraze" (3366) not far from their castle.[77] One of the women recognizes the man beside the road, telling her mistress that there was no better knight than Iwein:

> den ich sô swache sihe leben.
> im ist benamen vergeben,
> ode es ist von minnen komen
> daz im der sin ist benomen. (3403–3406)

[whom I see here in such a miserable condition. It is really hopeless, or it is because of love that his senses have been taken from him.]

At this moment, Iwein lies literally at a midpoint between worlds and between lives. The Arthurian court, as the setting of his previous life as a knight of the Round Table, represents one world. The forest offered a different world, supporting and sustaining Iwein since his attack of madness and providing a place in and through which he could gradually find his way back to the world of (civilized) humankind. Iwein's trajectory of becoming will take him finally to a third "world" represented by Laudine's court. In order to get to this other place, Iwein must negotiate a threshold space between forest and civilization and find his way to a new reality. He does this with the aid of the women who find him as they are out riding one day. After identifying the man they find as Iwein, the countess and her women heal him, provide him with clothing, and bathe him. The countess is the one, after all, who possesses the salve that can (and does) restore his mental faculties. They even provide him with the opportunity to prove himself by defending the countess and her land from the count of Aliers. In their care, Iwein is literally reborn, and he awakens the life he previously thought real but now remembers as though a dream, wondering "ist mir getroumet mîn leben?" ("Did I dream my life?" 3577) This time, the new Iwein is not merely fighting a joust or searching for *aventiure*; on the contrary, the threat to the countess is real. The women of Narison thus enable Iwein, as a result of his sojourn in their space, to start on his path toward eventual re-integration into courtly society.[78] An indication of Iwein's new path is the fact that, when he leaves the castle, he (like Erec and like Parzival) does not have a goal or a specific destination. He does not seek the adventures he comes across in this second part of the work, journeying through a geographically indeterminate area. Upon setting out, Iwein simply takes the first path he comes upon. This path leads him to the lion and ultimately, after further adventures, back to Laudine.

The appearance of the countess of Narison and her ladies marks the midpoint of the narrative, the turning point for Iwein, enabling Iwein to begin his journey out of uncivilized nature. Two other kinds of spaces, also occupied by women, likewise prove integral to Iwein's development. The first has to do with Lunete's role as messenger and with the relatively unrestricted freedom of movement she displays throughout the work. In her various capacities, as messenger and as "assistant" to both Laudine and Iwein, Lunete exhibits a unique ability to negotiate boundaries and space over the course of the narrative. She "stands out as a female figure who, for the most part, controls reality by directing the actions" of the men and women around her.[79] And her mobility is not her only outstanding characteristic. Not only is she mobile, but she can also speak the languages of at least two worlds, namely the Arthurian court and the court of Laudine, aiding Iwein in his quest(s) to do the same. As Laudine's messenger, it is she in fact who meets Iwein for the first time at his father's court, an incident that serves to illustrate Lunete's freedom of movement as well as her access to knowledge. (1181 ff.) Indeed, she consistently identifies Iwein when others around him cannot. It is Lunete, of course, who cares for Iwein after he slays Ascalon, presenting him with the protective ring that will render him invisible, supplying him with food and lodging, and finally arranging Iwein's marriage with Laudine.[80] The latter is certainly no easy task, the first time or the second. Lunete continues to accompany Iwein (literally and figuratively) on his journey, especially after she brings the errant knight the unwelcome message that he has neglected his responsibility in his promise to Laudine and that he has passed the year's deadline they both agreed upon for his return. (3052–3058) Performing a function similar to that of Cundrie in Book VI of Wolfram's *Parzival*, Lunete shames Iwein publicly (3110 ff.) in front of the entire Arthurian court, thereby maximizing the effect of her accusations and making it impossible for Iwein to refute them.

If Iwein's madness reveals "his lack of mental balance, his failure to live up to responsibility, his inability to face reality,"[81] then his adventures as the "der rîter mittem leun" (5502) gradually enable him to restore this lost balance, twice with the help of Lunete. Ferrante maintains that, just as woman as ideal exists in courtly romance, so also does woman as "realist, as debunker of male fantasies."[82] In this way, the figure of Lunete functions actively as Iwein's friend who shows him the reality of his situation, as opposed to Laudine, who is his passive love object. Part of this new reality involves helping others. To this end, Lunete becomes Iwein's second test of loyalty ("Treueprobe").[83] Iwein chances upon the fountain after freeing the lion and, at the sight of the stone and the chapel and a linden tree, he remembers his previous life:

> dô wart sîn herze des ermant
> wie er sîn êre und sîn lant
> hete verlorn und sîn wîp. (3933–3935)

[his heart was reminded of how he had lost honor, land, and wife.]

In his intense sorrow, he does not notice that his sword falls out of its sheath, wounding him. Lunete, however, hears his lament and brings him out of his reverie. Bound and imprisoned within the chapel, she has been blamed by Laudine for Iwein's infidelity and accused of treachery.[84] She can only be saved from the fiery fate that awaits her if Iwein agrees to prove her innocence in combat. (She had searched in vain for a champion earlier at Arthur's court: "und envant dâ nieman ze hûs/der sich ez wolde nemen an" 4166–4167; neither Gawein nor Iwein was to be found.) Eventually, Iwein does rescue Lunete, though he must first save Gawein's niece from the clutches of the giant Harpin. Finally, it is she who orchestrates the long-awaited final reunion between Iwein and Laudine, after Iwein at last finds his way back to the fountain:

> diu hete mit ir sinne
> ir beider unminne
> brâht zallem guot,
> als sî in ir muote
> lange hâte gegert. (8151–8155)

[Through her cleverness she had so managed it that only good came out of the conflict between them, as she had long hoped.]

Lunete has risked her own life in order to make this moment possible, a moment that she has long desired ("als sî in ir muote/lange hâte gegert") and that to all appearances heals the broken relationship ("ir beider unminne") between Iwein and Laudine.

The reference to "unminne" brings us to the controversial figure of Laudine. Laudine does not accompany Iwein on his journeys; on the contrary, she remains stationary in a sphere removed from those in which Iwein moves. This presents a marked contrast to *Erec*'s Enite, to whom scholars have often unfavorably compared Laudine. Wapnewski offers perhaps the sharpest criticism of her character; as opposed to the humble and selfless Enite, Laudine is "hart und anklagend, herrisch, blind und berechend" and her marriage to the murderer of her husband is "ein offenbar schwererer Verstoß gegen die *triuwe* als etwa später Iweins Terminversäumnis."[85] Blumstein, in *Misogyny and Idealization in the Courtly Romance*, also agrees that "this whole union [between

Iwein and Laudine] has been created in a way that is usually frowned upon as unseemly."[86] She concludes that Hartmann reveals himself as a misogynist in his portrayal of Laudine as a "wily and self-interested widow who uses men for her own ends,"[87] thus perpetuating stereotypes of fickle medieval widows. De Boor comments that Laudine's fickleness (like the solution at the end) appears to us as "oberflächlich und leichtfertig,"[88] though he does admit that the Middle Ages might have interpreted this in another way. Gustav Ehrismann sees Laudine's "Seelenlosigkeit" as reflective of her "ursprüngliche Dämonennatur": thus both of the major female figures in Hartmann's Arthurian romances appear opposite one another as fundamentally selfless and selfish archetypes, as human goodness and unnatural harshness, as loyalty and inconstancy.[89] Such negative assessments of Hartmann's Laudine did not begin with modern critics, however. In his *Parzival*, which is usually dated slightly later than *Iwein* around 1210, Wolfram von Eschenbach explicitly censures Laudine and her actions; she behaves "als wîp die man bî wanke siht." (253, 10 ff.) While Wolfram's criticism of Laudine may be justified in his comparison with Sigune, Kurt Ruh wrily notes: "die Forschung aber war fatal beraten, Wolfram darin zu folgen."[90] Ruh maintains that Laudine stands outside the moral norms, particularly because her character has fairy origins (from older sources) that allow her this freedom.[91]

Indeed, Laudine's castle and her fountain (the gateway to her kingdom) represent an alternative to the world of the Arthurian court, in a sense on the periphery of the familiar. Heide Göttner-Abendroth goes so far as to describe Laudine's realm as "magisch-matriarchal."[92] Certainly, the fountain represents a magical power associated with Laudine, whose fairy history has often been noted by Ruh and others.[93] One does not need to contemplate the supernatural, however, in order to describe Laudine's realm.[94] Clearly, Laudine has shared her land with her first husband Ascalon, and she later shares it with Iwein; nonetheless, the lands, as well as her hand, are unmistakably her own, even though she must negotiate the match with her chamberlain (*truchsæze*) and the rest of her court. (2388–2420) Lunete, in her speech upbraiding Iwein for his dishonorable behavior, refers to Laudine's freedom of choice and brings up the point that Laudine gave him her lands and her person freely, "mit vrîer hant" (3157) and trusted that he would protect them.

Laudine's responsibilities for her space are highlighted by the circumstances under which she consents to bestow her hand upon Iwein. Iwein decides after his first glimpse of Laudine that he must have her, seeming to possess her body with a glance and so moved by watching her do violence to herself in her mourning:

> daz im ir minne
> verkêrten die sinne,
> daz er sîn selbes gar vergaz
> und daz vil kûme versaz
> sô sî sich roufte und sluoc. (1335–1340)

[. . . that love robbed him of reason, to the point that he quite forgot himself and almost left his seat when she tore her hair and beat herself.]

To obtain her, Iwein solicits the aid of Lunete and together they confront Laudine with a dilemma that she absolutely cannot ignore, namely the safety of her land; it must be protected at all costs, especially since Arthur threatens it with his army. (1850–1862) At least this is the argument they use. Arthur never does attack, and Hartmann does not indicate that Laudine's land was ever in real danger. To keep her land safe, (2310–2331) Laudine capitulates and agrees to marry Iwein, not because of any frailty characteristic of woman, as the poet hastens to assure his audience, but because of her innate goodness and her concern for the welfare of her land and people.[95] Hartmann excuses her apparent fickleness,[96] saying that her goodness prompted her to make this correct decision and that none should criticize:

> er missetuot, der daz seit,
> ez mache ir unstætekheit:
> ich weiz baz wâ vonz geschiht
> daz man sî alsô dicke siht
> in wankelm gemüete:
> ez kumt von ir güete. (1873–1878)

[He who says it is because they are fickle is wrong. I know why they so often waver back and forth: it comes from their goodness.]

Hartmann also generalizes about women, insisting that he does not wish to speak anything but good of them. (1885–1888)[97] Laudine is portrayed as a responsible ruler in this situation,[98] capable of managing her own court. Hartmann also makes certain to verify her competence, allowing the audience to hear her thoughts as she and Iwein host the Arthurian company:

> alrêst liebet ir der man.
> dô ir diu êre geschach
> daz sî der künec durch in gesach,
> dô hete sî daz rehte ersehen
> daz ir wol was geschehen,
> und hete ouch den brunnen
> mit manheit gewunnen
> und wert ouch den als ein helt.
> si gedâhte 'ich hân wol gewelt.' (2674–2682)

[And for the first time, she became truly fond of her husband. When she had the honor of meeting the king because of him, she saw clearly that she had good fortune, also that he had won the fountain with courage and defended it as a hero. She thought: "I have chosen well."]

She has gained love and honor in bestowing her hand upon Iwein; obviously, she chose well.

Hartmann portrays the love-relationship and subsequent marriage between Laudine and Iwein in a positive manner; nevertheless, the poet does make clear that, at least initially, the Arthurian knight Iwein does not belong in the world Laudine rules.[99] This world is constructed not only as a threatened but also as a threatening space. Gawein gives voice to this threat, perceived as the danger that Iwein could lose himself and lose his knightly identity, by remaining in this world.[100] Drawing upon the example of Erec, Gawein succeeds in convincing Iwein that he must leave Laudine's court,[101] if only for a limited time, to avoid repeating Erec's mistake:

> geselle, behüetet daz enzît
> daz ir iht in ir schulden sît
> die des werdent gezigen
> daz sî sich durch ir wîp verligen.
> kêrt es niht allez an gemach;
> als dem hern Êrecke geschach,
> der sich ouch alsô manegen tac
> durch vrouwen Êntten verlac. (2787–2794)[102]

[Friend, watch out that you do not soon make the mistake of those who, because of their wives, are condemned for sloth. Don't turn wholly to a life of ease, as Sir Erec did, who was idle for a long time because of lady Enite.]

Through repeated references to imprisonment in the first half of the work, most notably during Iwein's first stay at Laudine's castle, Hartmann underscores Gawein's belief that Iwein's relationship to Laudine's space conflicts with accepted courtly (Arthurian) standards.[103] Iwein's imprisonment literally commences when the castle gates trap him in his chase after Ascalon:

> sus was mîn her Îwein
> zwischen disen porten zwein
> beslozzen und gevangen. (1127–1129)

[Thus was my lord Iwein locked and imprisoned between these two gates.]

Iwein is afraid and does not know quite what to do about his situation, since he can find no way out:

> dô suochter wider unde vür
> und envant venster noch tür
> dâ er ûz möhte.
> nu gedâhter waz im töhte. (1145–1148)

[Then he looked all around without finding with window or door from which to escape, and then began to wonder about what should be done.]

It is Lunete of course who releases him from this particular imprisonment, which threatens to take his life in a dishonorably female way. Iwein tells Lunete:

> Er sprach 'so ensol ich doch den lîp
> niht verliesen als ein wîp:
> michn vindet niemen âne wer.' (1169–1171)

[He said: "I won't lose my life like a woman; no one will find me defenseless."]

His attitude soon changes, however, when he glimpses Laudine in mourning as she follows the bier of her dead husband:

> da ersach sî der her Îwein:
> da was ir hâr und ir lîch
> so gar dem wunsche gelîch
> daz im ir minne
> verkêrten sine sinne,
> daz er sîn selbes gar vergaz. . . (1332–1337)

[Then lord Iwein saw her: her hair and her body were so beautiful that love robbed him of reason, to the point that he forgot himself . . .]

The sight of this beautiful woman tearing her hair in distress overwhelms him and robs him of his senses. As a result, when the funeral procession has concluded, Iwein remains a double prisoner:

> die porte wurden zuo getân,
> dâ sî durch was gegangen:
> und er was alsô gevangen
> daz im aber diu ûzvart
> anderstunt versperret wart.
> daz was im alsô mære,
> wan ob ietweder porte wære
> ledeclichen ûf getân,
> und wærer dâ zuo ledec lân
> aller sîner schulde
> alsô daz er mit hulde
> vüere swar in dûhte guot,
> *sone stuont doch anders niht sîn muot*
> *niuwan ze belîbenne dâ.*
> *wær er gewesen anderswâ,*
> *sô wolder doch wider dar.*
> *sîn herze stuont niender anderswar*
> *niuwan dâ er sî weste:*
> *diu stat was im diu beste.* (1704–1721, italics mine)

[The portals were closed, blocking the exit and making him again a prisoner. But he didn't mind that, for even if both portals had been opened wide and he had been freed of all guilt and permitted to go where he wished, he still would have had no other desire than to stay there. *If he had been someplace else, he would have wanted to return, for his heart would remain only where she was: that was the best spot for him.*]

The fact that the gates close behind her, locking him inside and preventing his escape, no longer troubles him. Even if he were free to go, he would not wish to leave, only desiring to remain where the lady is. In essence, Iwein's infatuation with Laudine holds him prisoner, though it is obvious that *minne* has effectively transformed his prison into a paradise he would not willingly leave. Later, Iwein himself expresses his desire to remain imprisoned, telling Lunete:

> sî vil sælec wîp,
> ich wil gerne daz mîn lîp
> immer ir gevangen sî,
> und daz herze da bî. (2241–2243)

[She is so lovely that I shall be glad for my heart and body to be her prisoners forever.]

To emphasize further the impropriety of Iwein's situation and his behavior, should he choose to remain with Laudine at her court, Gawein brings up the comparison with Erec. Thus urged into action, Iwein asks Laudine's permission to participate in tournaments and uphold his knightly honor; she acquiesces, granting his request under the condition that he return within a year's time. Unfortunately, he cannot keep his part of the bargain, missing the deadline, and the second half of the work is the result.

Despite the illusion of a happy end, *Iwein* concludes on a rather ambiguous note: Laudine requests (and receives) Iwein's pardon. (8122–8136) As if to underscore the ambiguity of the conclusion, the imagery of imprisonment returns at the conclusion; however, it is Laudine who is caught this time, having trapped herself by her oath to marry the knight with the lion. She admits: "der eit hat mich gevangen." (8092) This reversal suggests, placed as it is near the end of the narrative when all is ostendibly being put to rights, that it is more appropriate for women to be imprisoned, waiting to be set free by their knights, than vice versa. In this respect, we can see that the relationship between Iwein and Lunete is also righted, as Iwein releases her from imprisonment in the chapel, an inverse parallel to their first encounter following Ascalon's death. At the conclusion of the work, addressing him as "her Iwein, lieber herre mîn," Laudine asks forgiveness for causing him such pain and suffering:

> tuot gnædiclîchen an mir.
> grôzen kumber habet ir
> von mînen schulden erliten.
> des wil ich iuch durch got biten
> daz ir ruochet mir vergeben. . . (8123–8127)

[Sir Iwein, my dear lord, be kind to me. I have caused you great suffering and ask you for God's sake to forgive me . . .]

With those words, by her own admission captured ("gevangen"), she falls to her knees at his feet. Iwein, "der herre" (8132), then raises her up again and all is reconciled. This particular exchange does not occur in Hartmann's French source and is therefore an obvious addition to the German version. In his altered conclusion, Hartmann portrays at least the illusion of a stable relationship between Iwein and Laudine as a model for men and women who rule; this stable unit should, by extension, ensure social stability.

This program does not seem to succeed as well as it does in *Erec*, however. Even Hartmann's authorial intervention cannot conceal the fact that Laudine's realm remains her space. Laudine's space is not explicitly condemned and umistakably 're'patriated' as is the garden of Brandigan. Iwein becomes the knight of the fountain and does not return to the Arthurian court. His voluntary 'exile' from Arthur's world seems to allow the separateness of Laudine's realm to remain intact, despite the fact that the concluding scene appears to rob Laudine of her autonomy. One could interpret Laudine's court as a kind of courtly 'other,' positively valued in contrast to the impotent Arthurian court that cannot understand the true meaning of *aventiure*—this quality of 'otherness' is represented both figuratively and literally by the fountain, which must be 'overcome' in order for outsiders to gain access to Laudine's kingdom. And it is significant, showing Hartmann's critique of the Arthurian court, that Laudine's court is the place where Iwein remains at the conclusion of the narrative. These kinds of contradictions do not upset the harmony of the conclusion in *Erec*. Erec seems to have assimilated Enite's identity into his own by the end of their story. Enite remains silent after the concluding episode in the garden: her voice, as well as her potential for her own space (at least that potential symbolized by the garden), have been taken from her. Indeed, Hartmann states specifically that Erec has now learned to attend to Enite's wishes to the extent that it is good and appropriate for him to do so.[104] In *Iwein*, Hartmann presents a text with apparent inconsistencies and contradictions, a condition that Otfrid Ehrismann has positively associated with the postmodern (or the "praemodern" in Hartmann's case) "wenn man Plurivalenz und Offenheit nicht als Schwächen brandmarkt, sondern als textkonstitutiv annimmt."[105] This openness would seem literally to accommodate a greater number of possible scenarios for "becoming ."

And, in an intriguing way, it does. It is true that Iwein is really the only figure who is the focus of any kind of 'becoming ,' while Laudine remains a fairly fixed point and a somewhat ambivalent standard that Iwein must live up to. Her place is as 'other' as her self (as woman). On the other hand, she does not 'become' unambiguously re-incorporated into male identity: she is "diu künegîn" (8121), while he is "der herre." (8132) I would argue that they have their own titles, their own words, and their own selves. This vocabularly is part of an ambiguity (and perhaps the openness) that remains at the end . This ambiguity is reinforced by the spaces of the work's topography, which support the possibility that, despite Hartmann's concluding scene of reconciliation, Laudine (and Lunete) continue to defy incorporation into a rigid patriarchal space.

As Hartmann illustrates in *Erec* and *Iwein*, the romance offers the poet a unique opportunity not only to create and recreate worlds/patterns to delight the imagination of the audience but also to explore and evaluate possibilities in those worlds/patterns for the edification of that audience. In *Erec*, it is primarily the 'otherness' represented by the space of the forest allows both Erec and Enite to negotiate their roles and discover the appropriate balance. As we noted in the previous chapter, the first part of their shared journey forces Enite into situations in which she must make a conscious effort to speak at crucial moments. Because of Erec's command that she not speak, she confronts his threat of punishment each time she wrestles with the decision of whether or not to warn him of approaching danger. Unlike the Enite who kept silent because she feared losing her husband in Karnant, the Enite in the forest consistently speaks despite the risks of reprisal. Erec, during the second half of the work, directs his prowess toward helping those in need. Thus, both Erec and Enite learn to incorporate an appropriate measure of selflessness into their behavior, as befits those invested with the responsibility of rulership. Erec, of course, eventually asks Enite's forgiveness for his treatment of her; it was necessary to test Enite's mettle, just as one must purify gold:

> ez was durch versuochen getân
> ob si im wære ein rehtez wîp
> nû hâte er ir lîp
> ersihert genzlîchen wol,
> als man daz golt sol
> liutern in der esse . . . (6781–6786)

[It was done in order to test whether she were a proper wife for him. Now he was entirely certain of her, as one must purify gold in the kettle . . .]

The forest negotiations in *Erec* are ultimately focussed on testing and appropriately re-incorporating the feminine/female 'other' that threatens all masculine (male) selves. Enite represents woman, passion, danger to the greater social good. Part of her test involes keeping the reins of the horses that the couple takes with them from Karnant; Smits interprets these horses as an allusion to passion that can be traced to Saint Jerome.[106] The potential danger posed by Enite's behavior is illustrated most clearly by the parallel actions of Enite's cousin, the lady of Mabonagrin in the garden of Brandigan. The subversive space of the garden must be eliminated, and Erec and Enite find their way to positions strictly delineated by traditional gender roles, renegotiated to fix the couple into 'being' according to courtly social norms. Thus, although Hartmann illustrates at least a certain degree of agency on the part of his major female characters, this agency can only occur in 'other' spaces, placed outside of the court and thereby marginalized. The margins close in *Erec*, leaving only the hint of possibility behind. The isolated space of the garden 'disappears' as its inhabitants are reincorporated into the healthy social body; having learned its lessons, Erec and Enite no longer require the space of the forest to teach them how to fill their respective roles. In discovering her queenly identity, however, Enite loses the freedom of speech and the agency the forest allowed her during her sojourn in that space.

In *Iwein*, on the other hand, the negotiations through 'other' spaces form a different map; the margins remain 'open,' so to speak, to accommodate pockets of space whose possibilities encourage such traditional patterns as those offered at the conclusion of *Erec*. In contrast to Enite, Lunete and Laudine remain relatively static figures, while Iwein is really the only one who is the focus of any kind of 'becoming .' Laudine remains a fairly fixed point, but her place is as 'other' in her own domain. One also cannot ignore Lunete's unprecedented mobility or the integral part she plays in the work. Despite the fact that she is not noble, or perhaps for this very reason, she appears at significant times and places to steer the course of the narrative. Further, while the forest is designated as Iwein's space of 'becoming' in this work, the garden has been transformed into Laudine's realm. Laudine's space also possesses a subversive quality, particularly at the beginning of the work. Hartmann reveals this quality through the metaphor of imprisonment that dominates Iwein's first stay at Laudine's castle and that threatens to keep Iwein from the knightly way of life.[107] Unlike the garden of Brandigan, the space of Laudine's castle is not eliminated; on the contrary, it continues at the conclusion of the story. It is the place to which Iwein triumphantly returns; it is Laudine who is trapped by her oath. Though trapped, however, Laudine is not circumscribed by Iwein's identity as neatly as Enite becomes part of Erec (identified as his wife). Though Hartmann attempts to create a scene of harmony similar to the one that concludes *Erec*, the ending of *Iwein* seems contrived. Laudine's request for forgiveness, as she falls to Iwein's feet, rings hollow against her admission that she has been trapped by her oath. Even Hartmann seems to suggest that this (re)union might face an uncertain future, although the source of the instability remains ambiguous. Upon their reunion, the satisfied Lunete observes that they have come back together and they seem to have all the necessary ingrediants for a happy life: property and health, good sense and youth. If they wish to remain faithful to one another, and if God should grant them long life, then "diu gewinnet manige süeze zît" ("they will see many delightful days," 8147). One is not sure of the future. The possibility for "play," for the imagination of the audience, can remain in a kind of "gap" created by this ambiguity.

Notes

1. Michel Foucault, "Space, Knowledge and Power," *The Foucault Reader*, ed. Paul Rabinow (New York: Pantheon, 1984), 252.

2. "Hartmann, the man from Aue, oh how he decorates his tales both outwardly and inwardly with words and thoughts! How he forms the sense of the story with his language! How clear and transparently pure are, and ever will be, his cristalline words." Gottfried von Strassburg, *Tristan*, ed. Friedrich Ranke. 4th ed. (Berlin: Weidmannsche Buchhandlung, 1959) lines 4621–4630. All further references to *Tristan* will appear in the text.

3. One could say that epic, as 'history ,' has more rigid structural requirements. This is not the place to discuss the application of the concept of gender topographies to epic, although the applications are compelling. One could argue that, in the *Nibelungenlied* for example, both Brünhild and Kriemhild demonstrate a more negative dynamic between 'being' and 'becoming .' They seem them to defy courtly conventions by assuming opposite gender roles: Brünhild acts in an unmistakably male warrior role in her space of Island, while Kriemhild attempts to take control of her property, her destiny, and her vengeance in a decidedly un-womanly manner both at Worms and at Etzel's court. The freedom granted the women in these spaces enables them to step out of the roles conventionally ascribed to courtly ladies; obviously, they cannot remain there. They must move away from these spaces, characteristically accompanied by the men/husbands who would rehabilitate them, and their movement literally destroys them: Brünhild's journey from Island to Worms results in her assimilation into the male courtly world, while Kriemhild's subsequent passage from the court at Worms to the land of the Huns leads ultimately to her death at the conclusion of the work. Both women in the *Nibelungenlied* make ultimately unsuccessful attempts to take advantage of mobility through rigidly gender-marked 'spaces.' This mobility, in its process and in its effects, contrasts with the type found in romances.

4. Green, 254–255.

5. For a detailed structural and conceptual comparison of Hartmann and Chrétien, see Antonin Hrubý, "Die Problemstellung in Chrétiens und Hartmanns *Erec*," Hartmann von Aue, ed. Hugo Kuhn and Christoph Cormeau (Darmstadt: Wissenschaftliche Buchgesellschaft, 1973) 342–372.

6. Chrétien's were translated into Old Norse as well as Middle English in the mid-thirteenth century.

7. The freedom enjoyed by medieval poets to create their geographies with little regard for concrete 'reality' contrasts with the different 'spatial'

expectations of the early modern audiences, for example. According to Gerhard Wolf, early modern audiences demanded a kind of information that reflected an increase in empirical knowledge of the world. See Gerhard Wolf, "Das Individuum auf dem Weg zu sich selbst? Frühneuzeitliches Reisen nach Osten: Hans Dernschwam, Balthasar Springer und Fortunatus," in *Reisen und Welterfahrung in der deutschen Literatur des Mittelalters*, ed. Dietrich Huschenbett and John Margetts (Würzburg: Königshausen & Neumann, 1991), 210.

8. This is the opinion of de Boor, who maintains that the interaction between the center and the periphery illustrates by the hero's path to and from the Round Table is fundamentally all that happens in the Arthurian romance.

9. This is how Iser understands the primary function of fiction in courtly romance: "In diesem Falle funktioniert die Fiktion als die Beseitigung einer die Stabilität des Systems bedrohenden Gegebenheit." "Die Wirklichkeit der Fiktion," 310.

10. Auerbach describes adventure as a condition of "Auserwähltsein" (*Mimesis*, 132). Cormeau takes this condition of the "chosen" one step further, arguing that the relatively autonomous nature of the romance *aventiure* stands in opposition to the lack of autonomy to be found in the courts of the real world; the romance hero succeeds to an exceptional degree in the literary fiction ("Kunstwelt") where he cannot at an actual court that cannot grant him such opportunity/freedom. See Christoph Cormeau, "Artusroman und Märchen: Zur Beschreibung und Genese der Struktur des höfischen Romans," in *Wolfram-Studien 5*, ed. Werner Schröder (Berlin: Erich Schmidt, 1979) 78. The idea of the romance hero as "chosen" also supports allegorical readings of the romance journey as a process that leads the knight toward a specifically Christian goal. See Max Wehrli, "Strukturen des mittelalterlichen Romans— Interpretationsprobleme," in *Formen mittelalterlicher Erzählung. Aufsätze* (Zürich: Atlantis, 1969), 38. In his *Literatur im deutschen Mittelalter. Eine poetologische Einführung* (Stuttgart: Reclam, 1984), Wehrli terms the journey "einen Heilsweg in Analogie zum geistlichen Weg des einzelnen wie der Heilsgeschichte im großen. . ." (159)

11. Terkla, 169. Boklund comments that the order established by firm spatial and cultural boundaries must be reaffirmed continually "through a ritually controlled venture into chaos" (Boklund, 11) performed by the hero. In contrast to Terkla, however, Boklund attributes centrality to the internal order of the court rather than the external chaos. In general, the topographies of the MHG romances under consideration here support the centrality of the margins rather than the Arthurian court. The courts 'on the margins' (Karnant, Ascalon, Munsalvaesche) acquire the authority of

a new kind of centrality.

12. Terkla, 185–186.

13. Terkla, 221.

14. See Norbert H. Ott, "Zur Ikonographie der Reise. Bildformeln und Strukturprinzipien mittelalterlicher Reise-Illustrationen," in *Reisen und Welterfahrung in der deutschen Literatur des Mittelalters*, ed. Dietrich Huschenbett and John Margetts (Würzburg: Königshausen & Neumann, 1991), 40.

15. Ott, 53.

16. Ingrid Kasten, "Heilserwartung und Verlusterfahrung. Reisen als Motiv in der mittelalterlichen Lyrik," in *Reisen und Welterfahrung in der deutschen Literatur des Mittelalters*, ed. Dietrich Huschenbett and John Margetts (Würzburg: Königshausen & Neumann, 1991), 82.

17. Lilo Szlavek, "Der Widerspenstigen Zähmung in *Parzival*," in *Der Widerspenstigen Zähmung. Studien zur bezwungenen Weiblichkeit in der Literatur vom Mittelalter bis zur Gegenwart*, ed. Sylvia Wallinger and Monika Jonas, Innsbrucker Beiträge zur Kulturwissenschaft. Germanistische Reihe, no. 31 (Innsbruck: Druckerei G. Grasl, 1986), 46.

18. Michel Foucault, "Space, Knowledge, and Power," 252.

19. According to anthropologist Shirley Ardener, "the fact that women do not control physical or social space directly does not necessarily preclude them from being determinants of, or mediators in, the allocation of space..." Ardener considers this relative/relational aspect often typical of women's relationship to space. See Shirley Ardener, "Ground Rules and Social Maps for Women: An Introduction," in *Women and Space: Ground Rules and Social Maps*, ed. Shirley Ardener (Providence: Berg Publishers, 1993), 9.

20. Hartmann von Aue, *Erec*, ed. Christoph Cormeau, 6th ed. (Tübingen: Max Niemeyer, 1985) lines 8715–8729. All further references will appear in the text. The English translations are from *Erec*, trans. J. W. Thomas (Lincoln: University of Nebraska Press, 1982).

21. See also Derek Pearsall and Elizabeth Salter, *Landscapes and Seasons of the Medieval World* (Toronto: University of Toronto Press, 1973), 52.

22. The requisite components of a *locus amoenus*, according to Curtius, must at least include the following: one or more trees, a meadow, a spring or brook, birdsong, and flowers. More elaborate examples may also include a breeze. (Curtius, 195)

23. Pearsall, 53. See also Michael Camille, *The Medieval Art of Love: Objects and Subjects of Desire*. (New York: Abrams, 1998).

24. Erec completes this adventure while Enite remains outside. Her physical presence is not needed to inspire him with renewed strength and

courage during the battle:

> Êrec, ze swelhen zîten
> er gedâhte an vrouwen Ênîten,
> sô starcten im ir minne
> sîn herze und ouch die sinne,
> daz er ouch mit niuwer maht
> nâch manlîcher tiure vaht. (9182–9187)

[Whenever Erec thought of Enite, her love so strengthened his heart and his senses that he fought bravely with renewed vigor.]

25. See Karen Pratt, "Adapting Enide: Chrétien, Hartmann, and the Female Reader," *Chrétien de Troyes and the German Middle Ages*, ed. Martin H. Jones and Roy E. Wisbey, Arthurian Studies 26 (Cambridge: D.S. Brewer, 1993), 69.

26. Pratt, 80.

27. Pratt, 76.

28. Pratt also cites the work of Laurie Fink, who interprets the lady in the garden as the only active and powerful woman in the work, dangerous because she refuses to participate in the male system of exchange. (Pratt 71) Fink's research was presented in a paper entitled "Flesh Made Word: Constructing Sexuality in Chrétien de Troyes" at the Twenty-Second International Conference on Medieval Studies at Kalamazoo in May 1987.

29. Hugo Kuhn interprets Erec's fight with Mabonagrin as "ein Kampf um die rechte Minneform" because the joy (*Freude*) of this place "ist 'verschlossen,' unwirksam geworden." (144) The episode thus, for Kuhn, becomes an allegory of courtly joy.

30. The following is a brief overview of major works on medieval marriage and sexuality. For discussions of sexual equality within medieval marriage and its foundation in medieval canon law, see Elizabeth M. Makowski, "The Conjugal Debt and Medieval Canon Law," in *Equally in God's Image. Women in the Middle Ages*, ed. Julia Bolton Holloway, Joan Bechtold and Constance S. Wright (New York: Peter Lang, 1990) 129–144. See also James Brundage, "Sexual Equality in Medieval Canon Law," in *Medieval Women and the Sources of Medieval History*, ed. Joel T. Rosenthal (Athens: University of Georgia Press, 1990) 66–79; and Silvana Vecchio, "The Good Wife," in *The Silences of the Middle Ages*, vol. 2 of *A History of Women in the West*, ed. Georges Duby and Michelle Perrot. (Cambridge, MA: The Belknap Press of Harvard UP, 1992), 110–113.

31. See the context of these verses in 2948–2953:

swie schiere man die tische ûf zôch,
mit sînem wîbe er dô vlôch
ze bette von den liuten.
dâ huop sich aber triuten.
von danne enkam er aber nie
unz er ze naht ze tische gie.

[After they finished eating, Erec and his wife left the others and
fled to their bed, where the lovemaking was resumed. He did not
appear again until the evening meal.]

32. For a similar discussion of the semantics of lovemaking, see Frakes'
analysis of analogous scenes in the *Nibelungenlied*. (96 ff.) Frakes describes the "grammar" of the scenes in which Gunther and Siegfried consummate their relationships with Brünhild and Kriemhild, respectively, as
follows: "Whether one reads these metaphors as signifying romantic love
or more specifically the physical act of sexual intercourse does not alter
the fact that the phrases whose subject is male are transitive or have female verbal complements; the female subject has an intransitive verb with
a governing agentive complement for whose sake the action of the intransitive verb is performed: the man *acts on* the woman; she is *enacted* for the
sake of the man." (Frakes, 107) This "grammar" illustrates perfectly the
pronouncements of Aristotle and Aquinas on the nature of man and
woman.

33. In his treatise *Adversus Jovinianum*, Jerome equates excessive love
of one's wife with adultery. Jerome thus, as Brundage points out, identifies love with sexual relations and attacks "immoderate indulgence in sex"
by married persons. See James Brundage, *Law, Sex, and Christian Society
in Medieval Europe* (Chicago: University of Chicago Press, 1987), 90–91.

34. This attitude persisted despite the growing movement in the twelfth
and thirteenth centuries toward consensual marriage. Certainly the
courtly romance (particularly the German versions) promoted an ideal of
woman and man as partners in their marriage, having consented to their
relationship because of their mutual love for one another. This would result in another equally important balance between desire and reason: "Die
recht verstandene Liebe harmonisiert Trieb und Vernunft." (Köhler, *Ideal
und Wirklichkeit in der höfischen Epik*, 141) Yet, as Karina Kroj notes,
the relative 'equality' of this partnership remained problematic since
women's function in marriage remained primarily sexual: "denn als Ehefrau war [die Frau] Geschlechtspartnerin des Mannes, und als solcher war
ihr eher mit Mißtrauen zu begegnen." See Karina Kroj, *Die Abhängigkeit
der Frau in EhErechtsnormen des Mittelalters und der Neuzeit als Ausdruck eines gesellschaftlichen Leitbilds von Ehe und Familie. Zugleich*

eine Untersuchung zu den Realisierungschancen des zivilrechtlichen Gle-ichheitsgrundsatzes (Frankfurt: Peter Lang, 1988), 86.

Both Sharon Farmer ("Persuasive Voices") and Jo Ann McNamara ("The *Herrenfrage*"), among others, have pointed out that the reforms of the eleventh and twelfth centuries also placed increasing emphasis on (negatively) defining and categorizing 'woman' as a source of danger for both clerical and secular men, a source of societal disorder. Indeed, Paul's repeated reminders of the inferiority of women and Augustine's famous re-mark that God would have created a second man as a companion for Adam had there not been a need for offspring, were eventually given bio-logical justification through the work of Thomas Aquinas and his recep-tion of Aristotle. In addition, Farmer notes that it was not until the eleventh and twelfth centuries that Jerome's Adversus Jovinianum (see previous note) became popular. See Farmer, note 8, 519–520.

35. Leisch-Kiesl asserts that Eve developed as a systematic category for Christianity, becoming a constitutive element of male consciousness (an "other" necessary to define 'man'). See Monika Leisch-Kiesl, *Eva als An-dere: Eine exemplarische Untersuchung zu Frühchristentum und Mittelal-ter* (Köln: Böhlau, 1992) 27 and 146.

36. This comment seems rather incongruous in the context of the nar-rative thus far, since the audience has been given no explicit reason to sus-pect Enite's guilt in Erec's dishonor. It becomes clear, however, that both Erec and Enite feel that she deserves the blame he eventually heaps upon her.

37. Much has been made of the nature and extent of these tatters. The body must be appropriately clothed!

38. Erec, in his turn, is led away by other knights ("von den rittern enwec/ gevüeret besunder," 5117–5118) and cared for in male company. (5151 ff.) He remains among them until the queen comes to tend his wounds, healing being the province of women.

39. See Francis G. Gentry, "Hartmann von Aue's *Erec*: The Burden of Kingship," in *King Arthur Through the Ages*, ed. Valerie M. Lagorio and Mildred Leake Day, vol. 1 (New York: Garland, 1990), 161. Gentry points out that Enite is called "künegîn" by Hartmann at the successful conclusion of her trials in line 6732, *before* Erec receives his title from the poet. Enite's rulership role in the German version is moral rather than legal, however. Hartmann reinforces this by not allowing her the same off-ical coronation in the narrative that Chrétien's heroine receives.

40. Farmer discusses the proper and clerically sanctioned methods by which noble wives might exercise influence over their husbands in "Per-suasive Voices: Clerical Images of Medieval Wives," *Speculum* (1986): 521–526. Although a certain distrust of women and women's speech re-

mained, some medieval clerics (Farmer draws particular attention to the works of Thomas of Chobham in the early thirteenth century) attempted to find a greater good in women's powers of persuasion: "Through the cultural medium of spoken language, pious women, like evangelists, were agents of the civilizing process: they harnessed and brought under cultivation wild, savage men." (541) This is illustrated by Orderic Vitalis' account of Adele, wife of Stephen of Blois, who successfully persuaded her husband to embark on a second crusade. See Orderic Vitalis, *The Ecclesiastical History of England and Normandy*, trans. Thomas Forester, vol. 3 (London: Henry Bohn, 1854). Stephen was suffering reproach for having abandoned the siege at Antioch, and Adele was chief among those who urged him to undertake another crusade, "reminding him of it even amidst the endearments of conjugal caresses." (289) Vecchio also mentions Thomas of Chobham in a similar context. (Vecchio, 115–117)

41. Indeed, as Sterba points out, Enite will castigate herself later for having behaved like a gossip and for not having kept her thoughts to herself. See Wendy Sterba, "The Question of Enite's Transgression: Female Voice and Male Gaze as Determining Factors in Hartmann's *Erec*," in *Women as Protagonists and Poets in the German Middle Ages: An Anthology of Feminist Approaches to Middle High German Literature.*, ed. Albrecht Classen (Göppingen: Kümmerle, 1991), 61. Hartmann makes clear, however, that Enite *should* have spoken; she simply could not recognize the appropriate moment to do so. This is the essence of what she must learn during her journey in the forest.

42. See Hugo Kuhn, "Erec," in *Dichtung und Welt im Mittelalter* (Stuttgart: Metzler, 1959) 133–150. Kuhn states: "Wer sie, entgegen Hartmanns ausdrücklicher Versicherung, auch nur einer Mitschuld zeiht, versündigt sich an einer der reinsten Frauengestalten in Mittelalter und Neuzeit." (150) Ingrid Hahn concurs, asserting: "Enite ist am Ende die, die sie von Anfang an war, und sie muß deshalb auch—woran der Dichter keinen Zweifel läßt— ihrem Ehemann zu Beginn seines Weges überlegen sein." See Ingrid Hahn, "Die Frauenrolle in Hartmanns *Erec*," *in Sprache und Recht. Beiträge zur Kulturgeschichte des Mittelalters. Festschrift für Ruth Schmidt-Wiegand zum 60. Geburtstag*, ed. Karl Hauck (Berlin: Walter de Gruyter, 1986) 172–190. For Eva Tobler, Enite exemplifies Christian selflessness from the beginning. See Eva Tobler, "Ancilla Domini. Marianische Aspekte in Hartmanns *Erec*," *Euphorion* 80 (1986): 427–438.

43. Silvia Ranawake, "Erec's *verligen* and the Sin of Sloth," in *Hartmann von Aue. Changing Perspectives*, ed. Timothy McFarland and Silvia Ranawake (Göppingen: Kümmerle, 1988), 115.

44. Ranawake, 104.

45. See Rodney Fisher, "Erecs Schuld und Enitens Unschuld bei Hart-

mann," *Euphorion* 69 (1975): 160–174. Erec projects his own guilt onto Enite, hence his mistreatment of her. (162) And this is the origin of his fault comes from, not simply his *verligen*. (171) His fault has two parts: *verligen* and the misuse of his authority, both of which result from his immaturity. (173–174)

46. See Thomas Cramer, "Soziale Motivation in der Schuld-Sühne-Problematik von Hartmanns *Erec*," *Euphorion* 66 (1972): 97–112. Searching for a reason to explain Enite's obvious penance in the poem, Cramer explains the guilt problem in terms of Enite's poverty, a fault that (in Cramer's estimation) Enite never bothers to admit and never attempts to overcome.

47. Fisher, 163. Fisher neglects to mention in this context the status of Enite's father. He is an impoverished nobleman ("ein grâve rîche," 402) who has come into difficulty through a feud that was no fault of his own.

48. "Hartmann gibt nirgends zu verstehen, daß Enite eine ähnliche *wandelunge* erlebt wie Erec." (Fisher, 164)

49. Pratt, 83. And Pratt continues: "Thus Hartmann's narrator again exploits his authority in order to reinforce traditional stereotypes of women and to impose on his *matière* a unifying meaning which would appeal to twelfth-century patriarchal society." (84)

50. Hrubý, 350.

51. Hrubý, 355. For Smits, this "real marriage" is to be understood as an exemplary Christian one according to early scholastic doctrine on marriage. See Kathryn Smits, "Enite als christliche Ehefrau," in *Interpretation und Edition deutscher Texte des Mittelalters. Festschrift für John Asher zum 60. Geburtstag*, ed. Kathryn Smits, Werner Besch, and Victor Lange (Berlin: Erich Schmidt, 1981) 13–25.

52. Peter Wapnewski, *Hartmann von Aue* (Stuttgart: Metzler, 1962), 51.

53. Wapnewski, 53–54.

54. Petrus Tax, "Studien zum Symbolischen in Hartmanns *Erec*," *Zeitschrift für deutsche Philologie* 82 (1963): 43. Hahn actually sees desire as Erec's problem. This is illustrated through the use of the "Pferde–Motiv." Hahn interprets the horses as symbols of passion and pride (symbols which go back to Jerome), which Enite is able to harness and keep under control because of her *wîpliche senfte*. (Hahn, 183)

55. Bernard Willson, "The Heroine's Loyalty in Hartmann's and Chrétien's Erec" in Chretien de Troyes and the German Middle Ages, Ed. Martin H. Jones and Roy E. Wisbey, Arthurian Studies 26, (Cambridge: D.S. Brewer, 1993), 11.

56. Gentry, 164–165.

57. See Patrick M. McConeghy, "Woman's Speech and Silence in Hartmann von Aue's *Erec*," *PMLA* 102 (1987): 779–780.

58. "Von einem Raum-Reiz ist nichts oder fast nichts zu spüren, und ihn empfinden zu lassen, lag wohl nicht in den Absichten und Möglichkeiten des Dichters." Rainer Gruenter, "Zum Problem der Landschaftsdarstellung im höfischen Roman," *Euphorion* 56 (1962): 256.

59. This is, of course, the place where 'true' perspective is won—so that the hero (and heroine, in the case of Enite) can become what he (and she) are meant to be.

60. Klaus Hufeland, "Das Motiv der Wildheit in mittelhochdeutscher Dichtung," *Zeitschrift für deutsche Philologie* 95 (1976): 8.

61. See Lynn Thelen, "Beyond the Court. A Study of the wilde-Motif in Medieval German Literature," (Ph.D. diss., University of Pennsylvania), 1979. According to Thelen, Hartmann uses the attributes *wilde* and *kreftic* to convey the impenetrable nature of the forest. (32) In her study, however, Thelen establishes a rigid dichotomy between the civilized court and the uncivilized (and therefore uncourtly) wilderness. As a result, despite acknowledging that the wilderness plays an integral role in knightly adventure, Thelen fails to recognize the positive benefits of this liminal space.

62. Schmid-Cadalbert, 36. Interestingly, Hartmann also seems to represent a second type of forest. After Erec's first confrontation with Guivreiz, Hartmann says: "er kam in einen schœnen walt." (4629.08) Though the text around this passage seems corrupt in the ms., there seems to be agreement about this line. This forest is qualitatively different from the one in which the couple has spent so much time in the previous section. It is not *kreftic* but *schœn*; they encounter not robbers but king Arthur and the civilized court.

63. Likewise 6077–6083:

> sich teilte dô besunder
> von des jâmers grimme
> rehte enzwei ir stimme,
> hôhe unde nidere.
> der walt gap in widere
> vorhteclîch swaz si geschrê.
> dô lûte dicke: 'ouwê ouwê'!

[Her voice was divided into two parts by the force of her sorrow, into high and low. The forest reverberated with her cries; it resounded: "Oh and alas!"]

64. Wapnewski, 51.

65. See Gentry.

66. As when she takes Mabonagrin's lady aside after the combat has

ended.

67. McConeghy, 781. Sterba's argument is similar to that of McConeghy, based on Enite's acquisition of appropriate speech. She concludes that Enite must learn to speak for herself, while Erec must learn to become "other-directed" and to see beyond himself: "each partner's penance consists in recognizing their sexually and socially determined domains of strength." (Serba, 67) The main difficulty with Sterba's argument is that it contradicts itself; Hartmann's narrative, while it may indeed represent one answer to the battle of the sexes, continues to reinforce patriarchal gender structures.

68. See John W. Baldwin, "Five Discourses on Desire: Sexuality and Gender in Northern France around 1200," *Speculum* 66 (1991): 815. Baldwin expands his arguments in *The Language of Sex. Five Voices from Northern France Around 1200* (Chicago: University of Chicago Press, 1994). According to Willson, equality of desire was not Hartmann's goal, rather the portrayal of Enite as the ultimate example of Christian wifehood. Hartmann proposes a "more explicitly religious conception of Enite's wifehood" that Chrétien. (65) Bernard Willson, "The Heroine's Loyalty in Hartmann's and Chrétien's *Erec*," in *Chretien de Troyes and the German Middle Ages*. Ed. Martin H. Jones and Roy E. Wisbey. Arthurian Studies 26, (Cambridge: D.S. Brewer, 1993), 65.

69. See Gertrud Jaron Lewis, "*daz vil edel wîp*. Die Haltung zeitgenössischer Kritiker zur Frauengestalt der mittelhochdeutschen Epik," in *Die Frau als Heldin und Autorin.Neue Ansätze zur deutschen Literatur*, ed. Wolfgang Paulsen (Bern: Francke, 1979) 66–82. Lewis notes that the female characters in *Iwein* are more numerous than in *Erec*, (70) though her analysis focuses primarily on Laudine.

70. Hartmann von Aue, *Iwein*, ed. G.F. Benecke and K. Lachmann, rev. by Ludwig Wolff (Berlin: Walter de Gruyter, 1968) line 527. Unless otherwise noted, English translations are from *Iwein by Hartmann von Aue*, trans. and ed. J.W. Thomas (Lincoln: University of Nebraska Press, 1979).

71. McConeghy provides a more accurate translation for this verse.

72. The narrator says:

> wan sîn wort daz was ein eit.
> dô bat er als ein vrävel man
> daz er müese vüeren dan
> sîn wîp diu küenginne.
> daz hæte die sinne
> dem künege vil nâch benomen.
> er sprach 'wie bin ich überkomen!
> die disen rât tâten,
> die hant mich verrâten.' (4584–4592)

[since the king's word was as good as a formal oath. The arrogant fellow then asked to be allowed to take away the queen, his wife. The king was stunned. 'I've been tricked,' he cried, 'and betrayed by those who advised me!']

Gottfried's Marke makes a similarly impulsive promise to the knight Gandin, who demands Isolde as reward for his music. (*Tristan*, 13178 ff.)

73. This is the same term used to describe Mabonagrin's garden, suggesting a connection to that space, a space portrayed as female though improperly appropriated by a woman at the expense of her partner's honor. Gustav Ehrismann views the spring as part of Laudine's "Feenlandschaft" in Geschichte der deutschen Literatur bis zum Ausgang des Mittelalters, Zweiter Teil (Munich: C. H. Beck, 1927), 179. Indeed, the spring is the gateway to Laudine's court and to her heart. See also Robert E. Lewis, *Symbolism in Hartmann's Iwein* (Göppingen: Kümmerle, 1975), 65–70. The spring is not only the entrance to Laudine's kingdom but a symbol of Laudine as well. (Lewis, 68) Wehrli takes this image one step further. Both Laudine and the spring represent 'elements' to be conquered that are actually extensions of the self (which Wehrli implies is male). The elements of nature unleashed by the force of the fountain, the chaos unleashed by Laudine's rejection of Iwein— "sie beherrschen heißt sich selbst besitzen." Thus Wehrli negates Laudine's existence. Max Wehrli, "Iweins Erwachen," in *Hartmann von Aue*, ed. Hugo Kuhn and Christoph Cormeau (Wissenschaftliche Buchgesellschaft: Darmstadt, 1973), 506.

74. Thelen, 34.

75. Compare Wolfram's account of the siege at Pelrapiere in Book IV of *Parzival*, in which he describes the starving inhabitants in terms of the fat that is *not* dripping into their cooking pans.

76. " . . . rather, he is abandoned to fate and even in the state of madness represents one of the elect, guided on his way through the unaware and penitential state of madness to reach his second quest." (Saunders, 71) While Saunders refers specifically to the French Yvain, the same applies to Hartmann's Iwein.

77. Wehrli reads a bit much into this scene in "Iweins Erwachen" when he interprets it as a reference to Christ's resurrection at Easter, with the countess and her ladies representing the three Marys.

78. Carne describes this event as "die erste Treueprobe" for the new Iwein. See Eva-Maria Carne, *Die Frauengestalten bei Hartmann von Aue. Ihre Bedeutung um Aufbau und Gehalt der Epen* (Marburg: N.G. Elwert, 1970). 100 For Carne, these women show Iwein the selfless "Güte" of Hartmann's best female characters.

79. See Grace M. Armstrong, "Women of Power: Chrétien de Troyes's Female Clerks," in *Women in French Literature*, ed. Michael Guggenheim (Saratoga, CA: ANMA Libri), 39. She also compares Lunete's innate verbal acuity to that which Enite eventually acquires. Petra Kellermann-Haaf also praises Lunete's skill as a diplomat: with "ihre messerscharfen Analyse der politischen Situation," she possesses "eine Ader für alles, was politisch opportun ist." (Kellermann-Haaf, 51)

80. For Carne, Lunete offers a stark contrast to her mistress: "Gütig, unkompliziert und vernünftig ist sie der hilfreiche Geist des Werkes, der alles zum Guten führen will." (38) In fact, Carne goes so far as to say that Lunete's character embodies the same ideal of femininity for Hartmann that Enite does. (134)

81. Joan Ferrante, "Male Fantasy and Female Reality in Courtly Literature," *Women's Studies* 10–11 (1983/84): 90.

82. Ferrante, 67. And she continues: "The hero moves in a world of symbols and stereotypes, pursuing his own images of love and honor, but he must eventually face and come to terms with reality, and it is frequently a woman who forces him to do so."

83. Steiner points out that it is actually Lunete who becomes central to Iwein's adventures in the second part of the work, not Laudine as one might expect. See Gertrud Steiner, "'Unbeschreiblich weiblich .' Zur mythischen Rezeption von Hartmanns *Iwein*," in *Psychologie in der Mediävistik. Gesammelte Beiträge des Sternheimer Symposions*, ed. Jürgen Kühnel (Göppingen: Kümmerle, 1985), 251.

84. Laudine's unjust treatment of Lunete for Iwein's failure throws her own judgment into question, though Lunete does not seem to blame her, "welches allerdings mehr auf den Edelmut der Zofe schließen läßt als den der Herrin." (Carne, 68)

85. Wapnewski, 67.

86. Blumstein, 71.

87. Blumstein, 126.

88. De Boor, 82.

89. Gustav Ehrismann, 183.

90. Kurt Ruh, "Zur Interpretation von Hartmanns *Iwein*," in *Hartmann von Aue*, ed. Hugo Kuhn and Christoph Cormeau (Wissenschaftliche Buchgesellschaft: Darmstadt, 1972), 418. Others have made concerted efforts to rehabilitate Laudine and her reputation. Ojar Kratins, while he does not excuse Laudine's behavior, tries to offer one reason for these negative criticisms, namely that Hartmann (despite his asides with *vrou Minne*) tries to place Laudine "on the same level with Iwein, that is, on a level with which the audience can identify and feels free, therefore, to criticize." See Ojars Kratins, "Love and Marriage in

Three Versions of 'The Knight with the Lion ,'" *Comparative Literature*
16 (1964): 37. Göttner-Abendroth sees Laudine's realm as one of two
world orders in *Iwein*; the other is represented by Arthur and his court,
which she characterizes as "feudal-patriarchal." See Heide Göttner-Abendroth, *Die Göttin und ihr Heros. Die matriarchalen Religionen in
Mythos, Märchen, und Dichtung* (München: Frauenoffensive, 1980).
More recently, Otfrid Ehrismann goes so far as to attribute a certain
"postmodern" quality to Hartmann's depiction of Laudine, in that Hartmann demands that his audience accept her actions with a degree of openness: "Hartmann verschließt den alten Sinn des Motivs der leicht
getrösteten Witwe keineswegs, aber er macht ihn in gewisser Weise plu-
ralistisch rezipierbar." See Otfrid Ehrismann, "Laudine— oder: Hartmanns *Iwein* postmodern." in *Sammlung—Deutung—Wertung. Ergebnisse, Probleme, Tendenzen und Perspektiven philologischer Arbeit.
Mélanges de littéature médiévale et de linguistique allemande offerts à
Wolfgang Spiewok à l'occasion de son soixantiè annivsersaire par ses collègues et amis.* ed. Danielle Buschinger (Amiens: Université de Picardie.
Centre d'Études médiévales, 1988), 96.
　91. Ruh describes Laudine as "die feenhafte Quellenherrin." (419)
　92. Göttner-Abendroth, 183.
　93. "Wenn Laudine Herrin einer Gewitterquelle ist, so weist dies auf
ihren urpsrünglichen Feencharakter hin." (Ruh, 418) Whether Laudine's
character and her realm are remnants of matriarchal myth, as Göttner-
Abendroth would have it, is another question.
　94. See Volker Mertens, *Laudine. Soziale Problematik im Iwein Hartmanns von Aue* (Berlin: Erich Schmidt, 1978). Mertens sees Erec's situation mirrored in *Iwein*, for example, where Iwein must learn that a marriage based only on *minne* and desire is inadequate. (62) The difference
between the two works has to do with Hartmann's insistent references to
the social reality of the thirteenth century through his portrayal of Laudine as "Herrscherin." The Arthurian "Traumwelt" must yield to social
and political reality here. (68) In this context, according to Mertens, magic
has no role: "Trotz des mythologischen Apparats von Zauberbrunnen und
magischem Unwetter ist Laudines Welt die prosaische der Realität, und in
dieser finden beide ihr Glück, das eben deshalb nicht von der oft ver-
mißten Märchensicherheit, sondern nur *wænlich* sein kann." (65) Kellermann-Haaf agrees that Laudine's position as a widowed "Landesherrin"
is more "realitätsnah" than in any other courtly romance. (Kellermann-
Haaf, 42)
　For a withering but unjust critique of Mertens' analysis, see Gert
Kaiser's "'Iwein' oder 'Laudine'," *Zeitschrift für deutsche Philologie* 99
(1980): 20–28. Kaiser insists that the work is called 'Iwein' and not 'Lau-

dine' for a reason and that "der Beziehungshintergrund 'Situation der adeligen Frau' bietet keinen Schlüssel, um das Romangeschehen in seiner Komplexität zu deuten." (28) Perhaps the historical background is not the key to the work; however, it certainly adds to rather than lessens the complexity of Hartmann's endeavor.

95. See 1873–1878. Mertens makes a case for this as "Konvenienzehe," which Laudine would have felt compelled to agree to in her position as queen, to fulfill her obligations to her land. (Mertens, 36) For Carne, Hartmann's justification only serves to remind the modern reader of Laudine's immoral behavior. (Carne, 66) This is the type of judgment Mertens' analysis tries to rectify.

96. Her decision to find a husband to replace Ascalon obviously contradicts her earlier insistence at his burial that she could never commit such a sacrilege as to marry again.

97. Actually, it must be noted in Laudine's defense that she is coerced into making the decision in Iwein's favor, by Iwein and Lunete:

> diu maget und her Îwein
> begunden ahten under in zwein
> daz sîz noch versuochten baz,
> ob sî ir vrouwen haz
> bekêrte mit guote
> ze senfterem muote. (2003–2008)

[the maid and lord Iwein began to discuss between themselves whether they could better arrange it that she turn her lady's hatred to a more agreeable mood.]

98. She is not just the daughter of a duke, her higher rank illustrating one of Hartmann's most noticeable adaptations to his source. Mertens points this out (34–40) as does McConeghy in the introduction to his translation of *Iwein*. See Patrick McConeghy, ed. and trans., *Iwein* (New York: Garland, 1984).

99. In her analysis of spatial discourse in Chrétien's Yvain, Margaret Hostetler views Laudine's connection to both castle and fountain as creating a "division between [Laudine's] natural, violent passions and her social role as courtly lady." The locations of castle and fountain thereby "underscore Laudine's paradoxical position in the courtly love and marriage economies." See Margaret Hostetler, "Enclosed and Invisible?: Chrétien's Spatial Discourse and the Problem of Laudine," *Romance Notes* 37.2 (1997): 121.

100. Clearly there is a perceived threat to Iwein's identity as a knight and therefore as a man. In this context, it is also intriguing to consider Lau-

dine's fountain as a possible threat to Iwein's (or any man's) potency. This spring would thus represent an inversion of the "Fountain of Youth" that often graces the landscape of "Love's places" according to Michael Camille. See Michael Camille, *The Medieval Art of Love* (New York: Harry N. Abrams, 1998).

101. For Schwietering, Gawein's advice "stellt die erzieherische Idee der Dichtung programmatischer hin als Chrestien." See Julius Schwietering, *Die deutsche Dichtung des Mittelalters* (Hermann Gentner: Darmstadt, 1957), 159.

102. Gawein also convinces Iwein that, among other things, his wife can take care of herself. Faithful women need no other kind of *huote* besides their own honor. (2890–2893)

103. Ribard comments that barriers often appear at the beginning of romance adventures: "Au point de départ donc du roman. . .une situation de blocage—blocage réel, social ou psychologique . . ." (75) As illustrated in *Iwein*, these barriers frequently takes the form of imprisonment, physical (in towers and other enclosed places), and/or emotional (through the bonds of love).

104. *Erec*, 10119–10123. In contrast to Chrétien, where Erec and Enide are crowned at Arthur's court, Hartmann returns his couple to Karnant. The Arthurian court in *Erec*, while physically separate from Karnant, is institutionally the same. This treatment of the Arthurian court is unique to *Erec* and it changes considerably not only in *Iwein* but also in *Parzival*. Significantly, the Arthurian court does not figure at all in Gottfried's *Tristan*.

105. Otfrid Ehrismann, "Laudine," 97. And such pluralism and openness suit Hartmann, a poet "dessen Weltbild erschüttert und der mit klassischer Schlichtheit und ironischer Altersweisheit zu erzählen weiß: zu erzählen weiß von der Dekonstruktion der arthurischen Welt."

106. See Kathryn Smits, "Enite als christliche Ehefrau." *Interpretation und Edition deutscher Texte des Mittelalters*. Festschrift für John Asher zum 60. Geburtstag. Ed. Kathryn Smits, Werner Besch, and Victor Lange. (Berlin: Erich Schmidt, 1981) 13–25.

107. Of course, it becomes apparent that Iwein possesses a faulty understanding of the knight's role, at least as Gawein describes it to him and as it is practiced at the Arthurian court. But his freedom from the 'confines' of Laudine's court is necessary in order for him to discover the proper role.

CHAPTER 3

The Topography of Wolfram von Eschenbach

Spaces of "Becoming" and "Being" in Parzival

> *Even when gender seems to congeal into the most rei-*
> *fied forms, the 'congealing' is itself an insistent and in-*
> *sidious practice, sustained and regulated by various so-*
> *cial means.*
>
> —Judith Butler[1]

> *ich wil iu mêr von wîbes orden sagn*
> *man und wîp diu sind al ein*
> *als diu sunn diu hiute schein,*
> *und ouch der name der heizet tac.*
> *der enwederz sich gescheiden mac:*
> *si blüent ûz eime kerne gar.*
> *daz nemet künsteclîche war.*
>
> —Wolfram von Eschenbach[2]

Plot synopsis: Wolfram's *Parzival* is one of the most complex romance narratives, as a brief synopsis illustrates. Wolfram begins
with the story of Gahmuret, second son of the King of Anjou,
who goes east to seek his fortune. In the land of Zazamanc, he
marries the Moorish princess Belacane but leaves her to return to
his life of tourneying. (Book I) Their son Feirefiz, whose skin is
both black and white, is born after Gahmuret's departure.
Gahmuret then wins the hand of Herzeloyde, whom he can
marry because his first 'wife' was not baptized. Soon after,
Gahmuret is killed in a tournament (again in eastern realms),
Herzeloyde gives birth to their son Parzival. (Book II) In order to
keep him safe from the dangers of knightly life, Herzeloyde tries

to raise Parzival in a deserted place called Soltane; however, he eventually meets several knights from the Arthurian court and decides he must leave his mother. (Book III) After finding Arthur's court and killing Ither (the red knight), Parzival moves on; he receives training from the experienced Gurnemanz, rescues (and marries) the beseiged Condwiramurs (Book IV),and fails to ask the question of Anfortas on his first visit to the Grail castle Munsalvaesche (Book V). Hailed as a hero by the Arthurian court, he is nonetheless shamed before all by the hideous Cundrie for his failure at Munsalvaesche and he leaves to seek the Grail. (Book VI)

The next sections of Wolfram's narrative have a double focus. The story turns its primary focus to the adventures of Gawan, who leaves Arthur's court on his own quest at the same time Parzival departs (Books VII and VIII as well as Books X--XIV). Parzival meets the hermit Trevrizent in Book IX, where he learns his heritage and comes to recognize the sins for which he must take responsibility: the death of his mother, the death of Ither, and the failure to ask the question. The two strands of the narrative come together again in Book XV: after combat with Gawan, Parzival fights against an unknown knight, who turns out to be his half brother Feirefiz. They reach a truce and return together to Arthur's court, where (after more than four long years) Parzival is reunited with his wife and his two sons. They set off for the Grail castle, where Parzival has been summoned by the Grail messenger Cundrie and where he succeeds in asking Anfortas the question: "œheim, waz wirret dier?" (795,29) Parzival can take his appointed place as Grail king. Meanwhile, smitten by love for the Grail bearer Repanse de Schoye, Feirefiz has himself baptized. Leaving Parzival at Munsalvaesche, this couple travels east and they later become the parents of Prester John. The narrative ends with a brief version of the story of Parzival's heir, Loherangrin. (Book XVI).

In Book III of *Parzival*, the older knight Gurnemanz comes to the end of his catalogue of instructions for the young Parzival, and he exhorts his inexperienced pupil to seek favor with women:

> und lât iu liep sîn diu wîp:
> daz tiwert junges mannes lîp.

gewenket nimmer tag an in:
daz ist reht manlîcher sin. (172,9–12)

[Let women be dear to you, for that enhanced a young man's worth. Do not waver a single day toward them; that is true manly conduct.]

The conduct of "true men" should always reflect an understanding of what Gurnemanz calls "wîbes orden," which is really the essence of the relationship between men and women: "man und wîp diu sind al ein" (173,1) as the sun is to the day and "si blüent ûz eime kerne gar." (173,5) Man and woman, husband and wife[3] are one and they blossom from the same seed. Gurnemanz's explanation resonates with Wolfram's own views in the prologue to *Parzival*, where the poet leaves no doubt as to the importance he places on the role that both men and women will play in Parzival's story. The narrator promises that his tale will deal not only with "mannes mannheit alsô sleht" (4,12) but also with "wîplîchez wîbes reht." (4,11); this attitude is supported by Gurnemanz's advice is formulated in terms that support the prologue's apparently even-handed approach to the roles of men and women. Indeed, Gurnemanz' statement has often been interpreted Wolfram's as rather liberating attitude toward the relationship between men and women— i.e., they represent a kind of Platonic unity of two halves necessary for the successful functioning of a whole. One can infer a double meaning in the lesson here, however. On one level, Gurnemanz is simply speaking of the qualities attributed to womankind ("wîbes orden," the state of woman). But he seems to understand the state of womankind in particular to be distinguished by the fact that woman and man are one, suggesting that such union necessarily defines woman in a way that it does not define man.

Gurnemanz' subtle definition adds another layer of meaning to the prologue's discussion of "wîplîchez wîbes reht" and represents the fundamental contradiction (and the resulting ambivalence) that exists for Wolfram with regard to the question of woman[4]: women must both be included and excluded from society. This is the enduring paradox that literally places woman at the heart of Weigel's dialectic between the familiar (*eigenem*) and the other (*fremdem*). The dialectic accommodates not only the recognition of the necessity of marriage, expressed by Gurnemanz[5] as well as the "reht" attributed to women by the narrator in the prologue, but also the attitude (found in both literary and theological works) that women present a constant threat to order and to the world. The various spaces and forms of movement in Wolfram's *Parzival* illustrate Weigel's dialectic at work:

> Dabei werden die *Thesen* entwickelt, daß im Diskurs über die Wilden/die Fremde und im Diskurs über Frau/Weiblichkeit strukturanaloge Konzepte zu sehen sind, in denen die Dialektik von Eigenem und Fremdem aus der Perspektive des Einen im Blick auf das Andere organisiert ist und . . . durch ähnliche Vorstellungen, aber unterschiedliche diskursive Funktionsweisen zu kennzeichnen ist . . ."[6]

Wolfram literally expands the borders of the romance world far beyond the Arthurian court on several planes of existence. In so doing, he also widens the literary panorama of possibilities offered not only by the world of the Arthurian court but of two others: the Orient and the Grail castle. In terms of the processes that we discussed in *Erec* and *Iwein*, Wolfram's worlds offer their inhabitants a greater variety of places to 'be' and spaces to 'become.' Not surprisingly, process is of primary importance to Wolfram; he says so himself with respect to his hero: Parzival enters the story as a boy who grows beyond his *tumpheit* to become *træclîche wîs*. As Parzival goes through the process of acquiring wisdom and knowledge, he can 'become' the new model 'self' that Wolfram envisions for the perfect knight. This process is very complex, and in order for the audience to understand it along with the hero, Wolfram creates an equally complex and multi-layered narrative. On his long journey toward the Grail and eventual self-hood, Parzival has numerous encounters with a variety of 'others' as he traverses the spaces of the worlds Wolfram creates in the narrative. Wolfram also takes the audience on this journey, allowing them also to encounter 'other' worlds as well.

It becomes clear that the 'others' who inhabit these worlds and spaces can take a wide variety of forms ranging from giants, Moors, sorcerers, knights, kings, and hermits. One could say that these 'others' literally personify Weigel's theses (*Thesen*) that develop in a discourse on that which is wild or foreign (*die Wilden/die Fremde*). The spaces structure the interactions of the hero and the foreigners or outsiders, concretely forming "strukturanaloge Konzepte" to be interpreted by the audience. The spaces and the ideas that they structure also work to organize the dialectic between that which is one's own (*eigen*) and that which is foreign or strange (*fremd*) from the perspective of the self – looking at the other in another space. According to Weigel, the spaces that structure the discourse concerning the wild and the foreign similarly structure the discourse about women and the 'feminine' (often understood as the wild or foreign other with respect to the male self). *Parzival* clearly combines its version of both discourses in its topography: images of 'other' spaces, however many knights or monsters they include, *always* involve women.

Wolfram is roundly criticized by Gottfried for his expansive narrative. Gottfried, in the lines that follow his high praise of Hartmann (*Tristan* 4638–4690), describes Wolfram as "des hasen geselle" (4638) and a "vindære wilder mære." (4665) Indeed, perhaps like a hare jumping wildly over a "word-heath," Wolfram does expect his audience to follow him on a journey through the extraordinary geography he creates for the world(s) in *Parzival*. By creating at least three distinct worlds, Wolfram greatly expands the possibilities and the spaces for 'becoming' in his narrative. Wolfram's narrative style may appear disjointed and haphazard to Gottfried, but this style conceals a fairly unified design concept that Wolfram exhibits in the spaces he creates and the negotiations that occur in them. Even while displaying a wonderfully broad panorama of possibilities in *Parzival*, Wolfram does not allow them to get out of hand. They are in fact finally limited by the major addition that Wolfram makes to the Arthurian plot of Hartmann's romances—the Grail. As Parzival represents the exemplary king in Book XVI, in contrast to Arthur and other secular kings, so too does the story of the Grail seem to represent the search for the true order, to which all other stories and orders must remain subordinate. This addition of the Grail, because it has its own ideology that is (however creatively) tied to thirteenth century theology, necessarily privileges certain traditional models over others. Thus, as though to avert any of Hartmann's ambiguities, Wolfram attempts ultimately to fix the possibilities much more firmly into 'being' through a gendered topography structured more deliberately than Hartmann's.

WOLFRAM'S REACTION TO HARTMANN

In Book III, as Parzival nears Arthur's court, Wolfram directly addresses the poet who introduced the *matière de Bretagne* to German audiences, warning him to treat the new arrival well:

> mîn hêr Hartmann von Ouwe,
> frou Ginovêr iwer frouwe
> und iwer hêrre der künc Artûs,
> den kumt ein mîn gast ze hûs.
> bitet hüeten sîn vor spotte. (143,21–25)

[Sir Hartmann von Aue! To the house of your lady Ginover and
your lord, king Arthur, a guest of mine is coming. Please protect
him from mockery there!]

In speaking to Hartmann this way, Wolfram explicitly encourages
his audience to compare him and his story with his predecessor. In
his concern over Parzival's reception at Arthur's court as a place
where his fledgling hero must be protected "vor spotte," Wolfram
also seems to suggest the nature of his own later criticism of the
Arthurian court as shallow and concerned only with a knight's superficial qualities.[7] On a theoretical level, this represents another
instance of many in which Wolfram illustrates the nature of his
text as a process of "play" that (to use Iser's terms once more) will
produce meaning through the interaction of author, text, and audience.[8]

Wolfram's "play" becomes evident as he takes great care to integrate certain characters of *Erec* and *Iwein* into *Parzival*'s narrative.[9] Each character and situation resonate meaningfully in
Wolfram's narrative. Immediately after leaving his mother, Parzival
stumbles upon the lady Jeschute and treats her in a very uncourtly
manner. As it happens, Jeschute is Erec's sister, and the brutal treatment of her by her husband Orilus (to punish her apparent infidelity with Parzival) reminds the reader of Erec's treatment of
Enite. Wolfram uses the figure of the mournful and faithful Sigune
to comment negatively on the seemingly fickle behavior of
Laudine. On two separate occasions in *Parzival*, the poet indicates
in no uncertain terms that Sigune would not have given heed to
Lunete's advice to marry after the death of Ascalon. In Book V,
Parzival comes upon Sigune sitting in a linden tree. This tree symbolizes earthly love contrasts with the movement that Sigune is
making away from the temporal world. Wolfram says:

> ouch was froun Lûneten rât
> ninder dâ bî ir gewesen.
> diu riet ir frouwen 'lat genesen
> disen man, der den iwern sluoc:

> er mag ergetzen iuch genuoc.'
> Sigûne gerte ergetzens niht,
> als wîp die man bî wanke siht . . . (253,10–16)

[No thought had come to her as the counsel Lunete gave to her
mistress when she said: "Permit this man to live who slew your
husband. He can give you recompense enough." Signe desired
no such recompense as do women who are fickle . . .]

These verses, particularly the final line, secured Laudine's reputation for posterity as a primary example of woman's fickle nature,
and Wolfram's contrast is clear. Sigune's *triuwe* will not waver as
Laudine's did ("als wîp die man bî wanke siht"), and Sigune
chooses the life of an ascetic devoted to prayer and the memory of
her deceased lover rather than bestow her affections on another.

Parzival's encounter with Sigune outside her cell in the forest
at the beginning of Book IX gives Wolfram the opportunity for his
second criticism of Laudine. Here Wolfram praises the woman
who shuns another man's love while her own husband lives. If she
maintains her honor and her restraint following her husband's
death, the more praise she deserves:

> behelt si dennoch êre,
> sine treit dehein sô liehten kranz,
> gêt si durch freude an den tanz. (436,20–22)

[Yet if she still preserves his honor, she wears a garland brighter
than if she went, wreathed and merry, to the dance.]

Not a static queen with her own kingdom to bestow upon the
knight who would defend it and her honor, Sigune herself under-
takes a solitary journey in a space removed from courtly society,
traveling toward her goal of eventual reunion with
Schionatulander and God. In this way, Wolfram removes the conflict faced by Laudine from the arena of "actual" politics to a spiritual plane. Whereas Laudine decides to remarry following the
death of her first husband, Sigune refuses to be unfaithful to her
lover and Wolfram prefers to emphasize the indissolubility of the
bond shared between Sigune and Schionatulander.[10] Wolfram, at
least in the comparison between Laudine and Sigune, seems to
imply even consent alone can create an indissoluble bond between
man and woman, however one understands marriage.[11]

Wolfram's comparison of Sigune and Laudine exemplifies the way in which Wolfram incorporates Hartmann's work into his own and seeks to transcend it. Wolfram focuses on Sigune's *triuwe* and her *êre*, both of which must obey a higher law than Hartmann's *Realpolitik*, and on her spiritual journey.[12] Wolfram's criticism of Laudine specifically engages and refutes Hartmann's depiction of her role in *Iwein*. This criticism also illustrates that Wolfram, in contrast to Wand's assessment, does indeed go beyond factual narrative references and he engages in a more subtle discussion with his predecessor,[13] a discussion that can be charted through an examination of the gender topographies that shape the spaces of and between the various worlds of *Parzival*.

Relationships between men and women are certainly important for Hartmann; in *Erec* and *Iwein*, the relationships between the protagonists and their ladies play a pivotal role in the narrative. Wolfram emphasizes the centrality of these relationships on a broader social level. Throughout the work, Wolfram illustrates how unrequited or inappropriate love can have disastrous effects on various communities: Isenhart gives his armor away to prove his love of Belacane and he dies as a result of her 'test'; Clamide besieges Pelrapiere to force the hand of Condwiramurs, and she will not relent; Anfortas has caused the entire Grail world to suffer with him as a result of the wound he received in a duel for love. Courtly society is threatened with violent rupture if the proper courtly interactions between men and women are disrupted or prevented. As mentioned in Chapter 1, the scene which illustrates this most effectively occurs in Book XIII. (636,15–641,30) This scene shows the process through which Gawan 'heals' the rift that has persisted among the members of the court at the *Schastel marveile*, "sît si Clinschores kraft/mit sînen listen überwant." (637,19–20) The vengeful Clinschor has imprisoned his people within the castle gates, cursing them with the inability to communicate with one another in the language of standard courtly interactions: "daz si ze gegenworte/ nie kômen, frouwen noch die man." (637,22–23) A kind of Babel has resulted. Clearly, a society without proper contact between men and women can have no courtly interaction and thus can have no *minne*; this is a catastrophe. The people at Clinschor's court remain "ein ander unbekant" (637,20) until Gawan can reacquaint them once more, enabling the women and men of the court to function and interact as courtly society should: under the watchful eyes of Gawan, they gradually come together through eating (639,1–12), dancing (639,15–24), and conversation:

> Gar schiere ein ende nam der tanz.
> juncfrouwen mit varwen glanz
> sâzen dort unde hie:
> die rîter sâzen zwischen sie.
> des freude sich an sorgen rach,
> swer dâ nâch werder minne sprach,
> ob er vant süeziu gegenwort. (641,1–7)

[Shortly afterward the dance came to an end. The maidens in their bright beauty sat here and there, and the knights took seats at their side. He who pleaded for noble love, his joy took revenge on sorrow, and he received a gracious answer.]

Joy now takes its revenge on sorrow ("des freude sich an sorgen rach"), knights and ladies can now exchange words with one another ("süeziu gegenwort"), and *minne* has returned to this society; it is whole once more.[14] In its depiction of a harmonic whole, this scene anticipates the conclusion of the narrative, when Parzival finally heals Anfortas and Arthur presides over many marriages on the plain of Joflanze; like these later scenes, the effect of the one at the *Schastel marveile* is, of course, to represent the picture of society as it could or should become. Wolfram concludes all the narrative strands of his *Parzival* with scenes of "re-union," which seem to offer a vision of stability and harmony. The social body has been (re)constructed, as women and men have found their proper relationships to one another.[15] The establishing and the negotiation of these relations forms an integral part of Wolfram's program.

Love is at the center of these negotiations, of course. Just as Wolfram shows the *minne* as a crucial factor in the ultimate reintegration of society,[16] at least properly contained within the bounds of marriage, he also illustrates the illustrate the danger that manifests itself in *minne* as a potentially destructive force. As we have seen, this force wreaks havoc at the *Schastel marveile*, stemming from Clinschor's shame and ill will toward all men and women that results from his castration at the hands of a lover's angry husband:

> Durch die scham an sîme lîbe
> wart er man noch wîbe
> guotes willen nimmer mêr bereit;
> ich mein die tragent werdekeit.

swaz er den freuden mac genemn,
des kan von herzen in gezemn. (658, 3–8)

[For the shame done to his body he never again bore good will
toward anyone, man or woman, and when he can rob them of
any joy, especially those who are honored and respected, that
does his heart good.]

The source of Clinschor's ill will, *minne* appears here in an immoderate and selfish form. As a result of it, Clinschor has been literally
ungendered: Wolframs says he is neither man nor woman ("man
noch wîbe") and he essentially has no place in society. This is the
type of *minne* that also literally cripples the Grail society at
Munsalvæsche, physically represented by Anfortas' wound that cannot be healed; this love turned violent also motivates numerous military conflicts throughout the work and causes much suffering.[17]

Clearly, Wolfram believes that both women and men have
their respective parts to play, both in the game of *minne* as well as
in medieval courtly society at large. The conflicts and the suffering
that are caused by immoderate *minne* and that occur throughout
the narrative usually involve women who are threatened (beseiged,
as in the case of Condwiramurs or Belacane) or who are a threat
(to Clinschor and Anfortas, for example). These conflicts are invariably resolved by means of a male agent (Arthur, Parzival,
Gawan). In both the prologue as well as in Gurnemanz's advice,
Wolfram subtly associates the potential for conflict and disorder
with woman's particular role, betraying an unmistakable concern
for the behavior of women that undercuts the relative equality he
seems to advocate for both genders. Following the prologue's
rather convoluted introduction, in which he addresses his ideal
male audience (2,5–22), Wolfram changes his style and his tone in
the second part of his introduction. (2,23–3,24) He dedicates this
section exclusively to a longer and much more organized discussion of the "zil" (2,25) he envisions for women.

Dise manger slahte underbint
iedoch niht gar von manne sint.
für diu wîp stôze ich disiu zil.
swelhiu mîn râten merken wil,
diu sol wizzen war si kêre
ir prîs und ir êre,
und wem si dâ nâch sî bereit

> minne und werdekeit,
> sô daz si niht geriuwe
> ir kiusche und ir triuwe. (2,23–3,2)

[These various definitions are by no means directed at men solely; for women I will set up these same goals, Any woman willing to mark my advice shall know where to bestow her praise and honors, and, accordingly, on whom to bestow her love and respect, so that she will not rue the giving of her purity and devotion.]

Although he asserts that his goals for women do not differ from those he sets for men, Wolfram changes his tone. There is no play of images and no dialectical tension among concepts, "sondern klare, eindeutige, stufenförmige geordnete Aussage."[18] The new tone seems to imply that the message must be unmistakably clear for women, so that they will not misunderstand its meaning and perhaps go astray. Wolfram establishes this tone by focusing his goals for women concretely on the qualities of *kiusche* ("chastity," 3,2), *triuwe* ("loyalty," 3,2), and *stæte* ("constancy," 3,8). For Blumstein, the clarity of this message has the effect of relativizing the position of women and it is thus clear that, while Wolfram discusses man on a metaphysical level in the prologue, he maintains the discussion of woman on the secular social level.[19] He artfully contrasts his ideal of woman with a discussion of falsity ("conterfeit" in 3,12) that is generally read as an oblique and very negative reference to Gottfried's Isolde: "die lobe ich als ich solde/daz safer im golde." (3,13–14) It is true that, over the course of the narrative, Wolfram does stress repeatedly that these characteristics (*kiusche, stæte, triuwe*) properly belong to both men and women; nevertheless, it is significant that he feels the need to include them specifically his discussion of women from the beginning. In effect, Wolfram says from the start that these are the qualities that women must possess in order to 'be' women.

On the surface, Wolfram appears to be describing the characteristics of men and of women in a relatively neutral tone. Certainly, the context of the remarks supports this interpretation. One can, however, read a subtext of these statements that urges greater ambivalence, hinting that women are to be viewed with caution. Wolfram also reveals this ambivalence in Parzival's speech to Gawan as the two prepare to depart Arthur's court in Book VI. Parzival encourages Gawan to place his trust in women rather than in God, since God has obviously proven an unreliable object of service:

> friunt, ân dînes kampfes zît
> dâ nem ein wîp für dich den strît:
> diu müeze ziehen dîne hant;
> an der diu kiusche hâst bekant
> unt wîplîche güete:
> ir minn dich dâ behüete. (332,9–14)

[Friend, when it comes your time to fight, may a woman be your shield in battle and may she guide your hand—a woman in whom you have found both virtue and womanly kindness. May her love keep guard over you!]

Parzival's misguided advice only emphasizes his own inability to understand the situation. Eventually, he will learn that service to God is essential, and this will bring him (not Gawan) to the Grail. He must become aware and straighten out his priorities.

Parzival does become aware and he does become the Grail king. But the major interest of *Parzival* in the following lies not in the obvious (i.e. becoming worthy of the Grail), but rather in the topography of being that is represented by women in the story. Through the various processes of 'becoming' depicted in *Parzival*, Wolfram shows us various encounters with a multitude of 'others'—he shows us greater possibilities and greater play, yet ultimately greater restriction and a more concerted attempt to fix women particularly in to certain models of being: either they are part of man (as Gurnemanz suggests) or they are part of God (Sigune) or they remain positionally marginal and other. This is a fairly clear-cut program, one whose clarity belies the sometimes digressive nature of its presentation.

As he ranges far and wide over his "wortheide" in *Parzival*, however, Wolfram creates an extremely complex universe, impressive in its breadth and depth, in its cast of characters, and in its indictment of courtly society. This universe, which encompasses the far reaches of the Orient as well as the Arthurian court and the spiritual kingdom of the Grail, accommodates a broader variety of spaces for Wolfram's characters than we find in Hartmann's *Erec* and *Iwein*. Out of miscellaneous sources and traditional material, only some of which can be determined with any degree of certainty, Wolfram creates not only a unique but "a purely poetic geography which is consistent, symbolically meaningful, and artistically admirable."[20] Wolfram's expanded geography offers the audience's imagination a veritable playground of new and different places, and he suggests a variety of possibilities for the way in which 'other' beings (and other ways of being) may be encountered there.

WOLFRAM'S WORLDS

In *Parzival*, Wolfram creates three major worlds: the Orient, the Arthurian court, and the Grail world. These three worlds form the topographical framework of *Parzival*, remaining distinct from one another yet inextricably interconnected throughout the work.

The Orient provides the backdrop for the first two books, in which Gahmuret, as the second son of the house of Anjou, ventures eastward to seek his fortune. The Arthurian court provides the mainstay of the traditional courtly world, as it does in Hartmann, though Wolfram calls it more explicitly into question through Cundrie's public reprimand of Parzival before Arthur and his company in Book VI. In her greeting to Arthur, she offers a scathing indictment of the Arthurian society:

> Künc Artûs, du stüent ze lobe
> hôhe dînn genôzen obe:
> dîn stîgender prîs nu sinket,
> dîn snelliu wirde hinket,
> dîn hôhez lop sich neiget,
> dîn prîs hât valsch erzeiget.
> tavelrunder prîses kraft
> hât erlemt ein geselleschaft
> die drüber gap hêr Parzivâl,
> der ouch dort treit diu rîters mâl. (315,1–10)

[King Arthur, you were praised above your peers. But your rising fame is sinking, your swift renown now limps, your high praise is dwindling, your honor has proven false. The fame and power of the Round Table are lamed now that Sir Parzival has joined its company, though he also bears, as he sits over there, the outward signs of a knight.]

The court can only recognize the physical knightly perfection Parzival has attained, while they remain blind to the spiritual deficiency that this perfection masks. This blindness only reinforces the images of sickness and injury with which Cundrie describes the state of the Round Table's decay.

The Arthurian world, or perhaps more precisely the courtly world, encompasses other spaces as well. The castle of Gurnemanz, for example, and the places to which Gawan travels during his adventures in Books VII and VIII (as well as in Books X-XIV) can also be considered as extensions of the court, similar in ethos though differing in detail. Finally, the Grail world represents the culmination of Parzival's process of becoming. The society of Munsalvaesche is intended to portray the incorporation ✓ the courtly and the spiritual, located in a place that stands alone ("ein burc diu stêt al ein," 250,24) and that cannot be found by those who seek it:

> swer die suochet flîzeclîche,
> leider der envint ir niht.
> vil liute manz doch werben siht.
> ez muoz unwizzende geschehen,
> swer immer sol die burc gesehen. (250,26–30)

[He who diligently seeks it will not find it, alas. Yet many do search for it. He who shall see the castle unawares.]

Sigune, true to her function as namer, gives this information to the audience and to Parzival in Book V. (250,17–251,20) The domain that surrounds Munsalvaesche realm is called Terre de salvaesche, and it not only encompasses the Grail castle but also the forest where Sigune and Trevrizent retreat from the courtly world to the solitude of their cells.[21]

The variety of these spaces allows Wolfram opportunities to create and illustrate 'otherness.' Thus, the polarity between the strange and the familiar, the self and the other becomes more apparent in *Parzival* through Wolfram's spatialization of the text. He starts with the Orient.

THE ORIENT

Wolfram's Orient is a geographically determinate space, relatively speaking; as one of his most creative additions to Chrétien's *Perceval*, this space continues to intrigue critics. Gahmuret's story has been interpreted as, if not a reflection of the political situation of the house of Anjou in the late twelfth century[22] then certainly a "reale zeitgeschichtliche Situation."[23] Undoubtedly, eastern world of the Orient would have held a certain degree of familiarity for the thirteenth-century audience, living in the latter part of what scholars have traditionally referred to as "the twelfth-century Renaissance." During this "golden age of early scholasticism and of literary humanism"[24] that witnessed the disputes of Bernard of Clairvaux and Peter Abelard, the lyrics of the troubadors, and the spectacular failure of the second and third Crusades, the world was awakening to new intellectual as well as new geographic horizons.[25] Historians of geography describe an intellectual world quite literally extending its margins with the influx of Arabic learning after the advent of the Crusading era.[26] Translators in the Castilian capital of Toledo and the kingdom of Sicily expedited the recovery of ancient Greek and Arabic learning for the Christian West. Physical horizons also continued to expand in the direction of Africa and Asia, due mainly to the influences of international trade and the crusades.[27]

Typically, the culture Wolfram depicts in the East combines both the strange and the familiar, and there is no doubt that it represents the margin of the courtly world. Its relation to historical circumstances and medieval knowledge of geography remain subject to debate.[28] Generally, however, most critics agree that Wolfram's Orient is his own invention, despite any superficial similarities to actual history or geography. Thus, it seems reasonable to look for another meaning behind *Parzival*'s very elaborate introduction. Recently, Wolfram's representation of the Orient has been interpreted in terms of an attempt literally to incorporate the strange into the familiar and reappropriate it.[29] The fabulous wealth of the Baruch[30] is, of course, unparalleled in Europe. As the most powerful man in his part of the world, the Baruch is the first to whom the young Gahmuret offers his services as mercenary:

> im [Gahmuret] wart gesagt, ze Baldac
> wære ein sô gewaltic man,
> daz im der erde undertân
> diu zwei teil wæren oder mêr.
> sîn name heidensch was sô hêr
> daz man in hiez den bâruc. (13,16–21)

[He was told that in Baghdad there was a man so powerful that two-thirds of the earth, or more, was subject to him. To heathens his name was so great that he was called "The Baruch."]

The Baruch accepts Gahmuret's services, as any courtly lord would and should. Furthermore, as evidenced by the deeds of Isenhart and later Feirefiz in Zazamanc, the etiquette of knightly service to ladies prevails in this heathen culture just as it does in France and Wales. Their society is built upon the foundations of courtliness expected by the travelers from the west. The Baruch, for example, shows Gahmuret great favor ("dem wart der bâruc vil holt," 14,9) and rewards him as any generous ruler (European or otherwise) should. In return, Gahmuret hurries to aid him when news comes to Kanvoleis that the brothers Ipomidon and Pompeius are once again challenging the Baruch's authority. (101,21–102,22)

In general, the Middle Ages viewed the Orient as the geographic, cultural, and ethical antithesis of the Christian world and its values.[31] Wolfram is certainly too skilled a poet (and perhaps too much a realist more than a century after the first Crusade) to represent his Orient as merely the negative of western Christian courtly culture. Nevertheless, he makes the differences clear. Even though the Orient is unmistakably configured as "courtly" and peopled with the familiar cast of jousting knights and beautiful ladies, the world remains 'other' and outside: these people have a different skin color, they worship other gods, they live far from France. Wolfram reinforces the strangeness and the 'otherness' of this space by inscribing in it two female characters: the queens Belacane and Secundille. These two queens are effectively marginalized by their positions in distant Orient, not only geographically but thematically.[32] They themselves cannot be integrated into traditional courtly society, and their lovers/husbands (Gahmuret and Feirefiz, respectively) must desert them for more socially and culturally appropriate mates. This connection with potential mates differentiates the marginal status of Belacane and Secundille from the Baruch, who also very clearly inhabits the Orient with them. The Baruch happens to rule a faraway empire, but his wealth, his military prowess and his maleness temper his strangeness for Wolfram's audience. Wolfram makes no mention of any love interests where the Baruch is concerned.

Through their relationships, however, both queens have important connections to the rest of the narrative; thus they are placed in a dialectical relationship between the strange and the familiar, the margins and the center. Belacane provides a frame for the entire work. As Queen of Zazamanc, she is physically located on *Parzival*'s own geographic margins, and she is thematically present in Book XV, when Feirefiz reapppears to challenge Parzival. Geographically, her land represents the furthest point to which Gahmuret strays on his mercenary quests for power and wealth. This is also emphasized by the fact that Belacane herself is not related to anyone in the work, though she does become part of the structure of familial relationships through her son Feirefiz.[33] Secundille, on the other hand, remains totally outside. Although she herself appears only in Book I, Belacane's story has ramifications throughout *Parzival* because of the son she bears Gahmuret: Feirefiz, Parzival's speckled half-brother.

Following his adventures in Babylon and Nineveh (14,3 and 14,5), in Persia, Damascus, and Arabia, Gahmuret sets sail in the direction of the kingdom of Zazamanc, where he has heard of a queen under siege. Gahmuret and his crew arrive in the wake of a fierce storm:

> nu hœrt wie unser rîter var.
> daz mer warf in mit sturme dar,
> sô daz er kûme iedoch genas.
> gein der küngîn palas
> kom er gesigelt in die habe:
> dâ war er vil geschouwet abe. (16,19–24)

[Now hear how things went with our knight. The sea with such a storm cast him there that he barely escaped with his life, but into the harbor he came sailing toward the queen's great hall, from which he was observed by many.]

The kingdom of Zazamanc cannot be precisely located, unlike its more commonly known neighbors, nor is it ever described geographically. Wolfram does situate it in the context of the East and gives the place a name, thus lending the place credibility through the act of naming.[34] This place is far from "home," however, and the main indicator of the difference is reflected in the sudden importance of color; this provides the main signal to the audience that Gahmuret, along with his comrades, finds himself in another, rather unsettling environment:

> liute so vinster sô diu naht
> wârn alle die von Zazamanc
> bî den dûht in diu wîle lanc. (17,24–26)

[Black as night were all the people of Zazamanc, and he felt ill
at ease.]

The fact that all the inhabitants of this eastern part of the world
are Moors ("beidiu wîp unde man," 19,19) and have a different
skin color has never been mentioned before in the narrative,
though this certainly cannot be the first time that Gahmuret and
his companions have encountered people of color in their previous
service for the Baruch. The matter of skin color takes on increasing significance when Belacane appears, for color is the only physical characteristic that marks her as other. Unlike Cundrie, another
native of eastern realms, Belacane is not unbearably ugly; on the
contrary, she possesses the beauty of a true *Minneherrin*, a beauty
that inflames Gahmuret's passion.[35] Curiously, the matter of color
seems to be emphasized more with respect to the women:

> manege tunkele frouwen
> sach er bêdenthalben sîn:
> nâch rabens varwe was ir schîn. (20,2–4)

[many dark women he saw on both sides: their color was like the
raven's]

It is as though Gahmuret is surprised that their blackness does not
diminish the qualities he would normally associate with beauty. The
issue of color does not seem to affect Gahmuret; we are told: "Doch
was im [Gahmuret] daz swarze wîp/lieber dan sîn selbes lîp." ("But
the black woman was dearer to him than his own life," 54,21–22)
And yet it obsesses the narrator from the start; in fact, he can only
describe her using the negative of the familiar formulas, commenting "ist iht liehters denne der tag,/dem glîchet niht diu künegin." ("if
is anything lighter than the day, the queen did not resemble that,"
24,6–7) Not only does she resemble the night, but she is also "der
touwegen rôsen ungelîch." ("unlike the dewy rose," 24,10) Her
color is even a problem for Belacane, who reacts with uncertainty at
Gahmuret's arrival, unsure whether to bid him come to her castle or
to meet him herself, justifying her indecision with the remark: "er ist
anders denne wir gevar: ôwî wan tæte im daz niht wê!" ("he is not
of our color; if only that does not bother him!" 22,8–9)[36]
    The problem of color is also emphasized as Gahmuret makes
his escape from Zazamanc. The sailor from Seville, who offers a
way back to Europe, "was niht als ein Mor gevar." ("not colored
like a Moor," 55,2) This characteristic lends the man credibility, al-

lies him with Gahmuret as those of the same color in a world of a different hue, and gives the sailor the authority to suggest that Gahmuret leave Zazamanc. The major reason that Gahmuret gives for leaving Belacane has to do with religion, of course, and the fact that Belacane is not baptized, although this argument does not play a role until this point in the narrative. Clearly, Zazamanc is an inappropriate place for a courtly knight to stay;[37] the Orient remains a place on the edge of the known world, essentially a fantasy realm despite the realistic nomenclature that describes it.[38] The "marriage" between Belacane and Gahmuret serves its purpose, providing stability, resolving the military conflict, and producing Feirefiz. Like Gahmuret's later relationship with Herzeloyde, his union with Belacane is one based on passion. The alliance with Belacane is, however, not technically binding,[39] although (now that he is back in France) Gahmuret seems to think so.[40] The very determined Herzeloyde finally claims him for her own, demanding that he renounce the "mœrinne"[41] and proceeding to take him to court because he is obligated as winner of the tournament at Kanvoleis to become her husband. Though Belacane is never explicitly described in any way that would make her monstrous (except for her color), Wolfram implicitly criticizes the obvious erotic nature of her relationship with Gahmuret.[42] Since the Christian west cannot accept this erotic other world, Herzeloyde can therefore elicit the help of the legal system. Eroticism remains a defining feature of Gahmuret's relationship with Herzeloyde and so Wolfram's criticism will also extend eventually to her, although she possesses qualities that can rehabilitate her in a way denied Belacane. Susan Signe Morrison comments on the similarity between Gahmuret's two marriages, noting that in both cases "it is sexual difference which reveals what is alien and other," not religious and racial differences (which are eventually overcome).[43]

Despite her color and the impropriety of her relationship with Gahmuret from the western Christian standpoint, Wolfram insists that the Queen of Zazamanc "hete wîplîchen sîn." ("had a woman's manner," 24,8) And not only does she possess the essential attributes of woman, but these attributes offer the possibility of redemption (for Wolfram as well as for Gahmuret):

> Gahmureten dûhte sân,
> swie si wære ein heidenin,
> mit triuwen wîplîcher sin
> in wîbes herze nie geslouf.
> ir kiusche was ein reiner touf,

> und ouch der regen der sie begôz,
> der wâc der von ir ougen flôz
> ûf ir zobel und an ir brust. (28,10–17)

[Gahmuret reflected how she was a heathen, and yet never did more womanly loyalty glide into a woman's heart. Her innocence was a pure baptism, as was also the rain that wet her, that flood which flowed about her eyes down upon the furs about her breast.]

Her baptism by tears is an indication of her purity, despite her heathen heritage, and her tears also foretell the eventual baptism of her son Feirefiz. Her tears, her essence of womanhood and her role as *Minnedame* cannot transcend color, however, and this fundamental incongruity must remain. The courtly vocabulary in which the Zazamanc episode is couched serves to illustrate Belacane's connection to civilization and familiar culture, perhaps to allay suspicions of barbarism for Wolfram's audience. Any attempt at "höfische Vereinnahmung"[44] nevertheless remains incomplete, while the distance and the 'otherness' persist, powerfully symbolized by the black and white of Feirefiz's skin.

The second Oriental queen, Secundille, remains a figure of chronological and geographical distance with respect to the narrative; her realm of Tribalibot is as geographically ambiguous as the kingdom of Zazamanc.[45] She never speaks, nor does she physically appear, within the context of the main story line(s) in *Parzival*, though she does die on cue. Wolfram nevertheless assigns her a significant role in *Parzival*.[46] She maintains the connection of the main narrative with the Orient, introduced by Gahmuret's relationship with Belacane. The first reference to Secundille and her realm occurs in Book VI, when Cundrie reveals the existence of Feirefiz to Parzival before Arthur's court: Feirefiz, son of the queen of Zazamanc who has won for himself the queen of the land Tribalibot. Cundrie offers the heathen knight as a model for Parzival, simultaneously emphasizing that Parzival could have surpassed his half-brother, had he only asked the question at Munsalvaesche:

> wær ze Munsalvæsche iu vrâgen mite,
> in heidenschaft ze Tabronite
> Diu stat hât erden wunsches solt:

> hie het iu vrâgen mêr erholt.
> jenes landes künegîn
> Feirefîz Anschevîn
> mit herter rîterschefte erwarp (316,29–317,5)

[Had you but asked at Munsalvaesche—the city of Tabronit in heathendom has riches enough to satisfy all earthly desire, yet they cannot compare with the reward your question would have brought you here. The queen of that land was won in hard knightly combat by Feirefiz the Angevin.]

The queen of this land, whose riches could rival those of Munsalvæsche, is Secundille. She remains nameless, known only as the mysterious partner of the speckled knight until Book X (519,2–4), when Wolfram finally tells Cundrie's story. In this story, Wolfram reveals that Secundille reigns over a fantastic land:

> wan vil wazzer in ir lant truoc
> für den griez edel gesteine:
> grôz, niht ze kleine,
> het si gebirge guldîn. (519,14–18)

[For many rivers in her country ran precious gems instead of silt, big ones too, and by no means small, and she had mountains all of gold.]

Indeed, it is Secundille who has sent Cundrie (another of her wondrous possessions, together with Cundrie's misshapen brother Malcreatiure) to Anfortas as a gift, a token of her admiration for Anfortas' fame which has reached her:

> dô sagete man ir umben grâl,
> daz ûf erde niht sô rîches was,
> unt des pflæge ein künec hiez Anfortas.
> daz dûhte se wunderlîch genuoc. (519,10–13)

[Then she was told of the Grail, that there was nothing as precious on the earth, and how it was kept by a king named Anfortas. To her that seemed wondrous enough . . .]

This connection serves a double purpose, in that it further explains

Secundille's function in the narrative while it also subtly casts some doubt on her integrity. The gesture of gift-giving suggests a rather manipulative intent on the part of the queen, a perhaps inappropriate desire for power to know the man who controls the Grail and perhaps gain control of it herself:

> dô dâht diu edele künegîn
> 'wie gewinne ich künde dises man,
> dem der grâl ist undertân?' (519,18–20)

[Then the noble queen thought: "How shall I find out about this man to whom the Grail is subject?"]

The superiority of the Grail over Secundille and what she represents is proven on at least two other occasions. The first of these involves Secundille's figurative defeat by Condwiramurs in the duel between Feirefiz and Parzival that takes place in Book XV. During the first part of their duel, Feirefiz gains the upper hand, inspired by thoughts of Secundille and cries of "Tabronite!" (742,1 ff.) Finally Parzival seems to heed Wolfram's repeated exhortations to think of his wife, and Condwiramurs brings him the power of her love across four kingdoms. (744,4–6) This love, which is culturally and spiritually acceptable, prevails. Ultimately, as Cundrie says to Parzival in Book VI, even the earthly wealth of Tabronite cannot compare to that of Munsalvaesche; indeed, as if realizing this at last, Feirefiz has himself baptized, and marries the Grail bearer Repanse de Schoye. The report of Secundille's death reaches Munsalvaesche after their marriage confirms that this 'other' has been overcome.

The 'others' of the Orient are obviously differentiated from the courtly self of the audience: they have dark skin, they are fabulously and fantastically wealthy, and they are geographically remote. The stories of Belacane and Secundille guide the participation of the audience in the dialectic between the familiar and the strange (between "Eigenem und Fremdem"). The meeting with "monsters" ("das Ungeheuer") has been proposed as a defining characteristic of the Arthurian romance;[47] the monstrous and the 'strange' provided the medieval audience with "Gegen- und Zerrbilder," with images and counter-images that might offer ways in which to deal with conflicts "in den Beziehungen zwischen den Geschlechtern und Generationen."[48] The images and the otherness of Wolfram's Orient do not appear terribly threatening. As the audience travels further (yet closer to 'home') with the narrator, however, it becomes evident that "die Frau immer mehr den Platz des Fremden und Exotischen einnimt, daß sie sozusagen zum Territorium des Fremden in der Nähe wird."[49] In this way, one can begin reading the gender topography as a map that should lead the audience to a "correct" destination.

THE COURTLY (ARTHURIAN) WORLD

The Orient in *Parzival* provides a thematic and geographic frame for the work. Both Belacane and Secundille are located on its margins, geographically remote from, yet thematically linked to, the courtly "center" of the world. Although Wolfram situates the colorful figure of Herzeloyde[50] within more familiar Arthurian boundaries, her fate reveals a similar mechanism of marginalization, albeit under different circumstances and in different spaces. Unlike Belacane and Secundille, she does not belong "outside" the traditional borders of the courtly world; on the contrary, her kingdoms of Waleis and Norgals lie within the perimeters of Europe. As her brother Trevrizent reveals in Book IX, she herself had been sent by the Grail to become the wife of king Castis. (494,15–30) In a sense, she comes from outside the Arthurian world to take her place within it as queen, wife, and eventually mother.

Of all the characters that cross *Parzival*'s landscape, with the possible exception of Orgeluse, Herzeloyde has elicited the most varied responses from scholars, depending upon which of her three roles is under consideration: independent queen, Gahmuret's wife, and Parzival's mother. Not surprisingly, it is the latter role as widowed mother of the future Grail king that has been the primary critical focus. As Parzival's mother, Herzeloyde represents his biological and spiritual link to the Grail world.[51] Both her widowhood and her motherhood are traditionally interpreted as indications of her selflessness, humility, and passivity. For Gerhards, Herzeloyde's widowhood illustrates "den Typus der passiv duldenden Frau."[52] Schwietering praises the "selbstlose Hingabe" as "Mütterlichkeit" in the case of women like Herzeloyde (as well as Condwiramurs and Sigune),[53] while Ehrismann sees in Herzeloyde "ein menschliches Abbild der schmerzensreichen Mutter Jesu."[54] Gibbs also maintains that "it is at the birth of Parzival that Herzeloyde comes to perfect womanhood,"[55] citing the frequent association of Herzeloyde with the image of the Virgin Mary.

It must be recognized, however disillusioning this may seem, that Herzeloyde possesses the qualities not only of Mary but also of Eve.[56] Most critics react like Heise, who tries to excuse the characteristics that make Herzeloyde appear egotistical, insisting that the "Triebkräfte in Herzeloyde sind ihre Liebe und ihre Entsagung" and that she exemplifies "die Kraft der *triuwe*."[57] Lewis sees an illustration of Herzeloyde's "hybris" in her rather prideful association of herself with the Virgin Mary, which would shock Wolfram's audience if Wolfram had not previously shown them Herzeloyde's egocentric personality.[58] While Lewis' interpretation of Herzeloyde as an iconoclast exaggerates her character somewhat, it is undeniably true that she takes active part in what Walter Haug has described as "ein unentrinnbarer Kreislauf von Gewalt und Begierde," the defining feature of the Gahmuret books.[59]

As the queen who quite literally forces Gahmuret to become her consort, her motives and her passion for Gahmuret are not exactly ideal and pure.[60] On the contrary, its erotic undertones surface in at least two instances. The first involves the rather bizarre use of the shift with which Gahmuret covers his shield in battle. Although the shift, which has touched Herzeloyde's bare skin before Gahmuret leaves, is shredded almost to tatters ("zerhouwen," 101,15) by the swords of Gahmuret's opponents, Herzeloyde insists upon donning it again when her husband returns:

> daz leit ouch si an blôze hût,
> sô kom von rîterschaft ir trût,
> der manegen schilt vil dürkel stach. (101,17–19)

[and these she in turn laid against her naked skin each time her beloved returned from those knightly expeditions where he hacked many a shield to slivers.]

The second instance occurs after Parzival's birth, when Herzeloyde likens her child to her dead husband: "si dûht, si hete Gahmureten/wider an ir arm erbeten." (113,13–14) Earlier, immediately after she had received news of Gahmuret's death, Herzeloyde had consoled herself with similar thoughts, since at least Gahmuret's child remained to her: "ich was vil junger danne er,/und bin sîn muoter und sîn wîp." (109,25–26) These instances lead one to suspect that at least part of Herzeloyde's motivation to withdraw from court is a desire to keep Gahmuret alive.[61]

Wolfram criticizes the violence and desire rampant in the courtly world through Herzeloyde's eventual refusal to participate in it any longer.[62] Following Gahmuret's death, she retreats in mourning "zer waste in Soltâne." (117,9) While this place does not appear so exotic or remote as Zazamanc or Tribalibot, it is clearly set apart from the courtly world, located at its 'near' edge, so to speak:

> frou Herzeloyde diu rîche
> ir drîer lande wart ein gast: ...
> Sich zôch diu frouwe jâmers balt
> ûz ir lande in einen walt,
> zer waste in Soltâne;
> niht durch bluomen ûf die plâne.
> ir herzen jâmer was sô ganz,
> sine kêrt sich an keinen kranz,
> er wære rôt oder val. (116, 28–29 and 117,7–13)

[The powerful lady Herzeloyde became a stranger to her three kingdoms . . . This lady full of sorrow withdrew from her kingdom to a forest, to the clearing of Soltane, and not for the sake of flowers on the meadow. Her heart's grief was so complete that she cared for no garland, neither red nor faded.]

In her most controversial decision, Herzeloyde brings her son to this geographically indeterminate and deserted (at least from a courtly perspective) region in order to raise him far from "ritters leben." (117,25)[63] Herzeloyde endeavors to retain some aspects of civilization, bringing people with her who can farm the land and help her watch over her child. (117,16–28) Certainly, Herzeloyde's status as widow and queen would allow her this freedom of choice and mobility; among secular noblewomen, of all women in medieval society, widows quite possibly enjoyed the most independence.[64] While Wolfram does not explicitly condemn her move, for she is ostensibly mindful of the safety and future well-being of her son, he does call her motives into question. On the one hand, he says that Herzeloyde endures her joylessness in Soltane away from the court out of *triuwe* (116,19) and without *valsch*:[65]

> der valsch sô gar an ir verswant,
> ouge noch ôre in nie dâ vant.

ein nebel was ir diu sunne:
si vlôch der werlde wunne,
ir was gelîch naht unt der tac:
ir herze niht wan jâmers phlac. (117,1–6)

[Falsity had so utterly vanished from her heart that neither heart nor eye could detect it. To her the sun was a mist. She fled the world's delight. To her night and day were the same; her heart dwelt on sorrow alone.]

Yet Wolfram condemns her shortly thereafter for denying Parzival his heritage. (117,30–118,3) As Miklautsch puts it, Herzeloyde creates a "Sozialisationsdefizit" for her son in "einer ritter-feindlichen ausschließlich mütterlich definierten Welt."[66] Though Wolfram (and many scholars after him) insists on Herzeloyde's pious intentions for retreating to Soltane,[67] there is no word from Herzeloyde about her pious intentions for the care of her own soul at the beginning of Book III. The people she brings with her, de-spite the fact that she no longer holds court as she used to, indicate that she does not intend to lead the desolate life of a hermit/re-cluse. Her sole (and ultimately inappropriate) motivation for with-drawing to this place is to protect Parzival from the dangers of knightly life and to preserve of what remains of her life with Gahmuret. Selfishly she hopes that Parzival's fool's clothing will cause him sufficient embarrassment at Arthur's court so that he will return to her. (126,21–28) Such behavior suggests that motives for her retreat from the courtly world lie at least in part in a cer-tain self-centeredness of which Wolfram has shown her capable.[68] As if to support this suggestion, Wolfram comments upon Herzeloyde's death after Parzival's departure, saying that she would have been consigned to the fires of hell had she not become a mother:

ir vil getriulîcher tôt
der frouwen wert die hellenôt.
ôwol si daz se ie muoter wart! (128,23–25)

[Her death from sheer loyalty saved her from the pains of hell. Well for her that she became a mother!]

This rather drastic statement reinforces Wolfram's ambivalent por-trayal of her.[69]

Herzeloyde shares her self-induced isolation from the courtly sphere at least metaphorically with another exile—Sigune. Sigune also claims a separate space within the perimeters of the courtly environment, though her path moves her progressively further away from court and leads her ultimately to a non-courtly existence on another plane. Her position on this path marginalizes her; indeed, her path is the margin, placing her in the forest. A region that by its nature indicates to a medieval audience marginality on the outskirts of the civilized courtly world, this forest represents an area apart from Arthurian society. It is a place both real and symbolic that can depict a concrete geographic locality as well as a less tangible state of exile and/or escape.[70]

Szlavek interprets wilderness and nature as in *Parzival* as "das Gebiet des Weiblichen."[71] In fact, he comes upon the important women in his life unawares. The journey that brings him to Pelrapeire and his future wife leads through "vil ungevertes." (180,6 ff.) "Kom geriten ûf einen walt,/ine weiz ze welhen stunden," (435,4–5) he encounters Sigune in Book IX. Finally, Parzival comes to the Grail lineage through his mother and has the correct orientation from birth which he must follow in order to get there, since his path to the Grail itself cannot be geographically located.[72] Thus we may differentiate between "determinate" (Gawan) and "indeterminate" landscapes (Parzival), between well-defined localities and vaguely marked spaces.

While the forest in which Parzival encounters Sigune may be geographically indeterminate and while this area may be located on the edges of courtly society, it remains firmly within the jurisdiction of God. This is evident when one follows Sigune's development from mourning lover to saintly recluse.[73] Gradually, Sigune divests herself of all trappings of courtly appearance; Parzival notes at their second meeting that the conventional signs of courtly beauty have faded from her face and that she no longer looks very "minneclîch":

> owê war kom dîn rôter munt?
> bistuz Sigûne, diu mir kunt
> tet wer ich was, ân allen vâr?
> dîn reidleht lanc prûnez hâr,
> des ist dîn houbet blôz getân.
> zem fôrest in Brizljân
> sah ich dich dô vil minneclîch,

swie du wærest jâmers rîch. (252,27–253,4)

[Alas what has become of your red mouth? Are you Sigune, who told me who I was, without dissembling? And your head—it is bare—what has become of your wavy long brown hair? In the forest of Brizljan I saw you in all your loveliness though you were heavy with grief.]

As Jacobson notes, Sigune's loss of physical beauty in exchange for spiritual purity connects her with the figure of the Grail messenger Cundrie.[74] While Parzival hovers on the edge of Arthurian society during the time he spends searching for the Grail,[75] Sigune hovers on the edge of Parzival's consciousness. He encounters her alone in the forest at critical moments on his journey, which seems to indicate the significance of the role that Sigune has to play in it.[76] Critics have viewed Sigune as the epitome of the selfless, saintly Grail women. She is "the most beautiful creation . . . of Wolfram's poetic genius,"[77] a *memento mori*,[78] one of the most meaningful figures in *Parzival*,[79] and an example of the "essence of a human tragedy" that Wolfram could "extend and deepen until it took on a new significance"[80]—in short, "Wolframs wohl gleichermaßen faszinierendste wie auch änigmatischste Figur."[81] Bernhard Rahn ranks her with Parzival as a model for Wolfram's readers, since she represents the major figure in a type of "Legende,"[82] particularly because of her later role in Titurel.[83]

Yet at the end of the work, this remarkably vocal and exemplary model of selflessness has been silenced: she is dead. She is found, having died at prayer, by the company traveling to install Parzival as king at Munsalvaesche:

si riten für sich drâte
und funden sâbents spâte
Sigûnen an ir venje tôt. (804,21–23)

[They rode swiftly on, and late that evening they found Sigune in a posture of prayer, dead.]

This is her most public moment of the entire narrative, where she is surrounded not only by Parzival but by an entire company. In stark contrast to her previous encounters with Parzival, where she had to much to say, Sigune cannot speak a word here. She has reached the end of her physical and spiritual 'becoming,' parallel to Parzival's becoming worthy of the Grail, which is also now all but complete. Significantly, Parzival's first act as Grail king is to bury Sigune with Schionatulander, who now lies embalmed in a stone sarcophagus. Though Wolfram portrays this death as the culmination of Sigune's passage through *Parzival* as she slowly moves away from the courtly world, she remains excluded in her tomb from Wolfram's final vision of the future in the Grail world.[84] Both Herzeloyde and Sigune choose their isolation, as a consequence of their relationships with men; this isolation also results in their deaths, the ultimate marginalization from the courtly world.

One must remember, however, that *Parzival*'s early thirteenth century audience would probably not have interpreted the deaths of Sigune and Herzeloyde negatively. On the contrary, in the ultimately closed system Wolfram creates for *Parzival*, death leads to God and eternal life. For both Sigune and Herzeloyde, this is regarded as a privilege accorded them because of their exemplary conduct and their status. This "privilege" silences them on the plane of the narrative, however. The apparent contradiction between privilege and "reality" gives the reader cause to wonder about Wolfram's message, particularly in view of the women who remain at the end of the work.

The women who mark the margins discussed thus far (Belacane, Secundille, Herzeloyde, and Sigune) do not appear physically in *Parzival*'s final tableau, though all but Sigune are represented through a sort of male metonymy: Belacane and Herzeloyde[85] are present in the persons of their sons Feirefiz and Parzival, Secundille makes an "appearance" in the report of her death. In a very literal sense, through their absence, these women resist incorporation into the social body of the court(s) that Wolfram offers as models at the conclusion of *Parzival*. They have occupied key positions with respect to the narrative and with respect to the major male characters, liminal positions that allowed them a certain freedom from restrictions of speech and mobility (Herzeloyde and Sigune), of Christian doctrine (Belacane), in order that they might fulfill their purpose. Final (re)integration, however, is not allowed them; they have all perished. As Michael Camille phrases it, "the inversion and release of liminality works only for those in power, those who maintain the status quo and have something at stake in resisting change . . ."[86] Maintenance of the status quo in *Parzival* demands that these liminal positions remain as such. Their release would mean the collapse of the order that was, the order that is to be, and the balance between them.

Wolfram does offer a more temporary form of marginal status in the poem. He allows women to display unprecedented
mobility, locating them not necessarily in a particular space (like
Soltane or the forest) but following them quite literally through
it. This status belongs, most obviously, to the messenger
Cundrie. Cundrie traverses the boundaries of all of Wolfram's
worlds, in the process cutting across the geographical and ideological margins: from the exotic heathen queen Secundille to the
ailing Grail king Anfortas, from Munsalvaesche to Arthur's
court. In her capacity as a messenger who travels between the
Grail world and the Arthurian world, she belongs to neither
world completely. Cundrie's history is finally told in Book X
when Gawan encounters Orgeluse and her hideous servant
Malcreatiure, who happens to be Cundrie's brother. "Unglîch
menschen bilde" ("unlike human form," 517,24), the ugliness of
Malcreatiure and Cundrie[87] serves as a permanent reminder to
all who see them of the sin of Adam's disobedient daughters
(518,1–30), though Wolfram also mentions that people are indeed born like that in the land of Tribalibot[88] Cundrie also possesses another attribute that sets her apart: her knowledge.
(312,19–30; 782,1 ff.)[89] She thus occupies a doubly marginal position, as outsider and as messenger, which frees her from the restrictions of any particular code of behavior, as illustrated by her
disruptive yet critical appearance at the Arthurian court in Book
VI. Her position literally in-between worlds invests her with
great authority. She inspires wonder and awe when she arrives
at the Arhturian court; her accusations combine with her
hideous appearance to provide powerfully visible sign of
Parzival's failure at Munsalvaesche. Cundrie's 'otherness' highlights for Parzival in a way highlights his position as her
'other'—he must *become* as she *is* (and acquire the quality humility or *demut*). Cundrie's appearance before the Arthurian
court in Book VI recalls Lunete's public reproach of Iwein, and
Cundrie acts here with an authority unlike any other character
in the work, except perhaps for Sigune. It is no accident that
these two women (Cundrie and Sigune) figure most prominently
in Parzival's quest for the throne destined for him.[90] Both are
strange and alienating to the culture of the Arthurian court, and
they facilitate Parzival's eventual integration into the 'true' court
of the Grail king through a strategy works by means of the stark
contrast between their inner qualities of goodness and humility
and their outer appearance.[91] She remains an instrument, a

means, rather than an end in herself, unaltered by the changes she facilitates.[92] Cundrie's history, her appearance, and her knowledge maintain her separation from the Arthurian and the Grail worlds, although she is accepted in her capacity as messenger by each. Thus she retains her marginal position indefinitely and cannot be fully integrated into any of the societies she serves.

There is another mobile figure whose marginality, unlike Cundrie's, *can* eventually be overcome: Orgeluse de Logroys, Chrétien's nameless 'proud woman.' Incomparably beautiful,[93] she does not bode well for the hapless Gawan, whom she immediately presses into her service:

> Orgelûs diu rîche
> fuor ungeselleclîche:
> zuo Gâwân si kom geriten
> mit alsô zornlîchen siten,
> daz ich michs wênec trôste
> daz si mich von sorgen lôste. (516,15–20)

[The mighty Orgeluse behaved in unfriendly fashion. She came riding up to Gawan in such a bad temper that I would hardly be confident that she will banish my cares.]

Scholars have also offered varying opinions of Orgeluse: she has been described as haughty and aloof,[94] termed a caricature and a parody.[95] Sweeping across *Parzival*'s landscape in her quest for revenge against the slayer of her first husband, she leaves a trail of violence and ill-feeling and subdued men in her wake. Indeed, she interacts with most of the major male characters in the work at some point (i.e. Anfortas, Parzival, Gawan, Clinschor) The circumstances that have led her to her journey are told in Book XII. (612,21–619,27) She married the peerless Cidegast, in what was apparently a love match. As she describes their relationship, "ich was sîn herze, er was mîn lîp." (613,27) Their happiness was shortlived, brought to a premature end when Gramoflanz slew Cidegast. Desirous of Gramoflanz's death, Orgeluse accepts the services of "ein künec ders wunsches hêrre was" ("a king who was lord of what all men most desire," 616,13), Anfortas. The outcome of that collaboration proves disastrous, of course, not just for Orgeluse but for the entire Grail society:

> dô ich in minne solte wern,
> dô muos ich niwes jâmers gern.
> in mîme dienste erwarb er sêr.
> glîchen jâmer oder mêr,
> als Cidegast geben kunde,
> gab mir Anfortases wunde. (616,21–26)

[Just as I was of a mind to give him love, I found fresh grief instead. In my service he won suffering. A sorrow as great or greater than Cidegast had caused me, I endured from the wounding of Anfortas.]

She also has dealings with the infamous Clinschor, striking a bargain with him so that her knights may travel through his lands as they search for Gramoflanz. The knights too rich to serve for pay, she "allows" to serve for love of her, to keep her plot alive.[96] She only encounters one unwilling knight, Parzival (618,19–619,20), who frustrates her by resisting her wiles and her beauty.[97] Like the stories of Belacane, Herzeloyde, and Sigune, that of Orgeluse also connects the themes of love and violence, perhaps more so than any story in *Parzival*.[98] Unlike the former, however, Orgeluse illustrates that successful re-integration into courtly society is possible, in what Maria Bindschedler has called her 'recovery' through the persistent efforts of Gawan.[99]

THE GRAIL WORLD

Orgeluse survives Wolfram's narrative. On the plain of Joflanze, having been gradually worn down by the force of Gawan's love,[100] she forgives Gramoflanz and gives her hand to Gawan before the entire company (to the dismay of her mercenaries):

> dô sprach diu herzoginne
> daz Gâwân het ir minne
> gedient mit prîse hôch erkant,
> daz er ir lîbs und über ir lant
> von rehte hêrre wære.
> diu rede dûhte swære
> ir soldier, die manec sper
> ê brâchen durch ir minne ger. (730,15—22)

[Then the duchess spoke and said that Gawan had earned her love with deeds of high renown and that of right he was lord over her land and herself. These words were a heavy blow to her knights who had broken many a spear in their longing for her love.]

The other women of the *Schastel marveile* are also released from their imprisonment and live happily ever after.

The celebrations at Joflanze are echoed in Books XV and XVI by the rejoicing at Munsalvaesche. The Grail world is the world that Wolfram seeks to offer as a model for his audience at the conclusion of *Parzival*, in a sense representing the center of the universe which also includes the Orient and the Arthurian court. And it is here that Wolfram's topography of gender 'corrects' that of Hartmann, in much the same way that Wolfram uses Sigune as an example to 'correct' Laudine's behavior. Hartmann's representation of spaces suggest both the possibility of men and women 'becoming' together (*Erec*) and the possibility that the 'other' place inhabited by woman might not be entirely reincorporated into the domain of the male self (*Iwein*). When one observes the Grail world, it becomes apparent that these possibilities do not reappear in *Parzival.*

Wolfram welcomes two couples at the Grail castle, the two whose progeny carry the story of the narrative beyond the borders of the poem that is *Parzival*: the first consists of Parzival and Condwiramurs, the second of Feirefiz and Repanse de Schoye. Most scholars view Repanse de Schoye and, above all, Condwiramurs, as models of Wolfram's ideal of womanhood. Throughout *Parzival*, Repanse de Schoye appears as a silent beauty who radiates goodness and light, a woman who simply is. This is a feature that Gibbs sees as positive, in keeping with Repanse's image "as the archetype of queenly dignity and beauty."[101] Condwiramurs, as Parzival's wife and the future keeper of the Grail, has attracted much critical attention. Typical is Heise's statement that "Kondwiramurs ist es, die uns am leichtesten das Tor zu den großen Frauengestalten Wolframs öffnet," since she is always "present" in the work.[102] Her relationship with Parzival is viewed as the ideal combination of *minne* and marriage.[103] She is identified, of course, with Parzival's search for the Grail, since she accompanies him in thoughts during his five-year journey.[104] Condwiramurs herself, however, is described with few concrete details. Blamires explains this as part of the idealization of Condwiramurs—she is so perfect that she cannot be adequately described: ". . . Condwiramurs' appearance and character do not need to be limited by any details at all: they merely extend infinitely beyond the description of the other heroines."[105] Extending this exceptional status to all of the other female figures in the Grail world, Szlavek goes so far as to assert that only they show some kind of initiative in their own lives.[106]

These models of perfection are two of the "central" female characters of *Parzival.* Curiously, although they apparently belong at Munsalvæsche (or as part of its world), they bear little resemblance to those who have gone before them. While they certainly share beauty and virtue with the likes of Herzeloyde (indeed, Repanse de Schoye is Parzival's aunt), they remain silent observers in the world of the Grail: they look beautiful, they serve and perform other courtly functions, and they bear children, but they do not speak or act of their own accord in that environment. When Repanse de Schoye does say something, it is reported through a male speaker. In Book V, for instance, the chamberlain tells Parzival that Repanse has indicated that he should wear her cloak until other clothing has been made for him. (228,14—17) In contrast to many others in *Parzival's* large cast of charcters, these women are depicted as de-personalized and rather two-dimensional; they are also effectively desexualized, in that those desires typical of women (like Belacane or Herzeloyde) are subsumed by their perfect natures. These are the qualities which allow them to remain in the center, ultimately marginalized by their passivity, instead of being relegated to active negotiations that occur on the margins 'outside.' In telling the parallel adventures of Parzival and Gawan, Wolfram also encourages his audience to draw parallels between the Grail society and that of the *Schastel marveile.* In a recent analysis of the gender roles in both societies, Bumke compares the marriage of Feirefiz and Repanse de Schoye with the relationship between Gawan and Orgeluse. The comic circumstances of Feirefiz's hasty baptism and his marriage seem to show that, although Book XVI tries to define a new ideal (reflected in Parzival's success at Munsalvæsche), this ideal has its limits. The world of the Grail castle appears to remain more static than its Arthurian counterpart; perhaps this is an indication that the Arthurian society (as represented by Gawan and Orgeluse) might be superior to the Grail society in its re-establishment of gender roles at the *Schastel marveile* and its ability to change.[107] Certainly, the women of the Grail world represent models of 'being' rather than 'becoming.'

What does this discussion of margins and centers and 'becoming' reveal about a topography of gender in *Parzival?* Wolfram states in the prologue that he intends to deal both with women and with men in *Parzival*, and clearly gender roles and interactions play an integral part in the work. Pathak has said of genres that they "institute a reality and inscribe a subject."[108] According to Simon Gaunt, genres "represent constructed symbolic resolutions to social tensions and contradictions and thereby inscribe ideologies" and therefore "the construction and representation of gender within those ideologies is crucial to an understanding of how they function."[109] That the genre of courtly romance creates an "ideal" reality for its audience is beyond doubt. If, however, the social is the (secular) ideal and society is defined as a group which can communicate and interact, then it seems incongruous that the narrative relegates important female figures to its edges. Apparently, tensions exist, limits must be set, and boundaries must be established. Wolfram (like Hartmann) uses both static and dynamic characters to demarcate and traverse boundaries of his worlds, establishing examples for his audience of both being and becoming. The self-defining 'other,' most often depicted as female, must be contained metaphorically within these margins. Clearly, men must move in order to establish their identities: as warriors on the search for love and adventure (Gahmuret, Gawan), as the leader of a new spiritual knighthood (Parzival). Wolfram excels in variations on the movement of the courtly hero—movement of characters who change and 'become,' movement of characters who do remain essentially static. Throughout *Parzival*, Wolfram places women on both geographically determinate and indeterminate paths; they mark the routes and guide or accompany the travelers. In his essay "Wolframs Frauenlob," for example, Hugo Kuhn describes the function of women in *Parzival* as markers on this map, markers "von oft befremdlichen Gestalten des *bonum* weiblicher *triuwe*, zwischen denen gerade Parzival, wie auch Gahmuret oder Gawan, *seinen* Weg zu finden hat."[110] Women tend to remain static observers while the men travel their destined paths. Although the knights in *Parzival* do tend to move through their respective geography more than their female counterparts, the women are not static as observers, as the *bonum* of womanly goodness and loyalty— they do take part in the action of the plot. Indeed, not all of the women characters are static in terms of movement (Cundrie and Sigune) nor are they all static in terms of 'becoming' (Sigune and Orgeluse and perhaps Herzeloyde and Belacane). In short, the women who do not remain static are assigned pivotal roles in the narrative.

All of these women ultimately represent an anomaly, however, and they do not offer *Parzival*'s audience unequivocal and exemplary role models for "becoming." Despite her courtly qualities, for instance, Belacane belongs to a race of heathens. Cundrie and Siguna display the quality of *demut* that Wolfram admires so greatly; yet their lives as messenger, as recluse and later anchoress, do not offer unambiguous alternatives to the women of a courtly audience. Although Herzeloyde redeems herself through motherhood and partakes of the Grail family's 'pure' heritage, Wolfram's ambivalent depiction of her life as an independent queen does not recommend her as highly as his praise would indicate. Orgeluse must be rehabilitated in order to join the Arthurian society once more, for her revenge-filled existence creates a degree of instability that cannot be tolerated. The two women who "survive" and appear at the end to serve as exempla are Condwiramurs and Repanse de Schoye: beautiful, virtuous, stationary, silent wives and mothers.

To paraphrase historian Gerda Lerner, the process of creating ideals within the context of romance occurred in a form which marginalized women.[111] The spatial strategy of Wolfram's narrative thus allows the symbolic order to reassert itself, an order in which women must always occupy an ambiguous position. Medieval views of sex and gender could accommodate a certain degree of chaos, surprisingly enough *because* of the binary construct of medieval sexuality. The binary nature of the system enabled a certain flexibility in the application of the concepts of masculine and feminine. In fact, according to Cadden, the system survived precisely because it could incorporate such paradoxes as mother abbots and masculine women without compromising itself. In other words, medieval culture could accept a sense of gendered *duality* without a strict dichotomy.[112]

The system cannot be disrupted too far, however, for disorder regarding gender roles would indicate a parallel disorder of the social fabric. This brings us back to the essence of Erec's message to Mabonagrin after the latter has admitted defeat ("bî den liuten ist sô guot"), thereby ending the isolation that Mabonagrin had begun at the insistence of his lady and that threatened to undermine the social/sexual order in *Erec*.[113] Arthurian romance joined a variety of medieval discourses at the turn of the thirteenth century that were endeavoring to (re)structure relationships between men and women. While male activities certainly came under scrutiny, it becomes apparent that a primary interest remained in establishing parameters for woman's proper behavior. Woman remained an indispensable category that by its very indefinable nature consistently threatened to pull the social fabric apart.

In *Parzival*, Wolfram expands the social fabric into an elaborate tapestry, with a broad cast of characters who inhabit a wide range of places and who interact with one another on a variety of levels. In its scope and vision, *Parzival* adds a complex and eloquent voice to the medieval discourses attempting to negotiate the paradox of woman, to negotiate sexual difference and social roles. By the conclusion of his narrative, Wolfram has limited his expansive vision by focusing on the ultimate "true" vision that is the Grail. His attempts literally to synthesize or "fix" his worlds and their inhabitants (male and female, Christian and non-Christian) into 'being' also seem to restrict the possibilities of 'becoming' (at least for women) in *Parzival* by placing them primarily on the margins (literally and symbolically[114]). And yet, as one might expect, Wolfram's narrative defies reduction into simple dichotomies, "even when gender seems to congeal into the most reified forms" like those promoted by the medieval Church (to borrow the words of Judith Butler). Even if there is a "congealing" that occurs over the course of the narrative, it is indeed "an insistent and insidious practice" that is supported by the variety of spaces and places in *Parzival*, the complexity of the map(s) and the intricacy of the narrative. The narrative insists that the audience become part of the process.[115]

Notes

1. *Gender Trouble*, 33.
2. *Parzival*, 172,30–173,7: "I will tell you more about womankind. Husband and wife are one, as are the sun that shone today and the thing called day itself; neither can be separated from the other; they blossom from a single seed. Strive to understand this." As previously noted, all English translations of *Parzival* come from the translation by Helen M. Mustard and Charles E. Passage.
3. In Middle High German, as in modern German, these words can refer both specifically to wife/ husband and generally to woman/ man

(MHG *wîp/ man*; NHG *Frau/ Mann*).

4. An extreme example of this question can be found in Tankred Dorst's version of the Arthurian story *Merlin oder das wüste Land* (Frankfurt: Suhrkamp, 1981). Parzival questions his mother about the Arthurian court and asks whether women live there. Yes, his mother replies, and one must not even look at them. Parzival must turn his back on them because they are the threat of death: "Du mußt ihnen den Rücken zukehren...Sie lächeln und sprechen, aber sie sind eine Drohung des Todes." (65, scene 15)

5. It is interesting that Mustard and Passage emphasize this latent meaning; they translate "man" in line 173,1 as "husband," associating the "binding" nature of the union to the marital state. (95)

6. Weigel, *Topographien der Geschlechter*, 121

7. This anticipates Cundrie's speech before the court in Book VI, which states this criticism explicitly. (314,23–318,4)

8. "The Play of the Text," in *Languages of the Unsayable*, ed. Sanford Budick and Wolfgang Iser (New York: Columbia UP, 1989) 325–340.

9. For a detailed analysis of Wolfram's reactions and allusions to Hartmann, see Christine Wand, *Wolfram von Eschenbach und Hartmann von Aue. Literarische Reaktionen auf Hartmann im* Parzival (Herne: Verlag für Wissenschcaft und Kunst, 1989).

10. It is clear from Sigune's own words that she considers herself married to Schionatulander, one that again displays Wolfram's "play" with courtly conventions and also with current thirteenth-century discussion of the role of consent in marriage. Marlis Schumacher concludes that, although it is consensual and certainly valid in a spiritual sense, this "marriage" is "keine rechtliche Ehe" (60) mainly because it is not consummated. Wolfram's works. See *Die Auffassung der Ehe in den Dichtungen Wolframs von Eschenbach* (Heidelberg: Carl Winter, 1967), especially 48–64. Siegfried Christoph views the relationship as an example of *Kinderminne*, rather than marriage, and sees the relationship's immaturity as the cause of its tragic outcome. See Siegfried Christoph, *Wolfram von Eschenbach's Couples* (Amsterdam: Rodopi, 1981) 172–195.

11. On the rise of the indissolubility doctrine, see Georges Duby, *Medieval Marriage. Two Models from Twelfth-Century France,* trans. Elborg Forster (Baltimore: Johns Hopkins UP, 1978). See also Philippe Ariès, "Die unauflösliche Ehe," in *Die Masken des Begehrens und die Metamorphosen der Sinnlichkeit. Zur Geschichte der Sexualität im Abendland*, ed. Philippe Ariès und André Bejin (Frankfurt: Fischer, 1984; orig. 1982) 176–196.

12. Significantly, Wolfram leaves further details of Sigune's earlier courtly life and of Schionatulander's unfortunate demise to his later

Titurel fragment written c. 1220.

13. Wand, 207–208. While Wolfram shows obvious interest in Hartmann's work, Wand concludes that a "tiefgreifend[e] Polemik" is missing and that Wolfram's interest remains rather "unter sachlichen, erzähltechnischen Gesichtspunkten." I would suggest that the analysis of a topography of gender illustrates that Wolfram indeed engages in a polemical argument; however, he does this is a more subtle way.

14. As mentioned in Chapter 1 (p. 18), both Bindschedler and Bumke describe the way in which Gawan effects his reintegration of the isolated and divided court at the *Schastel marveile*. Bumke also describes the catastrophe of the loveless society at the *Schastel marveile* in an earlier article, "Die Utopie des Grals," in *Literarische Entwürfe,* ed. Hiltrud Gnüg (Frankfurt: Suhrkamp, 1982): 70–79. Renewed contact between men and woman initiates the courtly interaction that renews the all-important *minne*. Thus Bumke can say the "Wiedereinführung der Liebe wird hier als ein bedeutsamer Vorgang gesellschaftlicher Reintegration dargestellt." (77) This renewed love is fostered through courtly interaction.

15. The list seems endless, including Belacane and Gahmuret, Orilus and Jeschute, Obie and Meljanz, Orgeluse and Gawan, Clamide and Condwiramurs, among others. The last conflict is solved, of course, by matching the opponents at Pelrapeire to other mates: Parzival marries Condwiramurs while Clamide eventually requests the hand of Cunneware.

16. It is significant, however, that Wolfram has Trevrizent describe God not as *minne* but as *triuwe* in Book IX ("sît got selbe ein triuwe ist" 462, 19). God is not simply love but more importantly the loyalty that holds the social fabric together. The social prevails over the "personal." This is also the reason why, though there are several paths available for 'becoming' in romance (Enite, Sigune, Herzeloyde, even Orgeluse), women's 'being' remains ultimately fixed according to existing (and restrictive) cultural norms.

17. See Joachim Bumke, *Wolfram von Eschenbach,* 6th ed. (Stuttgart: Metzler, 1991). Bumke describes the rather grim situation: "Liebe und Tod, Liebe und Haß, Liebe und Krieg, Liebe und Gewalt: diese düstere Motivkette bestimmt die Liebesdarstellung im *Parzival*. Überall begegnen verzerrte, verkehrte und überzogene Formen der Liebe, die eine zerstörerische Wirkung nicht nur auf einzelne Menschen, sondern auf die ganze Gesellschaft haben." (133)

18. Ursula Heise, "Frauengestalten in Parzival," *Deutschunterricht* 9 (1957), 39.

19. Blumstein, *Misogyny,* 76 ff. Commenting on Wolfram's use of color symbols in the prologue, she notes that the black and white imagery is

used in reference to men and is a reflection of the state of the soul, whereas the "varwe" mentioned with respect to women in 3,21 "relates solely to the externalities a woman has to offer society." (86)

20. Mustard and Passage, xlix.

21. See Ernst S. Dick, "Fels und Quelle. Ein Landschaftsmodell des höfischen Epos," *Wolfram-Studien* 6, ed. Werner Schröder (Berlin: Erich Schmidt, 1980) 167–181. Dick describes the significant topographical characteristics of the places to which Sigune and Trevrizent withdraw, arguing that the place represented becomes "ein der Raumkonzeption des jeweiligen Werkes entsprechendes symbolisches Zentrum." (179) The symbolic meaning of the place is indicated by a stream of water issuing from rock: "Im *Parzival* wird der Ort, wo eine Quelle aus dem Felsen stürzt, zum Ort der Begegnung mit einer für den Helden schicksalhaften Gestalt." (171) Dick notes that the same landscape provides the setting for the fateful meeting of Orgeluse and Gawan.

22. Willem Snelleman, in *Das Haus Anjou und der Orient in Wolframs Parzival* (Nijkerk, Amsterdam: G.F. Callenbach, 1941), seeks to examine the third Crusade and its connections with the house of Anjou, as they manifest themselves in Wolframs Parzival.

23. Bumke, *Wolfram von Eschenbach*, 52. In fact, one no longer finds in Wolfram the fantastic motifs that the thirteenth-century audience would have known from the tales of Herzog Ernst and the Alexander legend.

24. David Knowles, *The Evolution of Medieval Thought* (New York: Vintage, 1962), 116. See also Charles Homer Haskins, *The Renaissance of the Twelfth Century* (1927; reprint, Cambridge: Harvard UP, 1957.) and the anthology edited by Robert L. Benson and Giles Constable entitled *Renaissance and Renewal in the Twelfth Century* (Cambridge: Harvard UP, 1982).

25. Indeed, as Jacques Le Goff demonstrates in *The Birth of Purgatory*, trans. Arthur Goldhammer (Chicago: University of Chicago Press, 1981), it is also at this time that the next world acquired a concrete geography as well.

26. See George H. T. Kimble, *Geography in the Middle Ages* (New York: Russell and Russell, 1938) and J.R.S. Phillips, *The Medieval Expansion of Europe* (Oxford, New York: Oxford UP, 1988), as well as Rudolf Simek, *Erde und Kosmos im Mittelalter. Das Weltbild vor Kolumbus* (München: C.H. Beck, 1992). Geographical writing, however, truly blossoms after the mid-thirteenth century with the reports of Marco Polo and the *Travels* of John Mandeville.

27. Phillips, 25. Kimble also discusses various contemporary explorations at length in chapters 5 and 6; however, he concentrates his efforts

on activities that occurred mainly after 1250, remarking that "in the early Middle Ages nowhere is the poverty of geographical knowledge more apparent than in regard to the Far East." (Kimble, 120) After the Ptolemaic era, which had reported on the Chinese silk trade, the boundary of Asia receded to the Ganges.

28. Paul Kunitzsch focuses on the actual geography of Wolfram's Orient and its correspondence to the knowledge of the time. See Paul Kunitzsch, "Erneut: Der Orient in Wolframs *Parzival*," *Zeitschrift für deutsches Altertum* 113 (1984): 79–111.

29. Bernd Thum, "Frühformen des Umgangs mit 'Fremdem' und 'Fremden' in der Literatur des Hochmittelalters. Der Parzival Wolframs von Eschenbach als Beispiel," in *Das Mittelalter—unsere fremde Vergangenheit. Beiträge der Stuttgarter Tagung vom 17. bis 19. September 1987,* ed. Joachim Kuolt, Harald Kleinschmidt, and Peter Dinzelbacher (Stuttgart: Helfant, 1990): 315–352. And also Burkhardt Krause, "Wolfram von Eschenbach. Eros, Körper-Politik und Fremdenaneignung," in *Kultur- und literaturgeschichtliche Studien zum Körperthema,* ed. Burkhardt Krause (Stuttgart: Helfant, 1992): 110–147.

30. According to Mustard/Passage, the Baruch is probably the Caliph of Baghdad.

31. Burkhardt Krause offers this summary: "Der Orient war also der sinnenfällige geographische, kulturelle und ethische Antagonist christlicher Welt und ihrer Werte schlechthin, die Negativfolie wahrer Moral, Ethik und rechter *conditio humana* überhaupt." (Krause, 119)

32. See Toril Moi, *Sexual/Textual Politics: Feminist Literary Theory* (London: Routledge, 1985). Moi describes Julia Kristeva's concept of woman as a border/limit, offering offers a way of viewing female marginality as *positionality*. (166)

33. Elisabeth Schmid offers a thorough structural analysis of familial relationships *Parzival* in *Familiengeschichten und Heilsmythologie. Die Verwandtschaftsstrukturen in den französischen und deutschen Gralromane des 12. und 13. Jahrhunderts* (Tübingen: Max Niemeyer, 1986) especially chapter 6.

34. According to Kunitzsch, the use of familiar place names is one way in which Wolfram aims to incorporate contemporary thirteenth-century knowledge of the Orient. These place names give Wolfram's Orient a concrete shape, particularly in the Gahmuret-books, because here the Orient is an organic part of the narrative. (Kunitzsch, 81) In this context, the unknown origin of Zazamanc remains incongruous.

35. Wolfram reports that Gahmuret finds the night after their first meet-

ing interminably long because Belacane has so excited him and he is frustrated by the fact that he will not see her again until daylight:

> . . . den helt verdrôz
> daz sô lanc was diu naht.
> in brâhte in unmaht
> diu swarze Mœrinne,
> des landes küneginne.
> er want sich dicke alsam ein wit,
> daz im krachten diu lit.
> strît unde minne was sîn ger . . . (35,18–25)

[The hero found it annoying that the night was so long, for again and again he felt his helplessness before the black Moorish queen of the land. He kept twisting like a willow branch so that his joints cracked. War and love were what he wanted . . .]

In this passage we find the juxtaposition of Belacane's color with her position as ruler and her effect on Gahmuret's emotions. Wolfram does not comment further, but his narrative leaves the reader to ponder the appropriateness of this relationship and of Gahmuret's passion. Gahmuret's own "hot" blood, in addition to dishonorable heathen knowledge ("gunêrtiu heidenisch witze," 105,16) eventually proves his undoing:

> ein ritter hete bockes bluot
> genomen in ein langez glas:
> daz sluog er ûf den adamas:
> dô wart er weicher danne ein swamp. (105,18–21)

[A certain knight filled a tall glass with a he-goat's blood and poured it on the diamond helmet; then the helmet became softer than a sponge.]

The hot ram's blood can be interpreted as a symbol of Gahmuret's passion; it softens Gahmuret's diamond helmet, allowing his opponent to deal him a mortal blow. For a recent opposing view, see Jutta Anna Kleber, *Die Frucht der Eva und die Liebe in der Zivilisation. Das Geschlechterverhältnis im Gralsroman Wolframs von Eschenbach* (Frankfurt: Peter Lang, 1992). Kleber interprets the ram's blood as the heathen libido, sublimated by the knightly ideal, that seeks revenge on Gahmuret. (197) Even though Gahmuret is defeated, his epitaph attests to his honor as a knight and as a Christian. (198) This view, however, ignores

Wolfram's own ambivalence toward Gahmuret's behavior.

36. Belacane's color seems to present more difficulties for Wolfram than Cundrie's hideous appearance. In all other respects, though, she behaves in a manner acceptable to the courtly world: she "was abr anders rîterlîch." ("she was otherwise noble," 24,9)

37. As the time nears for Gahmuret's departure from Zazamanc, references to Belacane's blackness increase in the text; thus the narrator seeks to reinforce the justification of the departure to the audience. (56,25 ff.) Ironically, in Book II, Gahmuret becomes known in France as the king of Zazamanc. According to Ebenbauer, Gahmuret's main reason for leaving Belacane is racial. Although Wolfram displays much sympathy for Belacane and her situation, she is not a suitable partner for Gahmuret because she falls short of the (white European) ideal. Alfred Ebenbauer. "Es gibt ain mörynne vil dick susse mynne. Belakanes Landsleute in der deutschen Literatur des Mittelalters." *Zeitschrift für deutsches Altertum* 113 (1984): 21.

38. Kunitzsch, 87.

39. Masser asserts that the union is not "rechtskonform." See Achim Masser, "Gahmuret und Belakane. Bemerkungen zur Problematik von Eheschliessung und Minnebeziehungen in der höfischen Literatur," in *Liebe und Aventiure im Artusroman des Mittelalters. Beiträge der Triester Tagung 1988,* ed. Paola Schulze-Belli und Michael Dallapiazza (Göppingen: Kümmerle, 1990), 128. Masser's main point is that Wolfram depicts the relationship between Belacane and Gahmuret in such a way that the audience could *not* misconstrue their union as a legitimate marriage according to the customs of the late 12th and early 13th centuries. In a time that laid so much value on proper forms and formalities, Wolfram portrays a "marriage" union constructed without those and thus implies that it is not valid.

Wolfram does, however, describe the "marriage" between Belacane and Gahmuret in terms standard for such courtly alliances, legitimate or not:

> diu ê hiez magt, diu was nu wîp;
> diu in her ûz fuorte an ir hant.
> si sprach 'mîn lîp und mîn lant
> ist disem rîter undertân,
> obez im vînde wellent lân. (45,25–29)

[She who was formerly called a maiden was now a wife, and as she led him forth by the hand she said: 'My person and my country are now subject to this knight, provided enemies will allow it so to be.']

Masser also overlooks the issue of religion. The heathen queen and the Christian knight would present an obvious mismatch to any medieval audience. According to canon law, a marriage between a non-Christian and a Christian may be "licit" (i.e. legal) under secular law but it is not valid in the eyes of the Church. And of course Gahmuret must find his way to Herzeloyde so that the story's (Christian) hero may be conceived.

40. His comments in Book II reveal his dedication to his Moorish wife, despite the fact that he did desert her and their unborn child. He protests to Herzeloyde: "frouwe, ich hân ein wîp:/diu ist mir lieber dann der lîp." (94,5) He longs for Belacane's love and transforms her blackness into his sun, (91,5–6) justifying his desertion with the excuse that he felt trapped by "der frouwen huote" (90,29) that kept him from knightly activities. Fear of this restrictive "huote" also becomes a defining feature of his marriage to Herzeloyde. See in this regard Danielle Buschinger, "Die Minne-Idee in Wolframs *Parzival*," in *Deutung und Wertung als Grundproblem philologischer Arbeit. Festkolloquium zum 60. Geburtstag von Wolfgang Spiewok vom 28.2–2.3. 1989 in Greifswald* (Greifswald: Ernst-Moritz-Arndt Universität, 1989), 113–114.

41. Herzeloyde brings up the religious argument once again:

> Ir sult die Mœrinne
> lân durch mîne minne.
> des toufes segen hât bezzer kraft.
> nu ânet iuch der heidenschaft,
> und minnet mich nâch unser ê. (94,11–15)

[You should renounce the Moorish queen because of my love. The blessing of baptism has more force. Therefore give up heathen ways and love me according to our religion's law.]

42. For Krause, Belacane represents an erotic other world where "Eros und Machtstreben unterschiedslos eins [waren]." (138)

43. See Susan Signe Morrison, "A Reader-Response to Wolfram von Eschenbach's Parzival: The Position of the Female Reader," in *Lesarten. New Methodologies and Old Texts,* ed. Alexander Schwarz (Bern: Peter Lang, 1990), 134. Morrison continues: "Since the woman is seen as an impediment to the propulsion of the male knightly code, she is constructed by the author as fictive and expendable. There is an openness in discussing Moorish 'otherness' but not gender otherness . . ." (134)

44. Thum, 334. Thum analyzes the Zazamanc episode in terms of its as-

similation of the "foreign" into language and actions familiar to Wolfram's courtly audience. (333–335)

45. Kunitzsch maintains that the name of her country, rendered by Wolfram as Tribalibot, derives from "Palibothra," a city on the Ganges whose name was transmitted from antiquity. Wolfram also retains the location of it on the banks of the Ganges.

Interestingly, Secundille's realm is connected to that of Belacane through a geographic discrepancy. In attempting to find an etymology of Zazamanc and its capital, Kunitzsch theorizes that, while Zazamanc seems to refer to a place in Africa, the city of Patelamunt refers to an Indian city. Such a conflation would certainly not be unusual, since many medieval geographers tended to view India as a land mass connected with Africa in the south. (Kunitzsch, 88) But, in the context of *Parzival,* this provides evidence of one more connection between these queens, between the margins that they mark.

46. See Karl Delabar, *Erkantiu sippe unt hoch geselleschaft. Studien zur Funktion des Verwandtschaftsverbandes in Wolframs von Eschenbach Parzival* (Göppingen: Kümmerle, 1990). Delabar takes a purely utilitarian view of the roles of minor female characters in Parzival. He comments that Secundille and other characters like Condwiramurs, Cunneware, and Liaze "sind . . . die 'Assistenten' der Protagonisten, auf diese hinkonstruiert und für deren Charakterisierung signifikant." (221) Delabar makes a valid point about these female characters: they are designed for a certain purpose connected with a male protagonist and then removed from the plot when they have fulfilled this purpose. (229) Unfortunately, Delabar's overall scheme draws too heavily from structuralism to provide more than a reductionist view of *Parzival.* Thus he cannot explore the gender issues that motivate Wolfram's treatment of Secundille and Condwiramurs, for example, attributing their roles and fates merely to the expediency of structure.

47. Petra Gilroy-Hirtz, "Begegnung mit dem Ungeheuer," in *An den Grenzen höfischer Kultur. Anfechtungen der Lebensordnung in der deutschen Erzähldichtung des hohen Mittelalters,* ed. Gert Kaiser (Munich: Wilhelm Fink, 1991): 167–209. See also Jeffrey Jerome Cohen, *Of Giants. Sex, Monsters, and the Middle Ages* (Minneapolis: University of Minnesota Press, 1999).

48. Helmut Brall, "Imaginationen des Fremden. Zu Formen und Dynamik kultureller Indentitätsfindung in der höfischen Dichtung," in *An den Grenzen höfischer Kultur. Anfechtungen der Lebensordnung in der deutschen Erzähldichtung des hohen Mittelalters,* ed. Gert Kaiser (Munich: Wilhelm Fink, 1991): 115–167, here 165.

49. Weigel, *Topographien der Geschlechter,* 121.

50. Because Herzeloyde displays a broad spectrum of emotions and acts in a variety of contexts, Gertrud Jaron Lewis has called her "das echte Charakterbild einer wirklichen dichterischen Persönlichkeit." See Gertrud Jaron Lewis, "Die unheilige Herzeloyde. Ein ikonoklastischer Versuch," *Journal of English and German Philology* 74 (1975): 485.

51. See David Blamires, *Characterization and Individuality in Wolfram's Parzival* (Cambridge: Cambridge UP, 1966). In his chapter on Herzeloyde, Blamires notes a sudden increase in descriptive passages following Parzival's arrival in the narrative. Blamires sees this "considerable elaboration" (71) as Wolfram's indication that Herzeloyde's main relationship is with Parzival.

52. See Gisela Gerhards, *Das Bild der Witwe in der deutschen Literatur des Mittelalters,* Ph.D. diss., Bonn, 1962, 220.

53. G. Ehrismann, 263.

54. Schwietering, 170.

55. See Marion Gibbs, *Wiplîchez wîbes reht. A Study of the Women Characters in the Works of Wolfram von Eschenbach* (Duquesne: Duquesne UP, 1972), 10.

56. See, for example, Walter Johannes Schröder, *Die Soltane-Erzählung in Wolframs Parzival. Studien zur Darstellung und Bedeutung der Lebensstufen Parzivals* (Heidelberg: Carl Winter, 1963) 58–59. See also Joachim Bumke, *Die Wolfram von Eschenbach Forschung seit 1945. Bericht und Bibliographie* (Munich: Wilhelm Fink, 1970) 140 ff. Most recently, Kleber depicts Herzeloyde's dual heritage "zwischen Lust und Busse." (163–215)

57. Heise, 60 and 62.

58. Lewis, 474.

59. Walter Haug, "*Parzival* ohne Illusionen," *Deutsche Vierteljahresschrift* 64 (1990): 201. Haug understands violence and desire as the underlying themes of the Gahmuret books (I and II), painting a rather grim picture of this inescapable cycle: "Männer, die nichts im Sinn haben, als mörderisch dreinzuhauen, Frauen, die die Männer in den Kampf treiben und auf die Sieger versessen sind, und immer dasselbe Ende: die Kämpfer geben keine Ruhe, bis man sie erschlägt, und den Frauen bleibt nichts, als an den Leichen ihrer Männer klagend zusammenzubrechen . . ."

60. Otto Springer offers a typically idealistic view of the relationship between Herzeloyde and Gahmuret. See Otto Springer, "Wolfram's *Parzival*," in *Arthurian Literature in the Middle Ages,* ed. R.S. Loomis (Oxford: Clarendon Press, 1959) 218–250. Springer believes that Herzeloyde "makes an ideal wife for Gahmuret because she combines her womanly affection with an understanding of her husband's prowess and

soldierly sense of duty." (245) Such an interpretation denies Herzeloyde's own very definite sense of self.

61. Bumke comments on Herzeloyde's reaction to Gahmuret's death: "Doch Wolfram wollte hier sicherlich keinen Wahnsinn darstellen, wohl aber ein Verhalten, das sich über alle gesellschaftlichen Konventionen hinwegsetzt." (*Wolfram von Eschenbach*, 58) To set oneself beyond societal conventions, however, does demonstrate a certain kind of madness that may not be acceptable. Herzeloyde touches the border of that madness.

62. For some reason, Haug overlooks this obvious critique, saying that Wolfram "idealisiert das rücksichtslose Haudegentum wie ungedämpfte Erotik in einem erstaunlichen Maße . . ." and that the poet's reaction is not "kritische Empörung" but "Klage." (Haug, "*Parzival* ohne Illusionen," 202)

63. Schröder observes that the *waste* of Soltane is actually best defined by what it is *not*: "Das Wort meint hier einen Ort, an dem es keine 'Welt' gibt, kein Rittertum. Herzeloyde geht 'aus der Welt,' sie lebt ohne Hofhaltung, ohne Festesglanz, ohne Minnetreiben und Turnier. Soltane ist also ein Ort ohne eigentliches Leben, ein Ort außerhalb des Daseins, das durch Streit und Kampf gefährdet ist." (12–13) It is an indeterminate place, like the forest in which Sigune and Trevrizent reside. The similarity of Soltane to the isolation of the forest seems to indicate that here Herzeloyde embarks on a path to salvation taken by others in her family. (Bumke, *Wolfram von Eschenbach*, 58) Her status remains more ambiguous than theirs, however.

64. McNamara and Wemple, 94.

65. For a convincing solution to the paradox that is Herzeloyde, namely the fact that Wolfram portrays her in an ambivalent manner yet finally leaves the audience with unequivocal praise, see David Duckworth, "Herzeloyde and Antikonie," *German Life and Letters* 41 (1988): 322–341. Duckworth explains that Wolfram emphasizes what he considers the overwhelmingly positive trait each woman possesses: Herzeloyde demonstrates *triuwe,* while Antikonie demonstrates *kiusche.* Though they are not *absolute* qualities, they indicate a lack of *valsch* in the respective context of each woman's life and behavior.

66. See Lydia Miklautsch, *Studien zur Mutterrolle in den mittelhochdeutschen Großepen des zwölften und dreizehnten Jahrhunderts* (Erlangen: Verlag Palm und Enke, 1991), 70. And, in the case of Soltane, the maternal world is not the best for the son. He must find his own way through knighthood, as a man, though his ultimate goal is the Grail, to which he is maternally connected.

67. Schröder's comment can be taken as representative here: "Herzeloyde flieht die Welt um ihrer Seligkeit willen, sie geht in die

Einsamkeit wie eine Eremitin . . . Als Witwe wählt Herzeloyde (wie später Signe) das Leben einer Nonne; als Mutter eines Knaben, der des Vaters *art* hat (118,3–6), entführt sie diesen in die Einsamkeit. Herzeloyde ist wieder *muoter* und *wîp,* ihr Verhalten wird religiös beleuchtet." (Schröder, 13)

68. Eders goes so far as to posit that Herzeloyde is trapped in her roles by her husband and her son. See Annemarie Eders, "Macht- und Ohnmachtstrukturen im Beziehungsgefüge von Wolframs Parzival. Die Herzeloydentragödie," in *Der frauwen buoch. Versuche zu einer feministischen Mediävistik,* ed. Ingrid Bennewitz (Göppingen: Kümmerle, 1989) 179–212. This is made clear by her dream. The dragon symbolizes both father and son (199–203), as it destroys her for trying to assert herself. Eders characterizes Herzeloyde as "nicht eine Frau, die passiv leidend einem weiblichen Masochismus verfällt, sondern sie hat intensive Wünsche und stellt Anforderungen." (195) And these wishes are thwarted first by her husband and then by her son.

69. Lewis offers an interpretation of Herzeloyde's death that is unique among *Parzival* critics. For Lewis, Herzeloyde's death represents her in total control one last time: "Als völlig egozentrische Frau, die allen Schicksalsschlägen durch ein Ohnmacht auszuweichen sucht, vermag sie den Verlust ihres größten Besitzes nicht zu überstehen." (482) In other words, she decides to die, rather than accept that she cannot have what she desires. This interpretation, while appealing, cannot be substantiated by the text.

70. Saunders, 19. This forest is also part of Terre de salvaesche, further linking Signe to the world of the Grail toward which she directs her cousin Parzival.

71. Szlavek, 44.

72. Szlavek, 46. As we have previously noted in Chapter I, one can distinguish between two particular types of localities through a comparison of Parzival and Gawan. The fundamental difference between the two knights "liegt darin, daß Gawans Abenteuer im Rahmen der Gesellschaft stattfinden, die Abenteuer Parzivals aber in der Wildnis oder am Rande der Gesellschaft." (58) Parzival's journey leads him through forests and wilderness, while Gawan's path "läuft in den Schranken der geordneten Gesellschaft, von Burg zu Burg, mit einem festen geographischen Ziel in einer bestimmten Zeitspanne."(45)

73. It is interesting that, of all the characters in *Parzival,* Signe (the embodiment of Christian saintliness) is metaphorically related to Belacane (the heathen queen whose only baptism was through her tears). Groos connects them through the image of the mourning turtledove, comparing Signe mourning in the linden tree to the turtledove image used to de-

scribe Belacane after Gahmuret's desertion. See Arthur B. Groos, "'Sigune auf der Linde' and the Turtledove in *Parzival*," *Journal of English and German Philology* 67 (1968): 631–646.

74. Jacobson, 9. See also Michael Dallapiazza, "Häßlichkeit und Individualität. Ansätze zur Überwindung der Idealität des Schönen in Wolframs von Eschenbach *Parzival*," *Deutsche Vierteljahresschrift* 3 (1985): 410 ff.

75. Jacobson, 7.

76. For a more detailed analysis of Sigune's role in Parzival's journey, see Sterling-Hellenbrand; "Women on the Edge in *Parzival*." See also Birgit Eichholz, *Kommentar zur Sigune- und Ither-Szene im 3. Buch von Wolframs Parzival* (138,9–161,8) (Helfant: Stuttgart, 1987). Eichholz comments on the similarities this scene shares with the earlier scenes involving both Herzeloyde and Jeschute. She notes that, like Herzeloyde, even Sigune attempts to show Parzival the wrong way to Arthur's court when he departs after their first meeting:

> si wîste in unrehte nâch:
> si vorht daz er den lîp verlür
> und daz si grœzeren schaden kür. (142,1—3)

[but she showed him the wrong direction, fearing he would lose his life and that she would thereby only sustain greater harm than before.]

77. Springer, 246.

78. Heise, 52. Coping with her fate, Sigune is "ein Bild leidender triuwe, das Parzival eindringlich entgegentritt und ihn formt." (56)

79. "Am tiefsten ist die Durchdringung von Minne und Gott in der Gestalt Sigunes vollzogen, die Wolfram aus einer Nebenfigur bei Chrestien zu einer der bedeutsamsten Gestalten des Werkes gebildet hat . . ." (de Boor, 112)

80. Gibbs, 38.

81. Dallapiazza, 410. Only Joseph Campbell has dared to suggest that Sigune's behavior is rather macabre, calling Sigune "that strange neurotic lover of a corpse." See Joseph Campbell, *The Masks of God: Creative Mythology* (New York: Viking Press, 1968), 477.

82. Bernhard Rahn, *Wolframs Sigunendichtung. Eine Interpretation der <Titurelfragmente>* (Zürich: Fretz & Wasmuth, 1958), 97.

83. "Wie Parzival steht aber auch Sigune in der göttlichen Gnade und findet dadurch den Weg zur Bereitschaft für die Erlösung. Indem ihre triuwe von Gott angenommen wird, bekommt sie auch eine neue, nun wieder mit vollem Leben gefüllte Idealität, die sie wie Parzival zum großen

Vorbild macht." (Rahn, 98)

84. In her recent study of the critical role of Perceval's sister in the Vulgate *Queste,* Janina Traxler could be describing Sigune's fate in her summary: "In the world of the Grail quest, not only is the best woman a dead woman, but the best woman is a dead virgin." Janina P. Traxler, "Dying to get to Sarras: Perceval's Sister and the Grail Quest." *The Grail. A Casebook,* ed. Dhira Mahoney (New York and London: Garland Publishing, 1999), 274.

85. Of course, Herzeloyde is also present as part of the Grail family, sister to Anfortas and Trevrizent (and Repanse de Schoye).

86. Michael Camille, *Image on the Edge. The Margins of Medieval Art* (Cambridge: Harvard UP, 1992), 127.

87. Wolfram also wryly notes in book 6 that no lances have ever been broken for Cundrie's beauty: "nâch ir minn was selten tjost getân." (314,10)

88.

> bî dem wazzer Ganjas
> ime lande Trîbalibôt
> wahsent liute alsus durh nôt. (517,28–30)

[By the waters of the Ganges in the land of Tribalibof people grow like that and cannot help it.]

89. Blumstein devotes an entire chapter to the topic of "Cundrie's Knowledge, Intellect and Ugliness." (88–105) Her argument is that Cundrie is "anti-courtly" in both her appearance and her knowledge and that Wolfram's depiction of her reflects his underlying misogyny: "He [Wolfram] is still under the influence of antifeminist prejudices to the extent that he upholds the notion that women *should be,* and always will be man's intellectual inferior." (104) Kasten makes a much more positive connection between ugliness and education, noting that Cundrie resembles Veldeke's Sibille in this regard.

90. On their combined roles in *Parzival,* see Evelyn Jacobson, "Cundrie and Sigune." *Seminar* 25 (1989): 1–11; James Marchand, "Honor and Shame in Wolfram's Parzival," in *Spectrum Medii Aevi,* ed. William McDonald (Göppingen: Kümmerle, 1983) 283–298; most recently, Alexandra Sterling-Hellenbrand, "Women on the Edge in Parzival," *Quondam et Futurus. A Journal of Arthurian Interpretations* 3 (1993): 56–68.

91. Ingrid Kasten sees her both as a "Metapher der Ausgrenzung" and as a strategy leading simultaneously "zu einem Verfahren der Integration." See Ingrid Kasten, "Häßliche Frauenfiguren in der Literatur des Mittelalters," in *Auf der Suche nach der Frau im*

Mittelalter, ed. Bea Lundt (München: Wilhelm Fink, 1991), 272. On the symbolic Christian level, the 'ugly' was traditionally marginalized by its association with sin: "wo das Häßliche für die Sünde, für die Körperlichkeit des Menschen, für den Tod steht." (Kasten, 276) This is precisely what Cundrie's goodness and humility overcome. In this way, she also offers a damaging critique of shallow courtly aesthetics. This is the essence of Dallapiazza's argument. In an interesting twist, this critique happens through the mechanism of a woman.

92. Indeed, Helmut Brall maintains that, in her strangeness, Cundrie offers "das wahre Portrait höfischen Kulturbewußtseins" because she stands on the border "zwischen den höfisch maskierten Wünschen und Träumen und den Mächten der Realität." (165) Brall's "cultural consciousness" is condemned to a liminal state in Cundrie's person, however.

93. Wolfram says only Condwiramurs can surpass Orgeluse's beauty: "âne Condwirnâmûrs/ wart nie geborn sô schœner lîp." ("except for Condwiramurs, no one had been born more beautiful," 508,22—23)

94. Springer, 240.

95. Buschinger states: "Orgeluses Charakterbild wird von Wolfram derart überzeichnet, daß man diese Kunstfigur nachgerade als eine Karikatur der Minne-Herrin deuten muß." (112)

96.

> die wârn ze rîch in mînen solt,
> wart mir der keiner anders holt,
> nâch minne ich manegen dienen liez,
> dem ich doch lônes niht gehiez. (618,15–18)

[Her wrath lay well nigh covered, and ever weaker had her anger grown while Gawan's embraces had awakened her.]

97. Because he is married and in love with his wife.

98. Haug, in "*Parzival* ohne Illusionen," takes Orgeluse's comparison of Cidegast with the unicorn (613,22–24) as a metaphor for the dark side of *minne*: "Es sind also die Katastrophen, die die Liebe zu Orgeluse mit sich gebracht hat, auf die die Wege beider Romanhelden, Gawans wie Parzivals, ausgerichtet sind. Und der Einhornvergleich gibt dieser Thematik einen scharfen Akzent . . ." (200)

99. Bindschedler views Orgeluse as an anti-Kriemhild, who illustrates that healing (of her desire for revenge) is possible through Gawan: "Kein Zweifel, daß Wolfram, der zwar für die Treue einer liebenden Frau, auch über den Tod des Geliebten hinaus (man denke an Sigune), die höchste Bewunderung zeigt, in Orgeluse die Verkörperung einer Anti-Kriemhild geschaffen hat. Denn Orgeluse läßt sich von ihrer Rachsucht 'heilen.'" (735) And the doctor who heals her is Gawan.

100. Wolfram lets us know that Gawan's embraces had weakened her earlier resolve:

> ir zorn was nâch verdecket:
> wan si het erwecket
> von Gâwân etslîch umbevanc
> dâ von ir zürnen was sô kranc. (723,7–10)

[Her wrath lay well nigh covered, and ever weaker had her anger grown while Gawan's embraces had awakened her.]

101. Gibbs, 102. Gibbs devotes an entire chapter to the character of Repanse de Schoye.

102. Heise, 45.

103. According to Buschinger, Condwiramurs fulfills the promise only hinted at with Herzeloyde: "Während in der Figur der Herzeloyde bereits andeutungsweise Wolframs Ideal der Ehefrau gestaltet wurde, wird diese Tendenz voll durchgesetzt bei der Gestaltung der Condwiramurs." (114) See also Kathryn Smits. "Einige Beobachtungen zu gemeinsamen Motiven in Hartmanns *Erec* und Wolframs *Parzival*," in *Festschrift for E.W. Herd,* ed. August Obermayer, Otago German Studies 1 (Dunedin: University of Otago Press) 251–262. Smits sees the marriage of Parzival and Condwiramurs beginning at "die Entwicklungsstufe, die Erec und Enite am Ende ihrer Geschichte erreichen" where the "räumliche Bewegungsfreiheit des Mannes" is understood from the very beginning. (258) This can be seen in the fact that Condwiramurs does not have to be physically present in order to inspire her husband. Indeed, she only appears in books 4 and 16. Blamires sees this as unequivocally positive.

104. "Und indem Condwiramurs mit dem Gral auf einer Ebene steht, ist der Bezirk 'Minne' aus dem Artusbereich gelöst, über ihn erhöht und vorbereitet, in den Gralsbereich aufgenommen zu werden." (de Boor, 101)

105. Blamires, 230. Blamires also maintains that Condwiramurs has an identity of her own apart from Parzival. (234)

106. "nur die Damen des Gralsbereiches zeigen etwas Initiative in ihrem eigenen Leben." (Szlavek, 61) This may be true of Herzeloyde, but Repanse and Condwiramurs do not seem as driven to take any initiative. Wolfram basically excuses them from having to do this on the basis of their innate goodness. In addition, as we have seen, one dare not call the indomitable Orgeluse a passive figure.

107. Bumke, "Geschlechterbeziehungen," 120.

108. Pathak, "A Pedagogy for Postcolonial Feminists," 432.

109. Gaunt, 16.

110. See Hugo Kuhn, "Wolframs Frauenlob," in *Liebe und Gesellschaft,*

ed. Wolfgang Walliczek (Metzler: Stuttgart, 1980), 51.

111. In *The Creation of Patriarchy*, Lerner discusses the process of symbol-making in the development of patriarchal societies as a process that marginalized women as it reinforced patriarchal symbols. The genre of courtly romance created its own symbols and ideals with similar results, marginalizing women even as it extolled their virtues. See also R. Howard Bloch,' *Medieval Misogyny and the Invention of Romantic Love* (Chicago: The University of Chicago Press, 1991).

112. Cadden, 202–213.

113. *Iwein* does not offer such an obvious example of potential disorder as Mabonagrin's garden. Laudine's repudiation of Iwein does, however, destabilize their relationship and leaves Laudine's realm vulnerable to attack once more since she has no husband/lord to defend it.

114. One could say that the flexibility of such female-gendered margins, created by male poets, illustrates desire at work. In "Sexual Difference," Irigaray describes desire as the change in an interval, "the displacement of the subject or of the object in their relations of nearness or distance." (8)

115. In a very concrete sense, *Parzival* engages the imagination of the reader or listener and creates the text out of interaction. In the final chapter of the *The Implied Reader* entitled "The Reading Process: A Phenomenological Approach," Iser views the reader/text interaction as essential to the creation of the literary work. (274–294)

CHAPTER 4

The Topography of Gottfried von Strassburg

Places to Play in Tristan

> . . . becomings are never indeterminate or generic; they
> are always becoming something . . . they are always a
> multiplicity
>
> —Elizabeth Grosz[1]

> If there is something right in Beauvoir's claim that one
> is not born but rather becomes a woman, it follows that
> woman itself is a term in process, a becoming, a con-
> structing that cannot rightfully be said to originate or
> to end. As an ongoing discursive practice, it is open to
> intervention and resignification
>
> —Judith Butler[2]

> diu valsche erwirbet valschen prîs.
> wie stæte ist ein dünnez îs,
> daz ougestheize sunnen hât?
> ir lop vil balde alsus zergât.
> manec wîbes schœne an lobe ist breit:
> ist dâ daz herze conterfeit,
> die lobe ich als ich solde
> daz safer ime golde . . .
>
> —Wolfram von Eschenbach[3]

Plot synopsis: After an introduction that recounts the parentage
and the early youth of Tristan, Gottfried focuses on Tristan's life
at the court of his uncle, King Marke of Cornwall, who has de-
clared the young Tristan his heir. In defending Marke's interests
against the Irish champion Morolt, Tristan is wounded with Morolt's poisoned sword. He must travel to Ireland so that the

maker of the poison (Morolt's sister the queen) can heal him. During this sojourn in Ireland, Tristan (known as Tantris) becomes the tutor of the young princess Isolde. Tristan returns to Cornwall, only to make another trip to Ireland at the behest of Marke to woo the princess Isolde in his name. The younger Isolde reluctantly follows the advice of her mother and Brangaene and puts aside thoughts of avenging her uncle's death in favor of accepting Marke's offer of marriage. The love potion (which had been made by Queen Isolde for her daughter's wedding night) is consumed by Tristan and Isolde on the fateful voyage back to Cornwall, and the intrigues begin with the substitution of Brangaene for Isolde on the latter's wedding night to deceive Marke. Despite the watchful and suspicious eyes of courtiers like Melot and Marjodo, Tristan and Isolde manage to conceal their affair in various situations: the assignation by the brook (where Tristan and Isolde convince the hidden Marke that they are not lovers), the flour strewn on the bedchamber floor, the ordeal, the little dog Petitcriu. Their escapades culminate in their banishment to the cave of lovers, the ultimate *locus amoenus*, from which they eventually do return to court. Finally, the lovers are caught together and Tristan leaves Cornwall. His travels take him to Arundel, where he meets Isolde of the White Hands. In the middle of Tristan's struggle with the memory of the Isolde he left behind, Gottfried's narrative breaks off.

GOTTFRIED AND HIS CONTEMPORARIES

We know nothing of the actual poet Gottfried, other than his name and the literary reputation he left behind. His name does not occur in the text of his poem (unlike Wolfram and Hartmann who name themselves)[4]—we actually have only the initial letter of the first acrostich (GDIETRICH), and some have interpreted this as a reference to the poet (at least the initial) and his patron. Gottfried's name does not appear in any other documents, unlike Walter von der Vogelweide, who is shown to have received a coat as a gift from a patron. Nevertheless, it seems reasonable from his association with Strassburg that Gottfried was probably writing in or around that comparatively urban center; unlike many of his contemporaries, he is not known to have been a knight or a *ministerial*. When one examines the ethical fabric of his narrative, and when one considers that his work received praise rather than excessive censure, it seems apparent that his audience had different expectations from those of Hartmann and Wolfram, as though "the moral and ethical considerations found in them did not play an important role in their own sphere of existence."[5] Indeed, Gottfried's own words indicate that he has little regard for Wolfram's art; he expresses his opinion in no uncertain terms in the passage known as the literary excursus (*Dichterexkurs*) in *Tristan*. It is generally agreed that Wolfram is the intended object of Gottfried's criticism of the anonymous poet in this passage. Referring to certain "vindaere wilder maere,/der maere wildenaere," (inventors of wild tales, hired hunters after stories," 4665–66) Gottfried accuses such poets of wildly leaping over the literary heath like the companion of a hare:

> swer nû des hasen geselle sî
> und ûf der wortheide
> hôchsprünge und wîtweide
> mit bickelworten welle sîn
> und ûf daz lôrschapelekîn
> wân âne volge welle hân,
> der lâze uns bî dem wâne stân (4638–4644)

[But if some friend of the hare, high-skipping and far-browsing, seeks out Poetry's heat with dicing terms, and lacking our general assent, aspires to the laurel wreath, let him leave us to adhere to our opinion that we too must have a hand in the choosing.]

Such poets certainly cannot deserve the laurel wreath awarded "dem Ouwaere," for their style is coarse and uncivilized when compared with Hartmann's cultivated language, which is even and smooth and aesthetically pleasing.[6] Wolfram seems to return these disparaging sentiments if we recall the discussion of falsity ("conterfeit") in the passage from his *Parzival* prologue mentioned in the previous chapter and cited in detail above: the praise and reputation of a woman who behaves in a dishonest or inconstant manner will decay as quickly as ice will melt under the hot August sun. Read aloud, the last two lines (particularly the "ich solde" at the conclusion of line 3, 14) might evoke the name of Gottfried's heroine.[7] The image is that of a common stone that cannot be made more valuable by a costly setting, and this image communicates the incomplete understanding that we have of love; in order to be worthy of inclusion in the audience of "noble hearts," we need enlightenment. According to Gottfried, the story of Tristan and Isolde should show us the shining example of their great love in the appropriate setting created for them by *minne*. (Not surprisingly, Wolfram finds more virtue in the reverse image, that of a precious ruby mounted in ordinary brass: "dem glîche ich rehten wîbes muot.")[8]

These allusions found in Gottfried and Wolfram are admittedly oblique; nevertheless, they highlight fundamental differences in ethos between the two poets that are revealing for our discussion of gender topographies in *Tristan*. Jaeger summarizes the contrast between Gottfried and Wolfram rather succinctly in the context of what he terms the "romantic dilemma."[9] Two principal tendencies develop in courtly narrative in an attempt to deal with this dilemma, the representation of a love that can ennoble those who experience it: "The first domesticizes sexual passion and the second mystifies it."[10] The first is represented for Jaeger by Wolfram von Eschenbach, who envisions the ideal in the chaste love of husband for wife and who takes the danger and the threat out of sexuality by returning it to child-like innocence.[11] For Wolfram, love acts as a "redemptive force in both social and religious experience.[12] In what by comparison is a "virtuoso act of conceptualizing," Gottfried represents the second solution, addressed to a new and different audience, which tries to integrate sexuality and love and to elevate the union of both to a new level. Gottfried makes love esoteric and exclusive, removing it to a "realm beyond reason" with a solution that we can perhaps attain but not comprehend.[13] A new audience, a new set of expectations, a new set of considerations, must also prompt the modern reader to speculate whether the possibilities suggested and represented in *Tristan* might also not have been offered as an alternative to the negative effects of increasing urbanization and restrictions on the activities of women of in the thirteenth and fourteenth centuries.[14] Clearly, as Gottfried's artistry charts *Tristan*'s domain for his audience, the work's topography operates as a creative vehicle through which traditional gender roles may be explored, questioned, and perhaps eventually transformed from those posited by Wolfram and Hartmann.

Gottfried's solution has led to much discussion of his place in the Arthurian canon, since he provides a striking and (to many) decidedly un-Arthurian illustration of what a secular alternative to Munsalvaesche might look like.[15] In a way that sets him apart from his contemporaries, Gottfried does try to accommodate sexuality in his new formula for romance; most recently, Jaeger compares Gottfried's attempt to a mixture of oil and water, with as much success, showing that the basic assessment of Gottfried's undertaking have not radically changed over the course of the last decade.[16] But, having radically altered Wolfram's focus, Gottfried's uniquely complex attempt to combine sexuality and virtue has intriguing ramifications for an examination of gender negotiations and performance. Gottfried redefines woman and man—which he does with the figures of both Tristan and Isolde. In allowing woman to give in to the sexuality that Christian teaching associated almost exclusively with women, Gottfried offers us indeed the term woman "as an ongoing discursive practice" that literally becomes for the audience "a constructing that cannot rightfully be said to originate or to end" and that suggests the possibility that it may be "open to intervention and resignification."[17] Actually the text itself has also remained open to many layers of interpretation, leading a rather "protean life" of its own.[18] In terms of the gender topographies we have examined in Hartmann and Wolfram, we will see that Gottfried's narrative uses its topographies as a process of further signification, to map what the poet considers to be model constellations of femininity and masculinity for his audience (both medieval and modern). As we have seen, "gender topographies" describe the metaphorical and discursive imprints left by the various places that men and women have occupied throughout the history of western culture. These imprints survive through the persistence of images that Weigel refers to as perceived images ("*Denk*bilder"), in contrast to actual images ("*Ab*bilder"). As they are mapped onto literary space by poets who attempt to make them comprehensible to the audience in the context of its own cultural and historical landscape, these perceived images are undeniably gendered; the topographies in which they are placed demarcate exemplary constellations of femininity and masculinity.[19] This mapping continues the process of "civilization" (or "Zivilisationsarbeit") that enables a culture to define itself.

Gottfried is a master of self-definition. His protagonists practice the art of self-definition constantly.[20] In an innovative way that separates him from his contemporaries, Gottfried plunders "the grand costume room and prop chest"[21] of Arthurian romance to create two exemplary protagonists (Tristan *and* Isolde) whose portrayal resists (or at least questions) the seemingly inevitable resolution of the "*Herrenfrage*" or the reevaluation of women's roles in a twelfth-century crisis of masculine identity.[22] This resistance is achieved through the ways in which Gottfried inscribes his characters in the space of his text. This inscription takes place quite literally within the forests and pastoral settings of the traditional romance/Arthurian landscape. In her 1963 monograph *Raum und Landschaft in Gottfrieds Tristan*, Ingrid Hahn examines the landscapes and spaces of Gottfried's narrative, trying to move away from a purely topical analysis of the rhetorical forms and traditions to a more complete understanding of the relationship between the landscapes and the meaning of the work as a whole. Not only does Hahn treat individual elements of landscape (the forest, the sea, the *locus amoenus* as represented both in the pleasure garden and in the cave of the lovers) but she also discusses spatial arrangements and landscape as forms of expression (not simply as geographic locations/places). Gottfried does mention real places; however, he is not concerned with accuracy.[23] The cave of the lovers has, of course, been a focal point of study and interest—a space unique to Gottfried's narrative and perhaps his most elaborate addition to his sources.[24] As we have seen in the previous discussions of Hartmann and Wolfram, romance offers a unique opportunity to explore the concept of gender topographies. Gottfried is no exception: in particular, the spaces of Ireland and Cornwall provide the outlines for the representational framework of the work, creating the gendered places and spaces in which and through which the gendered inscription can occur. Civilization, courtliness, defining life at court—these are of primary importance to Gottfried and, to treat them, he crafts a fascinating world in *Tristan* that scarcely resembles that of *Iwein* or *Parzival*. In the process, however, Gottfried creates a narrative in which topography and gender merge to show us a uniquely liberating landscape. The text of *Tristan* itself becomes a space itself where new significations are possible as Gottfried adopts and adapts the *Tristan*-story.[25] The central loci of Ireland and Cornwall epitomize Weigel's concept of gender topographies, illustrating that gender clearly plays an integral role in the arrangements of power and space in *Tristan*. These topographies of Gottfried's narrative go on to create unique spaces which suggest the possibility of potentially transgressive realities to the audience.[26]

A PLACE FOR NOBLE HEARTS

As we have seen in previous chapters, the creative act of "writing a world"[27] certainly describes the work of the poets who were composing medieval romance at the turn of the thirteenth century. This creativity was in part prompted by a developing concept of the fictional central to the "conscious structural experiment"[28] that is the courtly novel. This fiction did not, however, aim towards a concrete solution of the problems it described and elaborated. On the contrary, it is characterized by reflection upon the conditions of its own existence. This is perhaps nowhere more evident than in Gottfried's many asides and excursus wherein he reflects for his audience on the meaning of his own text. Such reflection offers the opportunity for a multivalent exploration of social and perhaps even individual identities on the part of audience and author.

In his prologue to *Tristan*, Gottfried von Strassburg shows that he understands the poet's role as a facilitator of such reflection, as a manipulator of textual space. First of all, Gottfried targets a very specific audience for his text:

> Ich hân mir eine unmüezekeit
> der werlt ze liebe vür geleit
> und edelen herzen z'einer hage,
> den herzen, den ich herze trage,
> der werlde, in die mîn herze siht. (45–49)

[Thus I have undertaken a labor to please the polite world and solace noble hearts—those hearts which I hold in affection, that world which lies open to my heart.][29]

These "noble hearts" comprise a select group: they alone possess the knowledge and experience necessary to comprehend the story Gottfried plans to tell them.[30] The poet himself also desires to take part in the special existence granted to this group: "der werlt wil ich gewerldet wesen,/ mit ir verderben oder genesen." ("to this life let my life be given, of this world let me be a part, to be damned or saved with it." 64–65) Gottfried offers his poem as the end of a journey, the desired destination of those noble hearts who seek such refined enlightenment: "von diu swer seneder maere ger,/der envar niht verrer dane her." ("Therefore, whoever wants a story need go no further than here." 123–124)[31] It is of course typical for a poet in the prologue to describe the public for which he is writing. Gottfried, however, develops a characterization of an audience that implies much more specific qualities or conditions.[32] Indeed, one of the purposes of the prologue is to develop this complex interrelationship between the author, the text, and the receptors of the text (i.e. the audience). The function of the reference to "edele herzen" is to make an explicit and further connection between the author, the audience and the title characters of the narrative. The audience must have a certain attitude toward love and life that is typical of an "edelez herz"—this term may have classical or mystical associations, as Speckenbach and others have noted, but Gottfried gives it his own specific meaning.[33] A heart is noble when it can accept in equal measure both desire and longing, pain and happiness, sweetness and bitterness.[34] The audience of this new 'elect' must accept the story of Tristan and Isolde—this is the transition point to the actual introduction of the narrative.

As Gottfried connects the story of Tristan and Isolde with the concept of the *edele herzen*, he develops the principle that Haug understands to be the poet's "entscheidende literaturtheoretische These."[35] Haug sees this revealed in the much discussed passage where Gottfried compares the tale told for the present audience to the experience of the eucharist, as it is the bread of the living. Gottfried is not trying to elevate profane eroticism to the level of eucharistic mystery, according to Haug. Rather, he is using familiar metaphors in an attempt to describe the possibility of genuine experience ("Sinnerfahrung") in the medium of literary fiction.[36] Gottfried gives his audience a great deal of responsibility to make sense out of the story—they can do this only if they belong to the elite group of noble hearts. They must navigate a complex relationship between words and sense, between speech/ language and reality:

> Das Wort, das nicht mehr auf einen außerhalb liegenden Sinnhorizont bezogen ist, eröffnet neue Möglichkeiten zur Täuschung und Lüge. Gerade die in sich selbst durchsichtige Sprache vermag zweideutig zu werden. Sie wird zu einem verfügbaren Mittel, das Tristan und Isolt in den Dienst ihrer Liebe stellen, die als höchste Instanz die Manipulation der Ausdrucksmittel, die, in dem sie die Ordnung in der Welt der Erscheinung auflöst, die Liebenden ins Verhängnis treibt.[37]

In that it serves the lovers Tristan and Isolde as a means of manipulating the world around them, language opens and explores new possibilities for deception and lying. Furthermore, in this language fraught with double-meanings, Gottfried's narrative plays consistently with the juxtaposition of the profane or pagan and the Christian, searching for a truth that seems to be a process in itself:

"es geht darum, die poetische Sprache zu klären und transparent und wirkungsmächtig zu machen, so daß sich in ihr selbst und aus ihr selbst eine Wahrheit darstellen kann, zu der sie in ebendiesem Prozeß auf dem Wege ist." After all, "die Wahrheit des fiktiven Romans" in the twelfth and thirteenth centuries is that of the literary experiment.[38] Clearly, Gottfried intends to construct his text and its worlds (both the narrative world and the world of the listeners themselves) so that they may serve as a means of identification; indeed, Gottfried takes great pains to convince the listener/reader that this means of identification has not been properly rendered into text until the present version of the poem.[39] To paraphrase Wolfgang Iser, Gottfried very self-consciously involves himself as well as the audience in an ongoing process that aims to produce meaning through interpretation.[40] Iser understands this process as a game, facilitated by "play" that invites the participation and interaction of the reader. While Iser attributes this type of play to modern, "performative" texts, we can anticipate a similar kind of performance from *Tristan*'s prologue, expecting that Gottfried will incorporate a certain degree of "play" in his text as he invites the participation of the readers/listeners in the world performed before them.[41] In this way, Gottfried displays his understanding of texts "as constitutive of reality rather than mimicking it—in other words, as cultural practices of signification rather than as referential duplications."[42]

"REAL" PLACES

The processes of "play" and cultural signification lead us back into the text and its topography, which literally and figuratively participates in both. First, Gottfried locates *Tristan*'s geography in familiar places like Cornwall and Ireland. In this way, the poet creates a frame of reference for his audience by recalling the characteristic outlines of Arthurian topography for the audience, even though here Marke takes the place here of Arthur as the central ruler figure. Marke wears the crown of Cornwall and has taken England under his protection at the behest of that land's fractious rival kings.[43] Furthermore, Marke resides at the castle of Tintagel, a place that resonates with Arthurian associations, notably that of cuckoldry: Tintagel is the site of Uther's brief affair with Ygraine. Nevertheless, in the first part of the narrative, Marke **is** Arthur for both Rivalin and Tristan—the exemplary king at whose court all good knights are made.[44] Gottfried repeatedly insists that Marke is a good king; indeed, in the first part of the narrative, he bears a close resemblence to Arthur. Rivalin comes to Cornwall at the time of a May festival,[45] seeking to improve himself at the court of this model king:

> er haete vil gehoeret sagen,
> wie höfsch und wie êrbaere
> der junge künic waere
> von Curnewâle Marke,
> des êre wuohs dô starke:

[He had often heard people say how noble and distinguished the young King Marke of Cornwall was, whose fame was in the ascendant]

Because he has a noble heart ("sîn edelez herze," 460), Rivalin goes to Cornwall to acquaint himself with the the manners of foreign lands ("vremeder lands site," 461) because he will thereby improve his own become famous himself ("selbe erkant dervan," 463) As Tristan is the result of Rivalin's affair with Marke's sister Blanscheflur, Marke is the "oheim" of Tristan (standing in the same relationship to him as Arthur to Gawan or Trevrizent and Anfortas to Parzival). Like Arthur, Marke also makes rash promises to challengers, as in the episode with Gandin, recalling similar blunders made by Arthur, as in *Iwein* or in Chrétien's *Knight of the Cart*. Thus Gottfried firmly anchors his story in Arthurian tradition, though some have interpreted the work as anti-courtly and in defiance of the a kind of Arthurian moral code, as represented by Parzival or Erec, especially since Tristan (the consummate courtier) thrives on the intrigues of the court. Indeed, the only direct allusions to Arthur are to be found in the scene with the cave, where the idyllic forest life of the two lovers creates a world of its own that surpasses any feast that might have been held at Arthur's court:

> ir zweier geselleschaft
> diu was in zwein sô herehaft
> daz der saelige Artûs
> nie in dekeinem sînem hûs
> sô grôze hôhgezît gewan,
> dâ mêre ir lîbe lustes van
> und wunne waere entstanden. (16859–16865)

[Their company of two was so ample a crowd for this pair that good King Arthur never held a feast in any of his palaces that would have given them keener pleasure of delight.]

The lovers seem to have no need of such feasts or such worlds any more; they are sufficient unto themselves and they have in their forest paradise no need for anyone or anything else besides Love herself. Indeed, Love is "ir hôhzît" ("their high feast," 16896) and "ir vröuden übergulde" ("their gilded joys," 18697) and it is she who brings them the equivalent of the Round Table each day:

> diu brâhte in durch ihr hulde
> des tages ze tûsent stunden
> Artûses tavelrunden
> und alle ir massenîe dar.
> waz solte in bessen lîpnar
> ze muote oder ze lîbe? (1689 8–16901)

[Their high feast was Love, who gilded all their joys; she brought them King Arthur's Round Table as homage and all its company a thousand times a day! What better food could they have for body, or soul?]

Tristan and Isolde, the new man and the new woman, have created an exemplary space together out of their love for one another. Gottfried offers here at least part of his answer to the decline of the Arthurian court that we have glimpsed in *Iwein* and that was made explicit in *Parzival*. He places "the civilized ideal of the [Arthurian court] against the embodied dream of the Cave of Lovers" where Tristan and Isolde can live out their ideal love "in the absence of, and in superiority to, the Round Table."[46]

THE FOREST TRANSFORMED

Gottfried also demonstrates his ability to manipulate not only the familiar "real" places but also the *topoi* that Curtius has used to characterize the ideal romance landscape, most prominent among them the forest and the *locus amoenus*.[47] Gottfried transforms the forest of Broceliande, so familiar to his audience from the works of his predecessors Hartmann and Wolfram, where it functioned as the backdrop for the travels of Iwein, Erec, and Parzival. The forest can be hostile as Gottfried shows us in Tristan's initial impressions of the Cornish landscape after he is set ashore by the merchants who kidnapped him.[48] The now homeless Tristan, the stranger without comfort ("der trôstlôse ellende," 2487), wrings his hands and prays for deliverance from his hostile surroundings:

> nu warte ich allenthalben mîn
> und sihe niht lebendes umbe mich.
> dise grôze wilde die vürht ich.
> swar ich mîn ougen wende,
> da ist mir der werlde ein ende.
> swâ ich mich hin gekêre,
> dane sihe ich ie nimêre
> niwan ein toup gevilde
> und wüeste unde wilde,
> wilde velse und wilden sê.
> disiu vorhte tuot mir wê. (2500–2510)

[I now look all about me and see no living thing. How I dread this great wilderness! Wherever I bend my eyes I see the end of the world, wherever I turn I see nothing but desert, wasteland, wilderness, wild cliffs, and sea as wild. How the terror of it afflicts me!]

Tristan also fears the wild animals who might come to devour him. As he rises from his despairing prayer, however, he draws his cloak around him, a magnificent piece of clothing "der was rîch/ und an gewürhte wunderlîch." ("magnificent and finely embroidered" 2535–2536) We are reminded that, though Tristan may have depicted a very menacing environment, the young man who now finds himself in this wilderness is a civilized and cultured and very resourceful man who will be able to survive whatever comes. He can think on his feet, as is shown by his lie to the pilgrims.[49] And, shortly thereafter, Tristan meets a hunting party and we are again treated to a display of Tristan's accomplishments, which we admire along with the astounded hunters. The purpose of the hunt scene is to show us what Tristan knows, as well as his relationship to and his perception by those who do not know what he does.[50] In this scene, as with the description of Tristan's comforting cloak, the emphasis is on beauty and courtliness and controlled order, in an exquisitely performed well-staged ceremony.

Thus, in Tristan's encounter with the hunting party, Gottfried transforms the hostility of the wilderness into the civility of courtly ceremony. He completes the ultimate transformation of the forest and the *locus amoenus*, however, later in the narrative when he creates the elaborate allegory that is the cave of the lovers . As Tristan and Isolde seek to conceal their affair from those around them, the forest offers more than a threshold; it becomes a destination in itself, the place where the lovers can be together, providing "both exile and idyll, pain and delight, the ideal yet the impossible escape."[51] The place is a grotto located very meaningfully (according to Gottfried) "als eine/ in dirre wüesten wilde" ("so secluded in the midst of this wild solitude," 17072–17073) . Love cannot be led into the streets ("ûf die strâze," 17076) nor found in the open country ("gevilde," 17077). Instead, Love lies hidden in the wilds at the end of a path that is hard and arduous ("arbeitsam und herte," 17080) and demands great effort from those poor sufferers ("uns martaeren allen" 17085) who would travel it. The successful effort is rewarded, however, with a sight beyond compare:

> swer aber sô saelic mac gesîn,
> daz er zer wilde kumet hin în,
> der selbe hât sîn arbeit
> vil saeleclîchen an geleit.
> der vindet dâ des herzen spil.
> swaz sô daz ôre hoeren wil
> und swaz dem ougen lieben sol,
> des alles ist diu wilde vol.
> sô waere er ungern anderswâ. (17091–17099)

[. . . whoever is so blessed as to reach and enter that solitude will have used his efforts to most excellent purpose, for he will find his heart's delight there. Whatever the ear yearns to hear, whatever gratifies the eye, this wilderness is full of it. He [or she] would hate to be elsewhere.]

Gottfried's treatment of the cave offers not only a refuge for banished lovers but also creates a complex and multi-layered allegory that finally completes the transformation of the forest. (16859 ff.)[52]

As he transforms the forest, Gottfried also charts new territory with respect to another aspect of romance topography—its function as a mechanism for the inscription of gender roles: "gender shapes bodies as they shape space and are in turn shaped by its arrangements."[53] These spatial arrangements can occur on several levels, perhaps best represented by the image of concentric yet interlocking circles. McDonald draws this analogy in his comparison between the endings of *Iwein* and *Tristan*.[54] Tristan does not become reintegrated into a court (like Erec or Parzival or Iwein)—all he is left with is a memory of fulfilled happiness at the Cave of the Lovers. This is an extreme form of the final romance separation of the hero from the Arthurian court. Whereas the movements of romance can be described as linear, the scenes in *Tristan* generate a circular map:

> Placed in a concentric world, the hero is necessarily constricted and circumscribed in his movements: Tristan-love is a conundrum of circularity . . . Narrative tension arises between the fixed center—the court of the monarch—and the margins, on which Tristan faces the constant flux of movement . . . he dare not learn to live outside the court, for that would mean the renunciation of his beloved.[55]

The centers and the peripheries are uniquely flexible in this narrative. This circularity has significant ramifications not only for the hero, as McDonald notes, but also for the hero's partner. Tristan moves in different ways than romance heros, and the movement of Isolde is different also; the circular repetitive nature of the trajectories keeps them coming back to and including her. Both Isolde and Tristan could be considered equals in this regard, because the circularity of the 'path' in this narrative also creates and supports and recreates her role. Isolde does not renounce courtly life for the forest, as Sigune does, nor is Isolde located at a court "outside" the center, where Laudine is placed. Regardless of how potentially disruptive Laudine's presence or absence may be for Iwein, her space remains physically separated from the Arthurian/courtly world that forms a "center" for Iwein. Isolde, on the other hand, always remains in and around the center, belonging at court just as Tristan does, moving as he does from one court to another (from Ireland to Cornwall) and also from the court to the forest and back.

IRELAND: A MOTHER'S PLACE, AN OTHER SPACE

Ireland is constructed as woman's space. It is not king Gurmun who is the focus of most of Gottfried's (and hence the audience's) attention but rather his wife and later his daughter Isolde. The connection between them and the influence (present and future) they wield is reflected in the fact that they both bear the same name. In fact, the daughter is also frequently referred to with the epithets Gottfried applies to her mother (9478).[56] We first hear of Queen Isolde's great knowledge as Morold taunts Tristan during their duel, after the latter has received a serious wound from Morold's poisoned spear.[57] No doctor in the world can heal Tristan; it is Morold's sister Isolde who alone possesses the knowledge of roots and all herbs ("wurze und aller crûte craft," 6949) as well as the medicinal learning ("arzâtlîche meisterschaft" 6950) to save his life: "diu kan eine disen list/ und anders nieman, der der ist." ("She alone knows the secret, and no other in the world" 6951–6952) If she does not heal Tristan, he will be past all healing. If she does not heal you, you will be past all healing. Repeatedly, she is referred to as "diu wîse Îsôt" ("the wise Isolde," 7291) and "diu sinnerîche künegîn" (" the well-versed Queen," 7299)[58] whose knowledge (*liste*) belongs to her alone. Indeed, as Hollandt points out, *wise* is the quality most often attributed to her.[59] As a queen who is not only well-versed in politics and diplomacy but who is an herbalist and a physician, the elder Isolde possesses knowledge that is usually associated in literature with magical female power (like that of Lunete or the Countess of Narison); in this way, Rasmussen connects Isolde's knowledge of the healing arts with the skill of other fairy/unmarried woman in medieval literature.[60] Indeed, Tristan must go to Ireland for healing rather than to the famed doctors in Salerno.[61] The elder Isolde holds the power of life and death over him, since she would have redirected all of her healing energy towards arranging his death had she known his real identity as the killer of her beloved brother. (7911 ff.)

Within the boundaries of this island space, the queen also wields considerable political authority, though she takes care to act (publicly) only with her husband's approval.[62] Her skills are particularly evident in the incident of the steward and the slaying of the dragon. Concerned to prevent her daughter from an unsuitable marriage, Queen Isolde uncovers the truth of the steward's deception and the slaying of the dragon through her hidden knowledge ("ir tougenlîche liste," 9301),[63] having conjured a dream in which she learned that all was not as it seemed (or at least as was told by the steward). Driven by the awareness that failure to find the truth would condemn the young Isolde to unhappiness as a result of her father's rash oath, both Isoldes discover the identity of the real dragon-slayer. It is the queen who, having taken Tristan under her protection, persuades her daughter to give up her desire for revenge, who presents the situation to her husband, who orchestrates the disclosure of the steward's treachery. Once again, the decision not to take revenge on Tristan for the death of Morolt shows considerable political acumen on the part of the queen, for if she were to take revenge, she would continue the enmity of Marke's people. Instead, she chooses to leave her brother's death unavenged for the greater good, so that her daughter can make a good match.[64]

And the queen, who is as beautiful as she is wise, takes great care in the education of her daughter, her only child. Since Isolde's birth, her mother has devoted all her energies ("alle ir vlîzekeit," 7721) to teaching the younger Isolde all that she can. In this, she is acting as a good queen should, to prepare her daughter as a kind of "matrimonial ambassador,"[65] literally "a marriageable object of exchange" whose mother has tutored her in a kind of "sexual apprenticeship."[66] As the older queen admits to Brangaene while preparing the prepares the infamous love potion for her daughter, "the better part of my life is bound up with her." ("an ir [Isolde] sô lît mîn beste leben" 11471).[67] The mother's love and care is evidenced in the fact the queen previously entrusted the education of the younger Isolde to the same accomplished priest who taught <u>her</u> as a girl. On the recommendation of this priest, who is forced to recognize in Tristan a man more accomplished than himself, the older Isolde engages the stranger (known to her as Tantris) as tutor for her daughter after he arrives in Ireland. (7979 ff.) Gottfried goes into great detail regarding the instruction that Isolde receives from Tristan with respect to *morâliteit* ("Sittenlehre"/ *bienséance*), or the behavior and decorum proper to the courtly sphere.[68] Describing the end result, Gottfried says:

> Sus haete sich diu schoene Îsôt
> von Tristandes lêre
> gebezzeret sêre.
> sî was suoze gemuot,
> ir site und ir gebaerde guot.
> si kunde schoeniu hantspil,
> schoener behendekeite vil:
> brieve udn schanûne tihten,
> ir getihte schône slihten,
> si kunde schrîben unde lesen. (8132–8141)

[Thus, under Tristan's instruction, lovely Isolde had much improved herself. Her disposition was charming, her manners and bearing good. She had mastered some fine instruments and many skilled accomplishments. Of love-songs she could make both the words and the airs and polish them beautifully. She was able to read and write.]

Tristan builds upon her previous education and refines her accomplishments to the point where rumor of them begins to spread beyond the borders of Ireland. He enables her becoming, in a rather atypical way for romance as we know the genre, from Hartmann and Wolfram. Tristan does not initiate Isolde's education (that is the task of her mother), though he expands and completes it, helping to mold Isolde into the perfection that corresponds to her inborn beauty. This is a reverse of the typical constellation in which the women enable the becoming of the hero (e.g. *Parzival, Iwein, Erec*).[69] The daughter, too, like her mother before her, holds the sword that means life or death for Tristan after she discovers that Tristan's sword is missing the fragment that her mother removed from Morold's body; however, young Isolde is a superior model of womanhood/ womanliness ("wîpheit"), and her great virtue will not permit her to commit murder. And it is finally the queen who asks that the king grant Tristan mercy and that Marke's request for Isolde's hand be given due consideration. The elder Isolde subsequently prepares the love potion ("tranc von minnen," 11435) that she hopes will ensure her daughter a happy and joyful life with her new husband, thereby securing the younger Isolde's political position. For Rasmussen, this is a key to the relationship between the two women: the mother's gift brings about the downfall of this carefully arranged marriage. The queen wants both love and political power to have a place in her daughter's marriage; the younger Isolde should have that love that is the "'glue' that holds patriarchal society together."[70] Nenno comments that the instance of the love potion prevents Queen Isolde from being portrayed as negatively as Feimurgan in *Erec*; Isolde's powers are limited "for, ironically, she is unable to control the specificity of the *minnetrank* ... Her magic is circumscribed, limited, and finite, for she is neither omniscient nor all-powerful. Any magical power she has comes from her knowledge and skill as a healer."[71]

In regard to the relationship between mother and daughter in *Tristan*, Rasmussen has said that Ireland appears to support a "mimetic feminine ideology" (Rasmussen's actual term is "mimetische Weiblichkeitsideologie") that the love potion is de-signed to perpetuate.[72] Indeed, the younger Isolde's marriage prom-ises even greater success than her mother's. As Marke's council points out, when they try to persuade him to seek Isolde's hand in marriage, Isolde is sole heir to the throne of Ireland (8501–8503); thus, her position reflects one commonly found among young women of her station. A marriage between her and Marke would end the conflict between Cornwall and Ireland and bring peace and wealth to both parties. Such a union would bring honor and fame to Marke for winning such a prize, and it would also bring Isolde considerable political power; eventually, she would wear the crowns of both lands. Indeed, the kingdom of Cornwall is her *Morgengabe*, the gift she receives on her wedding morning (11391 ff.). Queen Isolde is aware of the benefits of such a union, which is why she listens to Brangaene's suggestion of having Isolde go with Tristan after they uncover the truth of his role in Morolt's death. One is tempted to say "like mother, like daughter"; indeed, the knowledge (*liste*) of the young Isolde and her mother is matched only by that of Tristan himself.

The daughter, however, does not become the mother, defying the symbolism of their shared name.[73] The fateful journey from Ire-land to Cornwall certainly represents a transition from one world to another, though with an unexpected twist. The love potion pro-pels both Tristan and Isolde onto a new plane of existence, into a world hitherto unknown. The potion actually subverts Princess Isolde's 'instrumental function" and " has liberated her from the law of wifely obedience. "[74] This world is configured in a manner that differs fundamentally from any other Middle High German romance, for *Tristan* attempts to transform and transcend the Ger-manic code of ethics in the search for a higher truth. While the conventional game of *minne* seems to have encouraged women's passivity and to have left few acceptable alternatives to the strict code of noble behavior, Gottfried's path toward higher truth cre-ates for his female protagonist considerable space to act and to be/ to become. On a very literal level, this space is underscored by with Isolde's gradual inscription into the text, first as Gottfried de-scribes the skills that she learns under Tristan's tutelage. The sec-ond phase of the inscription occurs when Isolde is presented to the court in Ireland after the dragon has been slain. Her appearance is described in great detail, carving space out of the text for her body and for her actions that we all know will follow in the narrative:

die rehten haete sî gewant
hin nider baz, ir wizzet wol,
dâ man den mantel sliezen sol,
und slôz in höfschlîche in ein
mit ir vingere zwein.
vürbaz dâ viel er selbe wider
und nam den valt al z'ende nider,
daz man diz unde daz dâ sach,
ich meine vederen unde dach. (10940–10948)

[She had brought her right hand farther down, you know, to where one closes the mantle, and held it decorously together with two of her fingers. From there it fell unhampered in a last fold revealing this and that—I mean the fur and its covering.][75]

In her radiant beauty, Isolde rivals the sun, for so Gottfried has named her (led in to the hall by her mother the Dawn and followed by Brangaene the Moon).[76] Gottfried similarly inscribes Tristan at this point, describing his dress. Uniting the two soon-to-be lovers is the splendor of the gems that crown them in their exalted state. The narrator says of Isolde: "dâ lûhte golt unde golt, der cirkel unde Îsôt. ("Gold and gold, the circlet and Isolde, vied to outshine each other. 10977–10978). Her hair becomes indistinguishable from the golden circlet that adorns it. (10983–10985) And the chaplet on Tristan's head shines just as brightly, when Tristan enters in his turn:

ez haete im houbet unde hâr
clârlîchen umbevangen.
sus kam er în gegangen
rîch unde hôhe gemuot. (11138–11141)

[It (the chaplet) was bright and full of luster and made a ring about his head and his hair. And so he entered, magnificent and gay.] (Gentry 147)

The interplay of the gold and the light distinguish both Tristan and Isolde throughout the work. One can also see in these descriptions of the future lovers, Gottfried carefully inscribes both of them in the space of his text, using their clothing (in the words of Margaret Higonnet) as a "crucial marker in the system governing representation."[77] Not only is clothing a means of representation, but I see here in Isolde not simply a loving statue or image ("ein lebende bild") but a site of potential resistance, in the sense that clothing may also become (according to E. Jane Burns) a "generative force" that can be used "productively to make and mold a social body."[78] Isolde *becomes* her clothing, so seductively and imaginatively set in motion here, and in a sense refashions the male gaze in the next part of the narrative.

Here Tristan and Isolde represent nothing less than the apex of courtly society, literally crowned by their accomplishments and their character.[79] Isolde's match with Marke brings her power and wealth, neither of which she cares to relinquish over the course of the work. In addition, because of the (un)fortunate mishap with the love potion, Isolde enjoys with Tristan the "true" love that most considered possible only outside of marriage. This is the kind of relationship encouraged by Andreas Capellanus (at least in the first two books of *The Art of Courtly Love*) and the troubadours, the kind of relationship decried by Gottfried's contemporaries and mocked by Wolfram. And this is precisely the relationship that Gottfried celebrates throughout his poem, culminating in the elaborate allegory of the Cave of Lovers.

CORNWALL: A PLACE FOR TWO TO PLAY

In a sense both Tristan and Isolde go through a process of becoming in *Tristan*. In the first part of the narrative, we watch the young Tristan become the consummate courtier.[80] Tristan's education is described in detail, as is Isolde's later, and by the age of fourteen he has learned all the arts there are: "ein vierzehenjaerec kint/ kan al die liste, die nu sint!" (371 9–3720).[81] He astounds the members of the court at Cornwall and he comes to represent for Marke the perfect retainer, vassal, courtier:

> Der künec sprach: "Tristan, hoere her:
> an dir ist allez, des ich ger.
> dû kanst allez, daz ich wil:
> jagen, sprâche, seitspil.
> nu suln ouch wir gesellen sîn,
> dû der mîn und ich der dîn.
> tages sô sul wir rîten jagen,
> des nahtes uns hie heime tragen
> mit höfschlîchen dingen:

harpfen, videlen, singen (3721–3730)

["Tristan, listen to me,' said the King, 'you can do everything I want—hunting, languages, music. To crown it let us be companions. You be mine and I will be yours. By day we shall ride out hunting at night here at home we shall sustain ourselves with courtly pursuits, such as harping, fiddling, and singing."]

In return, Marke promises to give Tristan the one thing that the young "Wunderkind" lacks: the clothing and the horses and the weapons (sword, spurs, crossbow, golden horn) that a good vassal deserves to receive from his lord. Marke knows how to play the game of rulership ("sô kan ich spil" 3732) and he has the means to make Tristan's life in Cornwall "höfsch unde vrô." (3741) Tristan's process of becoming is finally completed when Marke invests him as a knight with a company of other young men, and he then returns to Parmenie to avenge his father Rivalin's death.[82] His life, however, is at the court in Cornwall and he returns there after installing Rual and his sons as the heirs of Rivalin's lands.

At this point in the text, Tristan seems to have reached the pinnacle of his development; Gottfried teases the audience by beginning the section immediately following Tristan's departure from Parmenie with "Waz leite ich nû mê hier an?" ("what fresh matters shall I now set in motion?" 5867) Of course, the audience who knows the basic story is also well aware of what the future (and the narrator) have planned for the hero who now represents *daz niuwe wunder* ("the new marvel," 6635), the term Gottfried uses to describe Tristan as he arms himself before the battle with Morolt; he has become (one could even say he now is) a kind of "New Man."[83]

The new man needs a suitable partner, and one can arguably consider Isolde a kind of "new woman." One can see in Isolde that the state of becoming woman is a kind of "escape from the systems of binary polarization of unities that privilege men at the expense of women."[84] Isolde is as much a courtier and a practitioner of *hövescheit* as Tristan. This distinct 'equality'[85] continues on the narrative level, as the miracle of the new man and the new woman show us indeed (literally in deeds and in words) the answer to the poet's question "what comes next?" Following the incident with the love potion, both Isolde and Tristan consistently create and re-create spaces for themselves in order to maintain their relationship:

> in was sanfte und alsô wol,
> alse zwein gelieben sol,
> den ir state unde ir zît
> ze staten und ze willen lît. (12969–12972)

[They were at their ease and as contented as a pair of lovers should be who can choose their meetings at their own time and convenience.]

They subtly 'hide' their love for one another from the public eye, proving adroit at manipulating words ("mit den si wunder kunden" (with which they could do marvellous things," 12991) and thereby appearances, artfully maneuvering their public conversation so that one could see Love's handiwork in their talk: "man sach dicke in ir maeren cleben/der minnen werc von worten." (12994–12995) They are so successful in their public secrecy and their "minnenspil" ("love sport" 13004) that no one has any idea their affection is anything other than that which would be appropriate given Tristan's close relationship with Marke.[86] In all of these situations, we see Isolde utilizing and exploiting her new space, and putting her numerous talents to use.[87] Well-trained by her mother, the younger Isolde shows a keen sense of political expediency:

> She responds to the two notions of *ere* which dominate Got-tfried's interpretation of the received narrative. The public personage in her answers to the ordinary world, the world about her, of diplomacy, malice, and intrigue—to the court. She answers with hypocrisy and pretence, with deception and betrayal, with ruthlessness and brutality. The private individual in her, howver, reacts to the world of love and to its particular moral code, to its *ere*, with total integrity, loyalty, devotion, and utter genuineness.[88]

Often it is Isolde's cunning (with the help of the indispensable Brangaene) that narrowly averts potential disaster when Marke is obsessed with doubt and suspicion.[89] They successfully play this game of wits:

> sus lôsete diu lôse Îsôt
> wider ir hêrren unde ir man,
> biz daz si'm lôsend an gewan
> beidiu zwîvel unde zorn

> und er wol haete gesworn,
> daz ir ernest waere.
> Marke der zwîvelaere
> der was dâ wider ze wege komen.
>
> (14004–14011)

[Thus wily Isolde dissembled towards her lord and husband till she had won him from his suspicion and anger with her tricks, and he would have sworn she meant it. Marke, the waverer, had found the right path again.] (Gentry 185)

Time and again, Brangaene and Isolde (and Tristan) successfully set "list/wider list" (13867–13868) and "sin wider sin." (13879)[90] Eroticism, adultery, betrayal, and love that consistently thwarts patriarchal-feudal convention characterize the new life of "lying truth"[91] that Tristan and Isolde lead at the court of Cornwall in a world, where that which is seen remains unseen. Their efforts culminate in commonly known as the "Assignation by the Brook" (*Baumgartenszene*) or the "Ordeal" (*Gottesurteil*).[92] Isolde in particular takes great care to call upon God to witness the various truths that she speaks to Marke and others. In the scene by the brook, she declares:

> nu weiz ez aber got selbe wol,
> wie mîn herze hin ziu stê.
> und wilein lützel sprechen mê:
> des sî got mîn urkünde
> und enmüeze ouch mîner sünde
> niemer anders komen abe,
> wan alse ich iuch gemeinet habe,
> mit welhem herzen unde wie (14752–14760)

[But God himself knows how my feelings stand towards you. And I will go a little farther. May God be my witness when I say it—may I never be rid of my sins by an other test than the measure of my affection for you!]

Indeed, in the scene of the ordeal, this ethic of lying truth seems to receive God's blessing. The penitent Isolde,[93] having had the foresight to give away her jewels and dress herself in appropriately humble attire, appears and is devoured by the eyes of those in the assembly watching her:

> manec herze und ouge nam ir war
> swâre und erbemeclîche
> ir gewandes unde ir lîche
> des wart dâ dicke war genomen." (1566 4–15667)

[Many eyes observed her, many hearts felt sorrow and pity for her. Her garment and her figure attracted much attention.]

In her recent analysis of courtly performance in the scene of Isolde's ordeal, Kelly Kucaba convincingly argues that Isolde and Marke, and God as well, share a similar view of what it means to be courtly (*hövesch*). It is not necessarily the case of Isolde alone manipulating the court, as some have suggested, nor does she manipulate God. Actually, in the context of Gottfried's world, they all wish to protect the same courtly interests. Kucaba understands the arrangement of the ordeal by Marke as yet another attempt by the king to continue the fiction of marital fidelity. He has shown consistently throughout the narrative that he does not wish to believe that his queen and his nephew are involved in a love affair. This interpretation ascribes a more active and conscious role to Marke in his own self-deception.[94] In this regard, he and Isolde become allies in the ordeal, which they use to support the deception even further. God's role in the ordeal has puzzled many readers of *Tristan*; after all, God has the last word, since He must sanction Isolde's oath and accept the 'truth' of it—and He does. The narrator seems rather taken aback[95] but praises Isolde's success:

> die generte ir trügeheit
> und ir gelüppeter eit,
> der hin ze gote gelâzen was,
> daz s'an ir ëren genas.
> und wart aber dô starke
> von ir hêrren Marke
> geminnet unde g'êret,
> geprîset unde gehêret
> von liute unde lande. (15747–15755)

[She was saved by her guile and by the doctored oath that went flying up to God, with the result that she redeemed her honor and was again much beloved of her lord Marke, and was praised, lauded, and esteemed among the people.]

In allowing God to accept the oath that Isolde has offered, Gottfried shows that the God of *Tristan* is a courtly God who can be as selective in perceiving the truth as Isolde can be in admitting it (though God presumably knows the entire truth).[96] From this perspective, God does not sanction the intention to deceitful; rather God sanctions Isolde's intention to behave in a courtly manner with respect to her king and her people, to repair that damage that has been done to her reputation and that of her lord. Isolde is not so arrogant as to believe that she can manipulate God, nor does Gottfried necessarily advocate the view of a God who can be "bought"; on the contrary, Isolde behaves in a courtly fashion that she believes acceptable to both Marke and to God that she believes they expect from her.[97]

When Marke's tolerance finally has reached its limit and he banishes the lovers from court, they seem to have attained their goal: they are together away from the court celebrating a love that seems sufficient unto itself[98] in a place that nourishes them through their love for one another and that provides them with all they need "ze wunschlebene" ("for a life of delight"):

> ouch muote sî daz cleine,
> daz s'in der wüeste als eine
> und âne liute solten sîn.
> nu wes bedorften s'ouch dar în
> oder waz solt ieman zuo z'in dar?
> si haeten eine gerade schar:
> dane was niuwan ein und ein. . . .
> dâ was doch man bî wîbe,
> sô was ouch wîp bî manne.
> wes bedorften di danne?
> si haeten daz si solten,
> und wâren dâ si wolten.
> (16847–16853; 16904–16908)

[Nor were they greatly troubled that they should be alone in the wilds without company. Whom did they need in there with them and why should anyone join them? They made an even number: there were simply one and one . . . What better food could they have for body or soul? Man was there with Woman, Woman there with Man. What else should they be needing? They had what they should have had where they wished to be.]

The lovers do, however, leave Brangaene behind to wait for an opportune moment to begin a reconciliation. Obviously, it is not in their plans to abandon their life at court entirely—their courtly identity, which in large part defines them, is at stake. And their courtly identity provides the reason for the rather puzzling decision of Tristan and Isolde to leave the cave of the lovers and return to the court, for, although the life of the lovers at the cave seems ideal (in that Isolde can devote herself to the man she loves, the bonds of her marriage having been effectively broken or suspended), the problem is that the lovers are exiles from society.[99] The later sun is the heat of discovery, the destructive heat of passion, an inappropriate light.Herzmann also views the return from the paradise of the cave as a "fall"; the lovers cannot avoid a certain "Hängen am Hof", evident in their preoccupation with courtly honor (*ere*) and in the gold that they brought with them. This shows that that they have not completely overcome the world outside; therefore they must suffer the consequence: "Rückkehr in die Trivialwelt und neues Leid und neue Irrwege."[100] Cole maintains that the lovers must leave because they cannot sustain "the perfection that the cave demands of its tenants." Whereas the lovers have previously had such success in perpetuating the ruse of their innocence before Marke, they seem to go too far in their desire to fool Marke in the cave. They cannot remain indefinitely in the cave on their because they cannot stop thinking about their other life at court; as a result, they seem to "desecrate the altar of love with deceit."[101] Their "honeymoon" inevitably comes to an end.[102]

As Tristan and Isolde tirelessly plan to meet and satisfy their desires for one another, they and their story constantly create space for themselves: space to be themselves, to act as they wish, to deceive, to escape.[103] When one compares Isolde with her Middle High German romance contemporaries (Condwiramurs, Laudine, and Enite, for example), one realizes that Isolde remains herself and maintains her own dual identities as wife and lover—she is not subsumed under the role of either man in her life. Indeed, Isolde seems to thrive on the challenge of keeping her life and relationships together, on the constant tension between love and sorrow, *liebe* and *leit*.[104] In a position that seems to hearken back to the queens of an earlier era, Isolde seems to have everything a woman of her station could desire. She is not the typical woman in the castle described by Gale Sigal as "a prisoner of the pedestal" who has "no voice and no choice."[105] She also has a double nature, transcendent, created by Minne.[106] Her autonomy, at its most radical, is visually underscored by the obvious female imagery of the lovers' cave as a sheltered womb-like space.[107] Isolde's freedom contrasts sharply with the subtle restrictions placed upon Wolfram's major (secular) female role model, Condwiramurs. Of course, Gottfried and Wolfram had completely different views of the world and how it should be. Gottfried refuses to praise Wolfram's poetry because Wolfram's meaning (*sin*) seems so obscured; this is unacceptable to one who wishes to raise the literary experience to the highest of all human truths.[108] Gottfried does appreciate Hartmann's crystalline words ("cristallînen wortelîn," 4629) but he ends up taking Hartmann's moral purpose and transforming it, in the final analysis, into an aesthetic of lying.

Gottfried's narrative style in general has been described as an art of lying, of lying for the sake of a deeper truth.[109] The priority that Gottfried places on this "lying truth" must finally cause the audience (both medieval and modern) to question the "truth" of the younger Isolde's role, which seems so liberating and anomalous when she is compared to her contemporary (literary) models. While Isolde enjoys the roles of queen, wife, and lover, she does not become a mother—she does not 'become' <u>her</u> mother. In this way, she continues to defy her conventional prescribed role; however, this also means her relationships remain essentially sterile.[110] She does not continue her matrilineal heritage into the future as she inherited it, although, she will be in the future in a different form as she becomes a memory for Tristan (a memory that he cannot live up to). This is how Dayan interprets Isolde's final monologue of farewell to Tristan, as a speech that "deepens familiar formulas":

> Here, the beloved lady presents perfect loving as a creative construction: the heart's desires (their present experience) become habits of the mind (the contemplative ideal). Through her recasting of sensuous attraction into cogitable concepts, she again demonstrates her perspicacity. More important, her ability to know emerges as a power to know in to the future; Tristan lacks such farsightedness.[111]

Isolde's memory, or rather the memory of her, becomes her legacy to the future—a more intangible self than that which Isolde's mother might have foreseen or hoped for, but perhaps ultimately more lasting.

EIN MAN MIT MUOTE

Destiny (and desperation)[112] force Isolde to become a memory for
Tristan by the end of Gottfried's narrative, as he is compelled to
leave Cornwall after Marke finally catches the lovers together in a
tight embrace. Actually, she is driven to arrange a meeting with
him because she has been robbed of her senses by "huote":

> diu huote daz vertâne antwerc,
> diu vîndin er minne,
> diu nam in alle ir sinne. (17848–17850)

[The ponderous load of cursed Surveillance weighed on their
spirits like a mountain of lead.]

After the incident at the cave of lovers, Marke has forbidden Isolde
to have any kind of relationship with Tristan, which of course
makes her desire to see him all the more. A lengthy excursus on
huote follows this passage, placed immediately preceding the scene
of Marke's final discovery and the lovers' parting. Gottfried maintains that, on the one hand, a woman requires constant surveillance so that she does not succumb to her baser sexual/sensual nature, the nature that is her legacy from Eve. On the other hand, a
virtuous woman will react badly to the watch set over her and she
will inevitably betray the man who initiates that watch. Although,
in a sense, the excursus actually seems to blame Marke for Isolde's
behavior, Isolde also seems to give in to these baser instincts in her
relationship with Tristan, particularly at this point—she is desperate, without any sense of moderation (*mâze*) and this is what leads
to the discovery of the lovers by Marke.[113] This excursus has received much attention in *Tristan*-scholarship. It has been variously
interpreted as: a "Frauenpreis,"[114] a defense of the lovers,[115] a version of the scholastic *quaestio* in which Isolde becomes a new
Eve,[116] an ideal (in the image of *daz lebende paradis*) that transcends "the concept of love outline in the prologue and experienced by Tristan and Isolde." [117] In her desire, of course, Isolde
shows herself to be a true daughter of Eve, as are all women[118]; as
Gottfried says, "Êve enhaete ez nie getân/und enwaere ez ir ver-
boten nie." ("Eve would not have done it if it had not been forbidden her." 1794 8–17949). Certainly, after a narrative in which
Isolde has displayed such unprecedented freedom to act and to become, Gottfried returns more explicitly to the long association of

sexuality and woman in Christianity "which saw sensuality as being more deeply rooted in the nature of woman than of man."[119] The new emphasis is on *mâze*, or moderation, which can productively facilitate the kind of loyalty and fidelity that *huote* attempts to preserve.[120] One must be true to one's self and to one's beloved, [121] and this genuine love will bring one to the new paradise, "daz lebende paradis" (18066): "Nicht ein Schranke, ein Gebot bestimmt das Verhältnis der aufeinander bezogenen Partner (Gott-Mensch in der Genesis, Liebender-Geliebte bei Gottfried), sondern jenes unbegrenzte Sich-ineinander-Versencken, das der Dichter in vielen Bildern verherrlicht."[122] What is most interesting, however, and something that even modern interpreters must come to terms with, is the fact that Gottfried at the end of the discovery scene does not criticize Tristan and Isolde for their actions. The lovers err mistake in allowing the truth to come to light. In fact, Marke might have preferred to remain merely suspicious, rather than to have those suspicions confirmed beyond the shadow of a doubt.[123]

Wharton interprets the Gottfried's ideal, that can be achieved by those living according to *mâze* and that can lead one to "daz lebende paradis", as " that of a lasting relationship between lovers, one which is entered voluntarily and is sanctioned by society—and this surely is in effect marriage based on affection."[124] In it, Gottfried seems to retreat from his celebration of Tristan and Isolde, suggesting that the only truly lasting love is that based upon the trust of a faithful husband and wife. He actually seems to echo Wolfram's sentiments, expressed in a dawn song that inverts courtly conventions:

> Swer pfliget oder ie gepflac
> daz er bî liebe lac
> den merkern unverborgen,
> der darf niht durch den morgen
> dannen streben;
> er mac des tages erbeiten:
> man darf in niht ûz leiten
> ûf sîn leben.
> ein offen süeze wirtes wîp kan sölhe minne geben.

[He who makes a habit, or ever did cultivate it, of lying at the side of his love unnoticed by the watchers, this man may not strive to leave that place, on account of the sunrise; he may await the break of day: one may not lead him hence upon his life. A sweet wife can give such love.] (translation mine)

As husband and wife, the lovers have all the right in the world to
enjoy one another's company without fear of any sort of reprisal
(as long as they do not repeat Erec's mistake). Clearly, one must
admit that adultery of the kind described and proscribed by Andreas Capellanus was probably more a literary indulgence than a
practical alternative for twelfth- and thirteenth-century noblewomen. Indeed, the game of courtly love finally serves the self-justification of an aristocracy that left women no room for self-development.[125] Gottfried's lovers suffer greatly because they seems to
play the game of courtly love too literally and too well, and they
are denied the luxury of Wolfram's dawn song. Gottfried's portrayal of Tristan and Isolde shows, however, a much more innovative topography of gender—precisely because he tries to circum-
vent Wolfram's solution to the familiar courtly conflict that arises
so often in the lyric. We can clearly see in *Tristan*, however, that
space plays a fundamental role in the exercise of power.[126] The
spaces that both Isoldes occupy, for example, allow them considerable power and place them in unique positions when compared,
for example, with their contemporaries in Wolfram von Eschenbach's *Parzival* or *Erec* and *Iwein* of Hartmann von Aue. An examination of the spaces in which and from which the two queens
act illustrates that these spaces function as mechanisms not only
for the construction but also for a possible *re*construction of gender roles at a time when such roles were becoming more rigidly established.

I suggest that Isolde plays just such a reconstructed role, exploring the possibilities offered by courtly romance and stretching
conventional boundaries. Both medieval and modern audiences
may perceive clerical elements in Gottfried's narrative in general
and particularly in the *huote*-excursus. In the middle of the excursus, for example, Gottfried actually seems offer a secular parallel
to the virtuous woman who achieves perfection and becomes a
man in the eyes of the Church:

> wan swelh wîp tugendet wider ir art,
> diu gerne wider ir art bewart
> ir lop, ir êre unde ir lîp,
> diu ist niwan mit name ein wîp
> und ist ein man mit muote. (17971–17985)

[For when a woman grows in virtue despite her inherited instincts and gladly keeps her honor, reputation, and person intact, she is only a woman in name, but in spirit she is a man!]

Despite Gottfried's references in the *huote*-excursus and centuries of interpretation to the contrary, Isolde is *not* Eve. As she tells half-truths and plans and acts and travels from courtly center to forest periphery and back, she becomes much like Tristan; she has (and makes use of) ample opportunity to exercise the traditionally masculine prerogative of choice. The love potion may affect her choice of whom to love,[127] just as her mother determined her "choice" of husband, but Isolde's other attributes remain unaffected. She need not deny her self nor need she act "wider ir art" ("despite her nature," 17971); in other words, she need not be a woman only in name in order to become "ein man mit muote" ("a man in spirit" 17985). Isolde "herzet sich mit manne" ("takes on the heart of a man," 17981) and becomes a woman who is also a man in spirit.

Johnson understands the attainment of *mâze* as a "synthetic moment" that is not necessarily an end in itself "but rather a new stage along a potentially endless path of self-development."[128] Such a formulation suggests that Isolde's (and indeed Tristan's) state of becoming remains constantly in process. This process of becoming does have a purpose (to become man or to become woman, for example) and therefore one can say that "becomings are never indeterminate or generic" for "they are always becoming something". In this state of continual becoming and almost potential possibilities, there is a "multiplicity"[129] that (to paraphrase Butler) has no beginning and no conclusion. In the story with Isolde of the White Hands, Tristan seems to slip into stereotype. Unable to be satisfied with only the memory of his Isolde, his senses are confused and he needs a physical reminder in the person of Isolde of the White Hands. He seems mired on the physical plane of existence. On the other hand, Isolde remains in memory, a figure who cannot be fixed into being, "a constructing that cannot rightfully be said to originate or to end." As frustrating as her character may be to a traditionalist like Wolfram, it is precisely her navigation of the fine line between counterfeit and truth that allows Isolde to remain a process "open to intervention and resignification."[130] In the perception of counterfeit there is uncertainty about the ideal, and in the space of that uncertainty Isolde can exist as both the blue paste in the gold and the gold in the brass. That twofold space provides the the freedom to "create a path, destabilize, energize instabilities"[131]—and to continue becoming.

Notes

1. Elizabeth Grosz, *Volatile Bodies. Toward a Corporeal Feminism.* (Bloomington IN: Indiana University Press, 1994), 173.

2. *Gender Trouble*, 33

3. She who is false shall win false praise. How durable is thin ice that gets the hot August sun? Just so quickly will her renown decay. Many a woman's beauty is praised afar, but if the heart within is counterfeit, I would praise her as I would praise a jewel of blue paste set in gold. (*Parzival*, 3, 8–15)

4. Hartmann names himself in the prologue to *Iwein*, speaking of a knight ("rîter") who was learned and who read when he had no better way to spend his time: er was genant Hartman/und was ein Ouwære),/ der tihte diz mære. ("He was Hartmann von Aue and the one who put this tale into verse"; *Iwein*, 28–30). Wolfram plays perhaps on this passage of Hartmann's when he names himself in *Parzival* at the end of Book II, announcing "ich bin Wolfram von Eschenbach, / unt kan ein teil mit sange" ("I am Wolfram von Eschenbach and I know a thing or two about poetry," 114, 1 2–13). In typically playful fashion, Wolfram goes on in this passage to make the (in)famous and much disputed statement: "ine kan decheinen buochstap" ("I don't know a single letter of the alphabet," 115, 27).

5. Gentry, "Introduction," *Gottfried von Strassburg. Tristan and Isolde,* xxii. Certainly, Gottfried seems to have written under much different circumstances from Hartmann and Wolfram. He is associated with a city (Strassburg) that was literally at the crossroads of Europe in the early thirteenth century, a center of artistic activity. Having its own charter, Strassburg was also one of the oldest independent cities in Europe and therefore very unlike the court of Heinrich of Thuringia, where Wolfram was probably located.

6. Gottfried continues, saying that he refuses to extend the honor of a laurel wreath to anyone whose style is not even and smooth:

> wir ensuln ez nieman lâzen tragen,
> sîniu wort ensîn vil wol getwagen,
> sîn rede ensî ebene unde sleht . . . (4659–4661)

[We shall not allow anyone to wear it whose words are not well-washed, his diction smooth and even.]

7. The use of the word "conterfeit" also resonates with Gottfried's use of it in the passage commonly known as the *minne*-excursus. This passage follows the scene in which love "ministers" to her patients Tristan and Isolde by bringing them together to consummate their relationship. Gottfried mourns the depths to which we have forced love to sink through our mediocre understanding of the true emotion:

> Minne, aller herzen künigîn,
> diu vrîe, diu eine
> diu ist umbe kouf gemeine!
> wie habe wir unser hêrschaft
> an ir gemachet zinshaft!
> wir haben ein boese conterfeit
> in daz vingerlîn geleit
> und triegen uns dâ selbe mite. (12300–12307)

[Love, mistress of all hearts, the noble, the incomparable, is for sale in the open market. What shameful dues our dominion has extorted from her! We have set a false stone in our ring and now we deceive ourselves with it.]

Gentry notes this reference and the possible connection with Wolfram in his translation of *Tristan* (see note 66, p. 262–263)
  8. The full passage reads as follows:

> ich enhân daz niht für lîhtiu dinc,
> swer in den kranken messinc
> verwurket edeln rubîn
> und al die âventiure sîn
> dem glîche ich rehten wîbes muot.
>   (*Parzival*, 3, 15–29)

[I count it no trifling thing if someone mounts a noble ruby, with all its magic virtue, in paltry brass. To such a jewel I liken a faithful woman's way.]

9. See C. Stephen Jaeger, *Ennobling Love. In Search of a Lost Sensibility* (Philadelphia: University of Pennsylvania Press, 1999). He describes

the romantic dilemma in his introduction. The tension between living virtuously and fulfilling sexual desire gave rise to the courtly literature of the twelfth and thirteenth centuries: "Virtue and sex formed a precarious union; it was constantly falling apart, showing its destructive nature, crushing those who claimed its ennobling force." (7) While Jaeger presents an erudite and rhetorically sophisticated argument in *Ennobling Love*, his discussion disregards at least two decades of feminist research in medieval studies.

10. *Ennobling Love,* 186.

11. Jaeger comments that "Parzival had told Gawan not to put his faith in God but in women, and women, as it turns out, loyally and chastely loved, function like God." (*Ennobling Love*, 190)

12. *Ennobling Love*, 190. This is also illustrated by Orgeluse and the way in which her love is turned into a desire for revenge and then into a force of reconciliation "that offers an answer tonoe of the great social problems of any warrior society, how to end cycles of revenge."

13. *Ennobling Love,* 191.

14. See Jo Ann McNamara, "City Air Makes Men Free and Women Bound," in *Text and Territory. Geographical Imagination in the European Middle Ages,* ed. Sylvia Tomasch and Sealy Gilles (Philadelphia: University of Pennsylvania Press, 1998) 143–159.

15. Subject of much discussion has been the relationship of Tristan to the standard Arthurian canon. Current scholarship, of which McDonald can serve as a representative example, accepts Tristan in the romance genre by considering it a more urbane (perhaps due to Gottfried's Strassburg milieu) anti-Arthurian romance. See William C. McDonald, "Gottfried von Strassburg: Tristan and the Arthurian Tradition." in *Tristan and Isolde. A Casebook*. Ed. Joan Trasker Grimbert. (New York: Garland Publishing, 1995)147–185. McDonald views Tristan as a parody: "The poet plays with traditional form and content, observing chivalry, courtliness and Arthurian ideals of love from the distance that irony and parody provide." (156) McDonald explains Arthur's absence from the narrative by saying that it is crucial Gottfried's argument "to establish Tristan's apartness from a code of (Arthurian) knighthood . . . it is not surprising that Gottfried excludes King Arthur from active participation in the story." (McDonald, 156– 57) Gillespie maintains that Tristan and the Nibelungenlied share a similar connection to Arthurian tradition. Both works are "the result of developments in a type of story-telling outside that of the Arthurian romance; yet they were composed in the same cultural milieu and exhibit much of the same concern with courtly manners and chivalric values apparent in the Arthurian epics." See George Gillespie "'Tristan- und Siegfriedliebe.' A Comparative Study of Gottfried's *Tristan*

and the *Nibelungenlie,"* *Gottfried von Strassburg and the Medieval Tristan Legend*, ed. Adrian Stevens and Roy Wisbey (Cambridge: D. S. Brewer, 1990), 162.

16. See Jaeger *Ennobling Love*. Helmut de Boor finds *Tristan*'s combination of the theological and the secular ultimately unsuccessful, though he does call the work "der kühnste und folgerichtigste Versuch, die hohe Minne als reales Erlebnis darzustellen, offenbar, wie weit sie von aller Realität abliegt." Helmut de Boor "Die Grundauffassung von Gottfrieds *Tristan*" in *Gottfried von Strassburg*. ed. Alois Wolf (Darmstadt: Wissenschaftliche Buchgesellschaft, 1973), 73. De Boor finds a kind of static 'thought' in *Tristan* because of Gottfried's reliance on his sources. (68–69)

17. Butler, *Gender Trouble*, 33. The same can be applied to interpretations of Gottfried's narrative as a whole, for this text has consistently resisted . Jaeger states it most plainly in his foreward to Gentry's 1988 revision of the Hatto translation: "If there are medieval categories into which the romance fits conveniently, they are yet to be found and formulated." (ix) Continuing research only serves to uphold this assessment.

18. This is the description that Picozzi gives, concluding her 1971 summary of *Tristan* scholarship with the statement that no interpretation of the poem can "realize all the potentialities of the text." Rosemary Picozzi, *A History of Tristan Scholarship* (Berne and Frankfurt: Herbert Lang, 1971), 154. McDonald echoes this sentiment by concluding that the poem is "an elusive, playful and often opaque tale about which the last world can never be said." (McDonald, 185) Frequently described as a limitless set of potentialities and possibilities, Gottfried's *Tristan* would seem to offer an apt illustration of Iser's definition of literature.

19. Weigel, *Topographien der Geschlechter* 11–12.

20. McDonald describes Gottfried's program of definition and determination on generic terms as well, in that the structure of the text reflects the incessant need for explication and signification "Through a collage-like interplay of image, situation and perspective, Gottfried conducts a remorseless inquest into chivalric romance...Gottfried delineates the radical self-determination that the lovers assert—their ranking of individual claims over recognized societal values—from within a well-defined tradition, the Arthurian romance, and invites us to see his figures in this constellation." (McDonald, 184)

21. Jaeger, "Foreward," in Gentry's translation (x).

22. Honeycutt offers further again reinforcement of the fact that the twelfth century was a time when there was a new awareness of 'subjectivity', that there were new discussions of gender roles in the context of the urbanization of Europe, monastic spirituality, and other changes. Gottfried would perhaps represent the area of urbanization. See Lois L. Hon-

eycutt, "Female Succession and the Language of Power in the Writings of Twelfth-Century Churchmen," in *Medieval Queenship*, ed. John Carmi Parsons. (New York: St. Martin's, 1993 and 1998) 189–203.

23. Gottfried fails to mention any kind of detail with regard to sailing technique, according to Hahn (in contrast to his careful descriptions of the hunt). In this, he actually stays very close to his sources. "Auch im Bereich der Geographie kommt es dem Dichter nicht darauf an, den sachlichen Gegebenheiten gerecht zu werden...Gottfried geht es einseitiger als Hartmann und auch Wolfram um Darstellung von Innenwelt." (Hahn, 37) Hahn goes on to describe Gottfried's "Stimmungslandschaft", which plays a much greater role in the narrative than in the more traditional Arthurian romance. Actually, there it is movement that creates the impression of landscape and space/place. Not so in Gottfried, who is much more psychological: "Der Grund dafür liegt in des Dichters psychologischer Schilderungskunst, mit der er subjektive menschliche Stimmungen erfaßt und szenisch im Raum verdichtet." (50)

24. Rainer Gruenter's essay is a detailed examination of the cave as Gottfried incorporates and transforms the classical *locus amoenus*. See Rainer Gruenter, "Das *wunnecliche tal*," ed. *Tristan-Studien*, Wolfgang Adam (Heidelberg: Carl Winter, 1993) 65–141.

25. Both medieval and modern interpreters have had difficulty dealing with the fact that Gottfried's narrative revolves around an adulterous relationship. In doing so, however, Gottfried discusses issues that are of primary importance to his society: the advantages and disadvantages of dynastic marriage, the matter of choice in one's destiny, and the possibility of finding love (especially, according to Andreas Capellanus, if love was not to be found in marriage). In this context, one must agree with Marianne Wynn: "Taking adultery as one of his major themes and treating it as a serious problem, describing and discussing the suffering it causes, and moreover insisting on the inevitability, indeed the necessity of it within the context of contemporary dynastic marriage was a move as innovative on the part of Gottfried as it was courageous." See Marianne Wynn, "Gottfried's Heroine," in *Gottfried von Strassburg and the Medieval Tristan Legend. Papers from an Anglo-North American Symposium*, ed. Adrian Stevens and Roy Wisbey. (Cambridge: D. S. Brewer, 1990), 141.

26. On the effects of urbanization in thirteenth and fourteenth century Europe on the roles of women, see Jo Ann McNamara, "City Air Makes Men Free and Women Bound." Gottfried's narrative seems to work against this trend, all the more interesting since Gottfried is considered a very urbane author, one who was a cleric in the city of Strassburg (as opposed to being a knight like Wolfram or Hartmann).

27. This is the metaphor for the essay collection edited by Barnes and Duncan (*Writing Worlds*).

28. "ein bewusstes strukturelles Experiment" Haug, 8.

29. Gottfried also takes care to specify who does *not* belong to this group:

> ine meine ir aller werlde niht
> als die, von der ich hoere sagen,
> diu keine swaere enmüge getragen
> und niuwan in vröuden welle sweben. (50–53)

[I do not mean the world of the many who (as I hear) are unable to endure sorrow and wish only to revel in bliss.]

30. See Speckenbach on the unique application of this term to an inner world where only certain people belong: "Daß hier nicht allgemein ein Mensch, sondern eine bestimmte Gruppe von Menschen mit *herze* bezeichnet wird, ist innerhalb der Dichtung einmalig, und auch in anderen Dichtungen ist mir eine eigene Welt von *herzen* oder gar *edelen herzen* unbekannt geblieben." Klaus Speckenbach, "Belege für *edelez herze* und die Textsituation". *Studien zum Begriff 'edelez herze' im* **Tristan** *Gottfrieds von Strassburg* (Munich: Eidos, 1965), 52. The term *edelez herze* is also used in connection with Tristan's education, as though he not only belongs to this group by virtue of his parentage but he is also educated to take his place in it. Speckenbach cites 4084–4094 as an example. (62) After the concept is gradually introduced and intensified through the beginning of the narrative, it is not necessary to repeat it so often after Tristan and Isolde drink the love potion: "Nachdem Tristan und Isolde die höchste Stufe der *edelen herzen* erlangt haben, wird die Entwicklung zu dieser Stufe nicht mehr dargestellt, sondern der Zusammenstoß der neugewonnenen Liebe mit der höfischen Welt." (67) They have achieved the level of the "noble hearts" at this point and the narrative focuses on the conflicts that arise between the lovers and the courtly world.

31. Speckenbach understands the term *edelez herz* as an analogy to the concept of the *edelen sêle* commonly used by early mystics. By focusing on the heart, the seat of emotion and embodiment of the "Gesamtheit des menschlichen Seins" (Speckenbach, 130), Gottfried expresses his intention to emphasize a more worldly love in his poem: "Innerhalb der Welt schuf er...eine weit gespannte, das Körperliche und Seelische umfassende Liebe, die von den *edelen herzen* Blanscheflur und Riwalin und im erhöhten Maße von Tristan und Isolde verwirklicht

wird." (131)

32. Grünkorn, 139. Gottfried goes on to elaborate in the literary exkursus that follows Tristian's knighting ceremony. Gertrud Grünkorn, *Die Fiktionalität des höfischen Romans um 1200* (Berlin: Erich Schmidt, 1994).

33. Gottfried wants to make his audience work at understanding accepting certain "Verstehensbedingungen...die die Rezeption nicht auf bloßes Textverstehen, sondern auf Widerspruch und Mehrsinnigkeiten und amit auf Sinnsuche und Reflexion festlegen." Meaning can only be found in the text with the participation of a competent and intelligent ("mitdenkenden") audience "das bereit ist, sich auf seinen poetischen Vermittlungsprozeß einzulassen." (Grünkorn, 150)

34. Haug, *Literaturtheorie*, 204.

35. Haug, *Literaturtheorie*, 209.

36. Haug, *Literaturtheorie*, 211.

37. This play on multiple levels is, of course, a characteristic of Arthurian romance that Gottfried's narrative shares with that of Hartmann and Wolfram, and others. (Haug, *Literaturtheorie*, 217)

38. Haug *Literaturtheorie*, 220–221. This experiment manifests itself, for example, in the rather fantastical view of knighthood that *Tristan* seems to present to the audience. Framing a question frequently asked of *Tristan*, McDonald wonders why the work seems to affirm such a fantastic world so remote from truth? The "fantasy" is part of a new kind of fictional "truth." The suggestion that Tristan cannot be shaped into a traditional Arthurian hero also implies that his lady will not fit the Arthurian mold either, and she does not.

39.

> Ich weiz wol, ir ist vil gewesen,
> die von Tristande hânt gelesen;
> und ist ir doch niht vil gewesen,
> die von im rehte haben gelesen (131–134)

[I am well aware that there have been many who have told the tale of Tristan; yet there have not been many who have read his tale aright.]

40. Wolfgang Iser, "The Play of the Text," 325. According to Iser, the author uses the existing world to create a text "made up of a world that is yet to be identified and is adumbrated in such a way as to invite picturing and eventual interpretation by the reader." (327)

41. Evelyn Birge Vitz presents a convincing argument for understanding medieval romances as performative texts in her recent study *Orality and*

Performance in Early French Romance. (Cambridge: D.S. Brewer, 1999). Her work underscores the applicability of Iser's theories to medieval romance.

42. Barnes and Duncan, 5.

43. The bloodshed in England ended when the Saxons placed themselves under Marke's protection; afterward, he became well-known as a good king:

> sît her diende ez im alle wege
> sô sêre und sô vorhtlîche,
> daz nie kein küicrîche
> eim künege mê gediende baz.
> ouch saget diu istôrje von im daz,
> daz allen den bîlanden,
> diu sînen namen erkanden,
> kein künec sô werder was als er. (44 6–453)

[From this time on, England served him so well and reverently in every way that no kingdom ever served king to better purpose. Moreover, this history tells of him that in all the neighboring lands where his name was known, no king was so esteemed.]

This image of Marke as a good ruler contrasts sharply with the king's image in his other role, that of Isolde's cuckolded husband.

44. Marke's reputation as king in the first part of *Tristan* has suffered among critics because of his part in the love triangle of the second part. Kerth advances the opinion that Marke is a purely literary king, who must be seen as a good king by the narrative although many of his actions would be incompatible with those of a historical ruler (like his decision not to marry, for example). It is thus a tribute to the artistry of the poet Gottfried "that we accept Marke as a king, and Cornwall and England as places." See Thomas Kerth, "Marke's Royal Decline." in *Gottfried von Strassburg and the Medieval Tristan Legend. Papers from an Anglo-North American Symposium*, ed. Adrian Stevens and Roy Wisbey (Cambridge: D. S. Brewer, 1990), 116.

45. It is at this celebration that Rivalin meets and falls in love with Blanscheflur.

46. McDonald 170.

47. See Schmid-Cadalbert, "Der wilde Wald. Zur Darstellung und Funktion eines Raumes in der mittelhochdeutschen Literatur." In *Tristan* we also see the typical placement of the *locus amoenus* in romance, for here too the cave lies on what seems to be the far side of the forest and that,

most importantly, the forest functions as a "threshold between the world on this side and the other place. (Saunders, 35). Actually, in *Tristan*, the forest provides an boundary area that helps to shelter if not seclude the lovers, though this area is traversed by other people such as Kurvenal and eventually Marke.

48. See also Hahn (*Raum und Landschaft*) on the initial hostility of the Cornish landscape.

49. As Gentry and others point out, unlike other lies, this one is not necessary.

50. See, for example, Margaret Brown and C. Stephen Jaeger, "Pageantry and Court Aesthetic in *Tristan*: The Procession of the Hunters." in *Gottfried von Strassburg and the Medieval Tristan Legend. Papers from an Anglo-North American Symposium*, ed. Adrian Stevens and Roy Wisbey (Cambridge: D. S. Brewer, 1990) 29–44.

51. Saunders, 94.

52. This allegory is, of course, one of Gottfried's most elaborate additions to his sources. I do not wish to diminish the importance of the cave as a unique transformation of the *locus amoenus* and a significant (in)version of the other gardens that we have seen in *Erec* (Brandigan) or in *Iwein* (by the fountain). As we shall see, however, the cave remains only one aspect of the gender topographies that are depicted in *Tristan*.

53. Ilich, 118

54. McDonald, 175 ff.

55. McDonald, 181–182

56. In fact, as Ann Marie Rasmussen points out, by the point at which Gottfried's narrative breaks off, it is difficult to distinguish between the mother and the daughter—the daughter does seem to have become her mother: "As the epic plays itself out, Princess Isolde acquires more of her mother's traits—her cunning, her wisdom. In the end...it is hard to know whether she is mother or daughter, for in a sense she has surely become both." See Ann Marie Rasmussen, "Ez ist ir g'artet von mir": Queen Isolde and Princess Isolde in Gottfried von Strassburg's *Tristan und Isolde*." in *Arthurian Women. A Casebook*, ed. Thelma Fenster. (New York: Garland Publishing, 1996), 50.

57. It is significant that we first meet the queen only "in absentia"; this has the effect of making her seem all the more intimidating and hostile, as the one who has the power to heal that poison of let it take its course. See Nancy P. Nenno "Between Magic and Medicine. Medieval Images of the Woman Healer," in *Women Healers and Physicians. Climbing a Long Hill*, ed. Lilian R. Furst. (Lexington KY: The University Press of Kentucky, 1997), 49.

58. The latter adjective ("sinnerîch") appears also in reference to Tris-

tan (5681), and thus significantly and thematically links the Queen and Tristan. See Gisela Hollandt, *Die Hauptgestalten in Gottfrieds Tristan. Wesenszüge—Handlungsfunktion—Motiv der List.* Heft 30. *Philologische Studien und Quellen.* Ed. Wolfgang Binder, Hugo Moser, Karl Stackmann. (Berlin: Erich Schmidt, 1966) 33, note 4.

59. Hollandt, 31, note 1. The adjective *wise* refers to three kinds of qualities associated with and displayed by Queen Isolde: 1. the magical fairy quality of her ability to heal ("Medizin und Magie"); 2. artistry and courtly skill ("Künste und Fertigkeiten"); 3. intelligence and judgment ("Scharfsinn und das besonnene Urteilsvermögen")

60. This knowledge "aligns Queen Isolde with the sorceresses who hold sway without male consorts on the margins of Arthur's world," like Morgan Le Fay in *Erec*, for example. (Rasmussen, "*ez ist ir g'artet von mir,*" 43). Nenno actually places Queen Isolde in the context of a gradual demonization of women's knowledge of the healing arts and comparing her in detail with Hartmann's Feimurgan in *Erec*. Queen Isolde's connection with the occult is tempered and her power is diminished, however, by her role as wife and mother, according to Rasmussen. Queen Isolde is 'in the world' and part of the patriarchal system: she is placed at the side of a man and she is the mother of a daughter. While she has taught her child many of her skills, she is ultimately preparing to give up her daughter in marriage to that patriarchal world. (Rasmussen, *Ez ist ir g'artet von mir*," 43)

61. The leprosy-stricken Heinrich, in Hartmann von Aue's *Der arme Heinrich*, is also directed to seek out the doctors in Salerno, who are the only ones who can help cure his illness. The fact that Queen Isolde knows more than these doctors further supports her special status.

62. See Petra Kellermann-Haaf's detailed study *Frau und Politik im Mittelalter. Untersuchungen zur politischen Rolle der Frau in den höfischen Romanen des 12., 13. und 14. Jahrhunderts* (Göppingen: Kümmerle, 1986). Also Rasmussen, "Ez ist g'artet von mir", 49: "For as is shown by the paradox of Queen Isolde's first exchange wit her husband, she knows, when she orders him in private to command her in public, that for a powerful woman the rule of love and the exercise of public power are inextricably linked." (49)

63.   unde alse ez nahten began
                diu wîse vrâgete unde sprach
                umbe ir tohter ungemach
                ir tougenlîche liste,
                von den wunder wiste,
                daz s'in ir troume gesach,
                daz ez niht alsô geschach,

als der lantschal sagete. (9299–9305)

[When night began to fall, the wise woman consulted her secret arts (in which she was marvellously skilled) on her daughter's distressful situation, with the result that she saw in a dream that these things had not happened as rumored.]

64. This kind of behavior is the mark of a good queen who understands her relationship to her daughter. Medieval queens understood the important role they played in persuading their daughters to accept a marriage: "A queen's persuasion of her daughter's consent could intensify that sense [of self] in them by emphasizing their consent as something of value to their parents, highlighting as well their choice to conform to their families' desires . . ." See John Carmi Parsons, "Mothers, Daughters, Marriage, Power: Some Plantagenet Evidence, 1150–1500," in *Medieval Queenship*, ed. John Carmi Parsons (New York: St. Martin's, 1993 and 1998), 78.

65. Parsons comments on the enormous importance of a royal mother's role in properly educating a daughter: "The role taken by such a mother in educating her daughters and preparing them for their adult careers is thus a pertinent consideration. To encourage their consent to an illustrious marriage she could stress prestige or wealth, representing the marriage as an opportunity for the exercise of power through patronage and other informal channels... An untrained daughter might prove incapable of managing her affairs after marriage, fail to establish an influential presence in her new home, and never develop the capacity to uphold her family's interests." Queens were also well aware that they could increase their own power through their daughters and they would therefore never deny an education to the daughters who would assuredly share the same destiny as their mothers. (73–74)

66. Rasmussen,"ez ist ir g'artet von mir", 43. In *Mothers and Daughters*, Rasmussen discusses this "apprenticeship" paradigm in greater detail particularly with respect to medieval German literature. "...The mother-daughter stories of medieval German fiction are socially, historically, and economically conditioned; versions differ, depending on genre, time, and class. Mother-daughter stories tell us something about competing modes of constructing kinship in the medieval aristocracy. They show us differing modes of sexualizing women. They embody the tensions between what is innate and what is learned, between compliance and disorderliness, between conformity and rebellion, between collaboration and resistance." (*Mothers and Daughters*, 25) The literature was, of course, written by men; therefore, it seems ultimately designed to show mothers how to construct for their daughters "a notion of female identity that depends on becoming and attractive and compliant object of male desire." (Rasmussen,

"*ez ist ir g'artet von mir,*" 43) The daughter Isolde could be said to embody (literally) an object of male desire; however, the topographies of *Tristan* illustrate her consistent resistance to this kind of objectification.

67. Zak observes that Isolde's "stylistic and thematic heritage is primarily matrilineal." See Nancy C. Zak, *The Portrayal of the Heroine in Chrétien de Troyes's 'Erec et Enide', Gottfried von Strassburg's 'Tristan', and 'Flamenca.'* (Göppingen: Kümmerle, 1983) here 69. For Rasmussen, this matrilineal heritage is the source of the younger Isolde's ability to resist.

68. See note 51 in Gentry's translation.

69. An analogy might be to the relationship between Gawan and Orgeluse, in the sense that Gawan is the instrument of her reintegration into courtly society.

70. "In other words, this epic is not only about a noblewoman's *knowledge* of her limited right to political power, and her manipulation of available resources. The mother's gift of the love potion means that while acquiescing in her daughter's (and her own) instrumental function, Queen Isolde still desires to give her daughter a measure of control over it." If her daughter cannot choose her husband, then she can at least love him. This love goes hand in hand with political power, as well. (Rasmussen, "*ez ist ir g'artet von mir,*" 49)

71. Nenno, 50. Nenno also gives an extensive comparison of the words used to describe Feimurgan and Queen Isolde, concluding that the Queen's power resides in her knowledge rather than in her force. (53)

72. Ann Marie Rasmussen, "Bist du begert, so bist du wert. Magische und höfische Mitgift für die Töchter," in *Mütter-Töchter-Frauen: Weiblichkeitsbilder in der Literatur,* ed. Helga Kraft and Elke Liebs (Stuttgart, Weimar: Metzler, 1993), 18. Rasmussen says elsewhere: "The goal of the mother's teaching is for the daughter to adopt and fulfill her mother's teachings, in other words, for the daughter to replicate her mother, to *become* her mother—for Isolde to become...Isolde." (Rasmussen, "*ez ist ir g'artet von mir*" 44) The mother/daughter relationship may be constructed conventionally to ensure continuity, to promote a concept of femininity that supports this continuity at the expense of a distinct identity; however, the teaching provides not only an ideal that one must live up to but also a "convention to be defied, a model to be subverted, and a protocol to be exploited." (Rasmussen, "*ez ist ir g'artet von mir,*" 43) The younger Isolde does just that.

73. Rasmussen, "Bist du begert, so bist du wert. 18.

74. "With the love potion, Queen Isolde passes her strength, her cunning, and her knowledge to her daughter, including the strength and the wit to defy the conventions that the mother herself embodies." (Rasmussen, "*ez ist ir g'artet von mir,*" 50).

75.   man sach ez inne und ûzen
                       und innerthalben lûzen
                       daz bilde, daz diu Minne
                       an lîbe und an dem sinne
                       sô schône haete gedraet.
                       diu zwei, gedraet und genaet,
                       diun vollebrâhten nie baz
                       ein lebende bilde danne daz. (1094 9–10957)

[One saw it inside and out, and—hidden away within—the image the
Love had shaped so rarely in body and in spirit! These two things—
lathe and needle—had never made a living image more perfect.]

Here, according to Jaeger, Gottfried seems to be looking at a statue
and describing it: "In the description of Isolde's clothing the aesthetics of
Gothic sculpture are of equal importance with literary conventions." See
C. Stephen Jaeger. *Medieval Humanism in Gottfried von Strassburg's* Tristan und Isolde (Carl Winter: Heidelberg, 1977), 111–116. Referring to
this gesture with which Isolde holds her mantle, Jaeger calls Isolde "stone
in motion" and the ultimate living image/picture: "Isolde's entrance represents the attempts to realize the aesthetic potential of the idea *daz
lebende bild.*" (113) In a way this is mimesis by means of art holding the
mirror up to art, showing Gottfried to be "the master craftsman." (115)
    76. Both Rasmussen ("*ez ist ir g'artet von mir*") and Zak note the im-
portance of Brangaene in this trio.
    77. Margaret Higonnet, "New Cartographies, an Introduction," in
Reconfigured Spheres. Feminist Explorations of Literary Space, ed. Margaret Higonnet and Joan Templeton (Amherst: University of Massachusetts Press, 1994), 6.
    78. In a fascinating study of the role of clothing in courtly literature
and the construction of gendered identity, E. Jane Burns has recently suggested a strategy she terms "reading through clothes". See E. Jane Burns,
"Speculum of the Courtly Lady: Women, Love, and Clothes," *Journal of
Medieval and Early Modern Studies.* 29.2 (Spring 1999): 253–292, here
280. In the context of courtly literature, "reading through clothes" means
"looking at women's attire as a possible means of resistance (albeit par-
tial) to those very paradigms of femininity used to objectify courtly ladies
either by peeling their clothes away to reveal highly fetishized white flesh
or by burying sexual difference beneath lavish layers of elegant garments."
(282) Burns is speaking mainly of women who are depicted looking at
themselves in a mirror and who literally change themselves: "Certainly the
inscribed female protagonists mentioned here are not free to do as they

please in shaping the concept of femininity, but the terms of the construction alter significantly when they move from being a mirror reflecting the
male lover's worth to women looking at themselves in the mirror." (283)
The younger Isolde could be considered a mirror of her mother, her name-
sake. Clothing creates the possibility of alternatives, according to Iris
Marion Young. The kind of female imagination encourages and supported
by the fashion world "has liberating possibilities because it subverts, un-
settles the order of respectable, functional rathionality supports domina-
tion. The unreal that wells up through imagination always creates the
space for a negation of what is, and thus the possibility of alternatives."
See Iris Marion Young, *Throwing Like a Girl and Other Essays in Feminist Philosophy and Social Theory*. Bloomington: Indiana University
Press, 1990, here 186.

79. Jaeger interprets the crown of virtues in the cave along with the
literary excursus. This resonates with gold and jewels, like the entrance of
Tristan and Isolde into the Irish court or Zak's exhaustive discussion of
Isolde and light on p. 7 1–72) as an indication of Gottfried's impulse to integrate the classical and the Christian tradition, the secular and the religious.

80. Gillespie compares the *Nibelungenlied* with *Tristan*, and Tristan
with Siegfried (Sifrit). In Gillespie's opinion, Tristan never changes, and
this static nature is what differentiates him from other Arthurian heroes.
(16 2–163) In the following, however, we will see that Tristan's character
is far from static.

81. Tristan's knowledge sets him apart, like Isolde (both mother and
daughter). In a sense, all three of these figures represent something alien
and other for the world of the narrative. This suggests interesting implications for an application of Weigel's dialectic between the familiar and
the strange, which would show a kind of "gender balance" that is not
found in Wolfram, for example (see Chapter 4).

82. Jaeger points out that Tristan actually has 3 fathers and receives
various qualities from each: Rivalin (*muot* and beauty); Rual (manners,
skill, learning, grace); Marke (*guot*). Jaeger says: "Of these three fathers,
none is by himself a whole man, non combines all those qualities which
make for integration of the inner and outer man." (*Medieval Humanism*,
42) The knighting is the completion of Tristan's development and his entrance into maturity. (49)

83. See Chapter III in *Medieval Humanism*, entitled: "The New Man:
Tristan's Development." On Gottfried's use of the adjective "niuwe" to describe Tristan, Jaeger comments: The use of 'new' here as a term of high
praise is a small indication of the spirit which predominates in the first part
of the work. No vernacular poet in the Middle Ages came closer to ex-

pressing the ideal of the 'new man' than Gottfried." (*Medieval Humanism*, 63). Certainly, no poet expressed it so self-consciously and so explicitly.

84. Grosz, 177. Grosz is discussing the theories of Delueze and Guatteri that overlap with feminist theories of the body: "These concepts seem loosely linked together in an attempt to reject or displce prevailing centrisms, unities and rigid status." (167) Grosz criticizes Delueze and Guatteri for supporting a rather universalist sense of becoming: "In short, the relation between 'being' (in all its ambiguities and impossibilities) and becoming is obscured; until it becomes clearer what becmoing woman means for those being who are women, as well as for those geings who are men, the value of their work for women and for feminism remains unclear." (182) Nevertheless, it is significant that Isolde's becoming is so prominent in *Tristan*.

85. This equality is literally inscribed in the text in the scene described earlier, in which Isolde and Tristan are "officially" (albeit separately) presented to the Irish court.

86.

> es gedâhte aber niemen niht,
> daz ir wort und ir geschiht
> an liebe haeten keine craft
> wan eine von der mâcschaft,
> die man sô grôze erkande
> under Marke und Tristande. (12997–13002)

[But nobody had any idea that their words or acts were inspired by any affection other than what came from the close kinship which all knew existed between Marke and Tristan.]

87. In "Gottfried's Heroine," Wynn presents a good review of the literature on Isolde up to 1990. According to Wynn, most of the research on Tristan has focussed on its ideological concepts rather than on individual characters. (129) The lack of material on Isolde is all the more remarkable since Gottfried changes his sources by extending the individuality of his heroine.

88. Wynn, 138.

89.

> er wante spâte unde vruo
> allen sînen sin dar zuo,
> daz er den zwîvel unde den wân
> gern haete hin getân
> und daz er mit der wârheit
> ûf sîn herzeclîchez leit

⟨vie⟩ gerne komen waere.

des was er gevaere. (13845–13852)

[Day and night he bent his whole mind to ridding himself of doubt and suspicion, and was most eager to arrive through proof positive at his own mortal sorrow. Such was his set intention.]

90. Gentry translates both of these verses as "cunning" matched against "cunning". The Middle High German word "list", as applied to the elder Isolde, also denotes knowledge; the word "sin" can be understood in this context on several levels as meaning, sense or intention.

91. See James F. Poag, "Lying Truth in Gottfried's *Tristan*," *Deutsche Vierteljahresschrift für Literaturwissenschaft und Geistesgeschichte* 61 (1987): 223–237.

92. There is always the question of who is served by the "ritualized performance that constitutes the proof" in the ordeal. See Peggy McCracken, *The Romance of Adultery. Queenship and Sexual Transgression in Old French Literature* (Philadelphia: University of Pennsylvania Press, 1998), 72.

93.

diu wîse, diu guote,

ir andâht diu was gotelîch.

si truoc ze nâhest an ir lîch

ein herte hemede haerîn,

dar obe ein wullîn rockelîn

kurz und daz mê dan einer hant

ob ir enkelînen want. (15654–15660)

[The wise, good lady's worship was most pious: she wore a rough hair-shirt next to her skin and above it a short woollen robe which failed to reach to her slender ankles by more than a hand's breadth.]

94. For Kucaba, the ordeal represents an example of a consummate courtly performance. "Der König besteht weniger auf eheliche Treue als auf Treue zu seinen höfischen Idealen. Oder anders gesagt: Die eheliche Treue an sich ist ihm nicht so wichtig, doch soll die *fiktion* ehelicher Treue aufrechterhalten werden." See Kelly Kucaba. "Höfisch inszenierte Wahrheiten. Zu Isolds Gottesurteil bei Gottfried von Straßburg," *Fremdes wahrnehmen—fremdes Wahrnehmen. Studien zur Geschichte der Wahrnehmung und zur Begegnung von Kulturen in Mittelalter und früher Neuzeit* ed. Wolfgang Harms and C. Stephen Jaeger with Alexandra Stein. (Stuttgart, Leipzig: Hirzel, 1997), 82.

95. Since God has apparently condoned this deception:

> dâ wart wol g'offenbaeret,
> und al der werlt bewaeret,
> daz der vil tugenthafte Crist
> wintschaffen alse ein ermel ist.
> er vüeget unde suochet an,
> dâ man'z an in gesuochen kan,
> alse gevuoge und alse wol,
> als er von allem rehte sol.
> erst allen herzen bereit,
> ze durnehte und ze trügeheit. (15733–15742)

[Thus it was made manifest and confirmed to all the world that Christ in His great virtue is pliant as a windblown sleeve. He falls into place and clings, whichever way you try Him, closely and smoothly, as He is bound to do. He is at the beck of every heart for honest deeds or fraud. Be it deadly earnest or a game, He is just as you would have Him.]

Kucaba presents a compelling interpretation of this bizarre passage, arguing for a figurative understanding of Christ as a kind of aesthetic potential that can recognize if not unite a literal and a figurative level the poem. The association of God's *logos* and poetic speech (*rede*) uniquely legitimizes Gottfried's narrative and its approach to truth. (Kucaba, 93)

96. Kucaba, 89.

97. Kucaba, 90.

98. Gert Kaiser, "Liebe ausserhalb der Gesellschaft. Zu einer Lebensform der höfischen Liebe," in *Liebe als Literatur. Aufsätze zur erotischen Dichtung in Deutschland*, ed. Rüdiger Krohn (Munich: C.H. Beck, 1983), 91.

99. See Janet Wharton, "'Daz lebende paradis' A Consideration of the Love of Tristan and Isot in the Light of the 'huote Discourse," in *Gottfried von Strassburg and the Medieval Tristan Legend. Papers from an Anglo-North American Symposium*, ed. Adrian Stevens and Roy Wisbey (Cambridge: D. S. Brewer, 1990), 150. Wharton offers a compelling analysis of the sun in the cave and the sun in the garden where the lovers are finally discovered. By comparison with the clear light of the cave, the later sun is the heat of discovery, the destructive heat of immoderate passion, and an inappropriate light. The comparison implies, among other things, that "the honor of love is diminished by lack of decorum, that is, if considerations of external honor are not observed." (153)

100. See Herbert Herzmann, "Warum verlassen Tristan und Isolde die Minnehöhle? Zu Gottfrieds *Tristan*," *Euphorion* 69 (1975): 227. The lovers thereby miss their opportunity to win the highest honor and virtue because they cannot free themselves from traditional understandings of honor and virtue. Herzmann draws provocative comparison to the young and naïve Parzival who gets to see the Grail before he is ready and fails to ask the question. Of course, Parzival receives a second chance. Despite the fact that we do have completed versions of the Tristan story from Gottfried's sources and continuators, Gottfried's own intentions must finally remain unknown.

101. See William D. Cole. "Purgatory vs. Eden: Béroul's Forest and Gottfried's Cave," *The Germanic Review* 70, no. 1 (1995): 6. Cole interprets Gottfried's cave as a Garden of Eden. Referring to lines 16974–16976, in which Gottfried describes the cave's green marble floor as an image of constancy (which should be as green as grass), Cole comments that "green and grass can signify constancy in only one place: the Garden of Eden, where springtime it eternal and nature allies itself with humankind." (7) Gottfried's courtly Eden has an Adam (Tristan) and an Eve (Isolde) as well as a serpent (in the form of the sword Marke sees between them).

102. For Ertzdorff, the love of Tristan and Isolde illustrates a new understanding of individuality and is therefore unsustainable because it must exist in conflict with the strictures of aristocratic courtly society: "diese Liebe ist nicht lebbar, weil sei in ihrer Absolutheit außerhalb der Zeit steht und im Tod nur Dauer hat." See Xenja von Ertzdorff, "Liebe, Ehe, Ehebruch und Tod in Gottfrieds *Tristan*," in *Liebe—Ehe—Ehebruch in der Literatur des Mittelalters*, ed. Xenja von Ertzdorff and Marianne Wynn (Giessen: Wilhelm Schmitz, 1984), 97. Even though the couple is faithful to one another, they are breaking the moral norms of God and society in their adulterous relationship—love must be bound within marriage. Therefore, the lovers must die. (96)

103. They literally embody what Jaeger terms 'the romantic dilemma'.

104. In this way, Isolde literally embodies the duality that permeates the entire narrative for Jaeger in *Medieval Humanism*. We find multiple expressions of this "two-foldness" in the work: interior and exterior aspects of the poem, inner and outer man, two courts (Marke and cave), chivalric honor and the honor of the *minnegrotte*, honor/love, *lip/muot*, body/ soul; Gottfried offers us a text that seems to exist suspended between the chivalric mentality with its heroic ideal and learned humanist tradition: "But these certainly are the two poles between which his literary activity is suspended, held there in an odd double position, which makes for the nearly inexhaustible ambiguities of his work." (Jaeger, *Medieval Humanism*, 18 9–190)

105. Gale Sigal, "Courted in the Country. Woman's Precarious Place in the Troubador's Lyric Landscape," in: *Text and Territory. Geographical Imagination in the European Middle Ages*, ed. Sylvia Tomasch and Sealy Gilles (Philadelphia: University of Pennsylvania Press, 1998), 203.

106. Zak says: "As the embodiment of aesthetic and artistic perfection, Isolde transcends time and space. She outdoes Helen of Troy. She is the most perfect of the goddess of love's creations." (77)

107. On the Cave of the Lovers, Jaeger says: "It is important to recognize that the cave of Lovers episode represents a secular spirituality . . . Gottfried then is the poet of spiritual love, and it is important to distinguish between this and divine love. He is an allegorist of the human spirit in its relationships with its parts and with the body, not with God." (Jaeger, *Medieval Humanism*, 177–178)

108. Clifton-Everest, 207 ff.

109. Clifton-Everest, 212.

110. It is certainly true that, before Isolde partakes of the love potion, her marriage to Marke represents " the possibility of replicating her mother's destiny, of becoming like her mother, of 'living up' to her name." (Rasmussen, "*ez ist ir g'artet von mir*," 48). But that trajectory of becoming does not take place; Isolde makes other choices.

111. See Joan C. Dayan, "The Figure of Isolde in Gottfried's *Tristan*: Towards a Paradigm of *Minne*," *Tristania* VI, no. 2 (1981): 32.

112. She wants to meet Tristan because she is frantic to see him: "und aber binamen Îsôte/der was ande und nôte." ("She was in a desperate plight," 17851–17852)

113. Gottfried goes on to say:

> Ezn ist al der dinge kein,
> der ie diu sunne beschein,
> sô rehte saelic sô daz wîp,
> diu ir leben unde ir lîp
> an die mâze verlât,
> sich selben rehte liebe hât. (18015–18020)

[Of all the things on which the sun ever shone, none is so truly blessed as a woman who has given herself and her life in trust to Moderation, and holds herself in right esteem.]

114. For Schnell, the excursus is essentially written in praise of woman: "Dessen Gültigkeit werden zumindest die weiblichen Personen Gottfrieds Publikum nicht in Zweifel gezogen haben." See Rüdiger Schnell, "Der Frauenexkurs in Gottfrieds *Tristan* (V. 1785 8–18114)," *Zeitschrift für*

Philologie 103, no. 1 (1984): 26.

115. Schröder sees it as a defense of the love of Tristan and Isolde: "Der *huote*-Exkurs ist—recht verstanden—nichts anderes als eine groß angelegte Verteidigung der Liebe von Tristan und Isolt, ihrer großen Leidenschaft, die den Inhalt des Romans bildet." Werner Schröder. "Zur Aussage und Funktion des *huote*-Exkurses im *Tristan* Gottfrieds von Straßburg," in *Text und Interpretation IV* (Stuttgart: Franz Steiner, 1993), 28. Of course, the true test of the "Tristanliebe" is the parting that follows the excursus.

116. For Thurlow, Isolde is "an Eve who flouts a *verbot* that Gottfried has shown to be wholly shameful and futile in his advice to husbands." See P. A. Thurlow, "Some Reflections on *huote* and *ere* in the 'Scheiden und Meiden' Episode of Gottfried's *Tristan*." *German Life and Letters* XXXV (1981–1982): 39) Even though Isolde acts as an Eve when summoning Tristan to the meeting in the orchard, she is still (in the words of the excursus) associated with the image of a good woman. Eve's disobedience, of course, began the whole story, establishing "a mode of behavior which will recur whenever a woman is subjected to prohibitions." (Wharton 144)

117. Wharton, 153.

118. "sus sint ez allez Êven kint,/die nâch der Êven g'artet sint." ("Thus they are all Eve's daughters, who are made in her image," 17961–17962)

119. Wharton, 145. For a discussion of one of the first juxtapositions of Eve and Mary, that occurs in the second-century writings of Justin Martyr, see Hilda Graef, *Mary: A History of Doctrine and Devotion* (London and Westminster MD: Sheed and Ward/ Christian Classics, 1985). Peter Brown examines the various and changing perceptions of the body in early Christianity in *The Body and Society. Men, Women, and Sexual Renunciation in Early Christianity* (New York: Columbia UP, 1988).

120. The purpose of *huote*, according to Hahn it is designed to prevent infidelity (Hahn uses the word "Untreue"). See Ingrid Hahn, "*Daz lebende paradis.*" *Zeitschrift für deutsches Altertum* 92 (1963): 18 4–195, here 185.

121. This is particularly necessary for the woman., who should reconcile her sensuality/nature as woman (*wîpheit*) with her innermost essence ("Wesenskern"), "daß sie zu lauterer Minne fähig wird. Diese verwirklicht sich in rückhaltloser Hingabe an den einen Geliebten und führt das *lebende paradis* herauf." (Hahn, 195)

122. Hahn, "*daz lebende paradis,*" 193.

123. See Hahn, "*daz lebende paradis,*" 194, and Kucaba. Kucaba suggests that it is of secondary importance "daß Isold Tristan liebt; von viel

größerer Wichtigkeit scheint es, *wie* sie damit umgeht: Wenn sie ihre Liebe nur zu *helen* wüßte—so die Implikation dieser Aussage—wäre kein Anstoß gegen Ehe oder Ehre vorhanden." (Kucaba, 81).

124. Wharton, 149.

125. See Bumke, "Liebe und Ehebruch in der höfischen Gesellschaft," 40.

126. Foucault, "Space, Knowledge and Power," 252.

127. Obviously, the same holds forTristan with regard to the love potion and the matter of choice.

128. Laurie Johnson, "Reading the Excursus on Women as a Model of 'Modern' Temporality in Gottfried's *Tristan*," *Neophilologus* 82 (1998): 254. Johnson points out the significance of the fact that Gottfried does not say explicitly that all women are Isolde; instead, he states that many Isoldes exist: "The contention that these 'types' are embodies in countless real individuals . . . as well as the insistence that these individuals can live in a new way . . . implies that the synthesis of the opposition between *sensualitas* and *ratio* must occur in countless individual situaitons." (254) Although Gottfried does not reject rhetorical tradition in his excursus on women (his recourse to traditional rhetoric has sparked much of the discussion of this particular passage), he "differentiates himself from patristic writers by weaving fictive constructions and ideas about individuality, autonomy, and creativity into given structures." (255) This is further evidence of the extent of Gottfried's fiction.

129. Grosz, 173

130. *Gender Trouble*, 33

131. Grosz, 172.

CHAPTER 5
Conclusions

> *A sign is a thing which causes us to think of something beyond the impression the thing itself makes upon the senses.*
>
> —Augustine[1]

> *These are the ways in which reading literature gives us the chance to formulate the unformulated.*
>
> —Wolfgang Iser[2]

The stylized landscape of medieval literature functions primarily like the sign Augustine describes above, drawing the audience's attention more toward an implied meaning that lies behind it than toward the landscape itself. Among other issues, this implied meaning betrays a concern on the part of the poets with appropriate gender roles. The "actual" landscape of romance impresses the senses of its audience as a composite of the *topoi* with which Curtius characterizes the ideal landscape, locating the main action of its narratives in such typical places as the forest and the *locus amoenus*. Upon this landscape, however, medieval poets superimpose other topographies necessary to draw a complete picture of the world of the poem. One kind of topography that figures prominently in the romance involves gender. As Sigrid Weigel has pointed out in *Topographien der Geschlechter*, various topographies of gender function in literature to map model constellations of femininity and masculinity for the audience.[3] These constellations of gender embed themselves in cultural memory through written and spoken language over time; they provide for successive audiences literary blueprints that inscribe and delineate gendered ways of becoming and being specifically appropriate to a given cultural order, as this order has been perceived and received throughout its history.[4] Furthermore, these constellations do not simply convey, for example, a medieval understanding of gender constructions and relations in literary or textual form to a modern audience. These traditional images of men and women also function as vehicles that can produce other meanings that are then communicated, not unlike Augustine's sign, on other levels of any given narrative: "Nicht nur ist das Wissen über *vergangene* und *andere* Geschlechtsmuster und –verhältnisse (*gender*, verstanden als kulturelle Konstruktion) weitgehend in textueller Form überliefert, sondern auch andere Bedeutungen werden mit Hilfe tradierter Frauen- und Männerbilder produziert."[5] Taking gender as a cultural construction, as Weigel and others have done, this study has examined gender topographies as an mechanism for the construction and inscription of gender roles in the major Arthurian romances written in the German-speaking area in the latter part of the twelfth and early part of the thirteenth centuries.

The spatial arrangements of the narratives reveal much about how the poets constructed and portrayed gender roles for the men and women in their audience through the creation of gendered spaces, advocating certain ones while excluding others. In this way, the poets could use the versatile metaphor of topography to encourage the acceptance of model behavior among their listeners. Since the literal landscape of the romance is not bound by the same strictures as the "real" landscape, or the landscape of the epic, the metaphor became particularly effective in the fictional context of Arthurian romance and thus provided a vehicle through which this form of socialization could occur. Thus, the romance genre permits a flexibility that we see manifested both literally and metaphorically in its topography. Spaces away from the court, especially the forest, offer a liminal area where men come to terms with their identity, and where women can also exhibit an unprecedented degree of agency and responsibility. In fact, women seem to own a certain magical space in this domain, in which they are not constrained by normal time or space. This magical, and potentially subversive, space is exemplified by the garden of Brandigan in Hartmann's *Erec*, a space that must be eliminated because it threatens the social order. Hartmann does, however, present a more moderate version of this space in the forest through which Erec and Enite must travel as she learns the virtues of appropriate speech and he learns the value of appropriate action. Since Erec and Enite eventually find their way to positions strictly delineated by traditional gender roles, it is clear that Hartmann does not attempt a permanent restructuring of boundaries in *Erec*. Nevertheless, the poet does stretch the margins to accommodate his narrative, which calls for at least a certain degree of agency on the part of his major female characters, if only in these marginal spaces.

While the margins close in *Erec*, leaving only the hint of possibility behind, the margins of *Iwein* expand and remain 'open,' so to speak, to accommodate pockets of space whose boundaries do not seem as rigid as those drawn at the conclusion of *Erec*. Lunete's mobility literally steers the course of the narrative. Although the forest is designated as Iwein's space in this work, the garden has been transformed into Laudine's kingdom, which continues to possess a subversive quality, particularly at the beginning of the work, when Hartmann repeatedly emphasizes Iwein's literal and metaphoric imprisonment in that place. And this space is not eliminated; on the contrary, it is allowed to continue at the conclusion of the story, despite the fact that Hartmann attempts to create a scene of harmony similar to the one that concludes *Erec*.

In contrast to Hartmann, Wolfram creates a much more expansive world than that of *Erec* or *Iwein* for his *Parzival*, incorporating the Orient, the Arthurian court, and the Grail world (as well as traditional romance spaces like the forest) into the landscape of the narrative. This elaborate world map with its extensive geography proves ultimately—and ironically—more restrictive than Hartmann's topography, particularly with respect to the construction of gender roles. Evidence for this can be found in Wolfram's positioning of *Parzival*'s key female characters on the margins, literally and symbolically: Belacane and Secundille in the Orient, Herzeloyde in Soltane, Sigune in the forest, and Cundrie forever in transit as Grail messenger. And they remain on those margins, despite the importance of their roles for the narrative. Those exemplary female characters who are located at the centers of the world and the work do not display the same degree of agency as their positionally marginalized counterparts; yet they are the models finally advocated by Wolfram at the conclusion of *Parzival*. In his desire for closure, Wolfram attempts to tie up all loose threads of his narrative at the conclusion, illustrated most notably by Feirefiz's hasty baptism and the fortuitous report of Secundille's death. Throughout his narrative, Wolfram depicts negotiations between margins and centers, and he offers suggestions for the resolution of the encounters with the 'other' that are essential to these negotiations. The resolutions attempt to reincorporate the 'other' and they have the effect of effacing 'other'-ness from the narrative. In this way, Wolfram demarcates the margins of his textual world, as well as the spatial and ideological boundaries of this world, more precisely than his contemporary Hartmann.

The variety of spaces and places in *Parzival*, the complexity of the map(s) and the intricacy of the narrative invite the audience into the story and into its process, in a way that resonates strongly with Iser's concept of *Leerstellen* and audience imagination; Wolfram's audience must work to understand. In a very concrete sense, *Parzival* engages the imagination of the reader or listener and creates the text out of interaction.[6] Wolfram's attempts literally to synthesize or "fix" his worlds and their inhabitants (male and female, Christian and non-Christian) into 'being' throw into relief the unique variety of the modes of male 'becoming' in *Parzival*. Hartmann allows some ambivalence, some spaces that can be understood as other for both men and women (*Erec*) in which both go through an appropriate process of becoming, or as other and apart ("separate but equal") in *Iwein*. The spaces of Wolfram's narrative represent an interplay of spaces for 'becoming' and for 'being.' In so doing, he maps onto the geography of his world a fairly clear topography of gender that ultimately fixes gender roles into 'being' more restrictively than the comparatively modest geographical scope of Hartmann's narratives. Wolfram underscores his ambivalence toward women through the structure of these spaces in the topography of *Parzival*, a structure that frames complex and varied negotiations regarding the spaces themselves, the power and knowledge they can impart and ultimately the roles of the men and women in them, creating a study in contrasts between men's becoming and women's being. Indeed, there are only two women who can be said to participate in any process of becoming in *Parzival*: Sigune and Orgeluse. Sigune, of course, removes herself from the courtly sphere and therefore also from the earthly (or earth-bound) sphere as she completes a spiritual journey toward 'becoming' one in God with her beloved Schionatulander in God. Orgeluse's trajectory directs her away from her single-minded quest for vengeance and brings her into a peaceful union with Gawan. She can be reconciled with those who had wronged her, and her marriage (along with her ability to forgive) facilitate her reintegration into courtly society. Her model contrasts with that of the static Grail world where, aside from Parzival's successful journey, it does not appear the society has changed at all in its behavior or outlook.

Many analyses have corroborrated Foucault's simple but profound observation that space plays a fundamental role in the exercise of power.[7] Wolfram ultimately limits the spaces for women in *Parzival*, for instance, fixing the most impressive examples of female power into an immutable state of 'being': Sigune is dead, as is Herzeloyde, while Orgeluse is married and Cundrie permanently inhabits the margins of each world she moves in. These women therefore cannot pose any destabilizing threat to the new world order with which Wolfram concludes his narrative. Disruption cannot be avoided completely, however. The penultimate verses of the narrative tell the story of Parzival's son Loherangrin, who offers his help to the princess of Brabant and who is eventually driven away from that country (despite a happy life there) by the princess' forbidden question. (824,1–826,29)

The threat of destabilization is nowhere more evident, however, than in Gottfried's *Tristan*. The topograpy of *Tristan* continues to pose a significant contrast to that of Hartmann and Wolfram, particularly because female space and power play such an integral role in constructing the narrative. The island of Ireland can be distinctly understood as female space, for example, due to the presence of both Isoldes: the elder queen and her daughter. The younger Isolde also displays considerable authority and autonomy after she arrives in Cornwall, skillfully managing her relationship with Tristan and manipulating appearances and reality to suit her purposes—exercising the traditionally male prerogative of choice. More than any other woman in the Arthurian cast of characters, Isolde represents woman who "as a term in process, a becoming, a constructing that cannot rightfully be said to originate or to end."[8] The topographies of *Tristan* outline the contours of a multivalent and distinctly unconventional (at least in terms of the Arthurian tradition represented by Chrétien, Hartmann and Wolfram) narrative, inviting the audience to explore the possibilities that courtly romance offered and to stretch the conventional boundaries that left women no room to develop.[9] The fact that Gottfried was writing in the comparatively urban center of Strassburg (unlike many of his contemporarites he was not a knight or a *ministerial*) must also prompt the modern reader to speculate whether these possibilities might also not have been offered as an alternative to the negative effects of increasing urbanization and restrictions on the activities of women of in the thirteenth and fourteenth centuries, recently described by McNamara.[10]

As we have seen, literary space becomes a formidable tool in the hands of its poets. Through their respective topographies, Hartmann, Wolfram and Gottfried mapped their worlds, offering their audiences a variety of possibilities for 'becoming' and 'being' – they staged and enacted multiple performances of gender, as it were. Of course, certain possibilities ultimately had to be rejected in favor of others. Since these romances were well-known to audiences of the early thirteenth century and later audiences as well, it is tempting to imagine that, while exploring a range of possibilities in their works, these poets exercised considerable influence over which of those possibilities could finally be accepted, at least ideologically. Certainly their images and their imagined landscapes have inscribed for successive audiences varied places and spaces for men and women to 'be' and to 'become'. It is not surprising that the poets generally advocate trajectories of becoming that support the status quo of the courtly society for which they write; they could not have done differently, as much as modern feminists and theorists might wish otherwise. But these medieval poets also intentionally created worlds of depth and complexity that, in depicting the relationships between men and women in courtly society, could not fail to take up and continue the dialogue concerning gender roles that had begun in the middle of the twelfth century.

In each work that we have discussed (Hartmann's *Erec* and *Iwein*, Wolfram's *Parzival*, and Gottfried's *Tristan*), we have seen that gender topographies provide the romance poet with a framework that can structure explore many aspects of human relationships (gender roles chief among them) and finally integrate them into a meaningful whole. The goal of such integration, achieved by each poet with varying degrees of success, underscores a program of socialization that can be seen at work in the romance genre. For modern eyes, medieval Arthurian romance masks its social function with fantasy and imagination, but as literature it has a distinctly historical place, "always enmeshed in circumstance, time, place, and society."[11] *Erec, Iwein, Parzival,* and *Tristan* remain texts that are in the world and of the world, texts that have something to say about the worlds of their writers and of their audiences (past, present, and future). In this way, romance can be viewed with other literary works

> . . . as social documents that intervene in the material world through their form; they display, embody, and allegorize the social tensions of an historical moment in polyphonic and often contradictory ways. They can invoke the spirit of subversion and rebellion only to contain it again at the end.[12]

Various spatializations and constellations occur as poets map for their audiences different patterns of 'becoming,' explorations of various possiblities; certainly some possibilities are accepted while others are rejected. Indeed, there seem to be more instances of becoming male than of becoming female in the romance genre, perhaps as a result of the answer to the *Herrenfrage*. The most fascinating aspect of romance, and (I suggest) a reason for its enduring popularity then and now, is the way its "virtual reality"[13] captivates the imaginations of its audiences. Romance might 'play' with subversion only in order to contain it again in the last verse; nevertheless, as long as we pursue the question "wie man zer werlte solte leben," the 'play' is a major part of both the message and the fun.

Notes

1. Augustine, *On Christian Doctrine*, trans. D.W. Robertson (New York: Liberal Arts Press, 1958) 34, Book 2.I.1.
2. Iser, "The Reading Process," in *The Implied Reader*, 294.
3. Weigel, *Topographien der Geschlechter*, 11–12.
4. Weigel views the relationship between gender and cultural memory as an area that demands further examination: "In kulturgeschichtlicher Perspektive aber eröffnet sich hier ein anderes weites Untersuchungsfeld, in dem es um den Zusammenhang von 'Geschlecht' und 'kulturellem Gedächtnis' geht: um die in Sprache und Schrift erinnerten Gechlechter-verhältnisse und um die geschlechtsspezifischen Symbolisierungsweisen der kulturellen Ordnung." See Sigrid Weigel, "Geschlechterdifferenz und Literaturwissenschaft," in *The Graph of Sex and the German Text: Gendered Culture in Early Modern Germany 1500–1700*, ed. Lynne Tatlock

(Amsterdam: Rodopi, 1994), 24.

5. Weigel, "Geschlechterdifferenz und Literaturwissenschaft," 23.

6. I refer once again to the final chapter in *The Implied Reader* entitled "The Reading Process: A Phenomenological Approach." (274–294) where Iser views the reader/text interaction as essential to the creation of the literary work.

7. Foucault, "Space, Knowledge, and Power," 252.

8. Butler, *Gender Trouble*, 33.

9. According to Bumke ("Liebe und Ehebruch in der höfischen Gesellschaft"), the game of courtly love finally serves the self-justification of an aristocracy that left women no room for self-development.

10. McNamara, "City Air Makes Men Free and Women Bound."

11. Edward Said, *The World, the Text, and the Critic* (Cambridge: Harvard UP, 1983), 35.

12. Anton Kaes, "New Historicism and the Study of German Literature," *German Quarterly* 62.2 (1989): 213.

13. Iser, *PMLA*, 311.

Bibliography

Primary Literature

Andreas Capellanus. *The Art of Courtly Love.* With introduction, translations, and notes by John Jay Parry. New York: F. Ungar Publishing, 1959 [c 1941].

Augustine. *On Christian Doctrine.* Trans. D.W. Robertson. New York: Liberal Arts Press, 1958.

Chrétien de Troyes. *Arthurian Romances.* Trans. D.D.R. Owen. London: J.M. Dent, 1988.

Gottfried von Strassburg. *Tristan.* Nach dem Text von Friedrich Ranke. Neu herausgegeben, ins Neuhochdeutsch übersetzt, mit einem Stellenkommentar und einem Nachwort von Rüdiger Krohn. 3d ed. Stuttgart: Reclam, 1984.

————. *Tristan.* Ed. Gottfried Weber. Darmstadt: Wissenschaftliche Buchgesellschaft, 1967.

————. *Tristan.* Trans. A. T. Hatto. Ed. and Rev. Francis G. Gentry. New York: Continuum, 1988.

Hartmann von Aue. *Erec. Mittelhochdeutscher Text und Übertragung.* Ed. and Trans. Thomas Cramer. Frankfurt: Fischer, 1972.

————. *Erec.* Ed. Christoph Cormeau. 6th ed. Niemeyer: Tübingen, 1985.

————. *Erec.* Trans. Michael Resler. Philadelphia: University of Pennsylvania Press, 1987.

————. *Iwein.* Ed. G.F. Benecke and Karl Lachmann. Revised by Ludwig Wolff. Berlin: Walter de Gruyter, 1968.

————. *Iwein.* Ed. and Trans. Patrick McConeghy. New York: Garland, 1984.

————. *Iwein.* Trans. J. W. Thomas. Lincoln: University of Nebraska Press, 1979.

Ketsch, Peter. *Frauen_im Mittelalter: Quellen und Materialien.* Vol. 1. *Frauenarbeit im Mittelalter*; Vol 2. *Frauenbild und Frauenrechte in Kirche und Gesellschaft.* Ed. Annette Kuhn. 1st ed. Düsseldorf: Schwann-Bagel, 1983/1984.

Das Nibelungenlied. Nach der Ausgabe von Karl Bartsch. Ed. Helmut de Boor. F.A. Brockhaus: Mannheim, 1988.

Orderic Vitalis. *The Ecclesiastical History of England and Normandy.* Trans. Thomas Forester. Vol. 3. London: Henry Bohn, 1854.

Thomasin von Zirclaria. *Der wälsche Gast.* Ed. Heinrich Rückert. Berlin: Walter de Gruyter, 1965.

Walther von der Vogelweide. *Gedichte.* Ed. Karl Lachmann. Berlin: Walter de Gruyter, 1965.

Wolfram von Eschenbach. *Parzival.* Ed. Karl Lachmann. Berlin: Walter de Gruyter, 1965.

————. *Parzival.* Trans. Helen M. Mustard and Charles Passage. New York: Vintage Books, 1961.

General Secondary Literature: Medieval

Ariès, Philippe. "Die unauflösliche Ehe." *Die Masken des Begehrens und die Metamorphosen der Sinnlichkeit. Zur Geschichte der Sexualität im Abendland.* Ed. Philippe Ariès und André Bejin. Frankfurt: Fischer, 1984 (orig. 1982), 176–196.

Ashe, Geoffrey. "Topography and Local Legends." *The New Arthurian Encyclopedia.* Ed. Norris Lacy. New York: Garland, 1991 and 1996, 455–458.

Auerbach, Erich. *Mimesis. Dargestellte Wirklichkeit in der abendländischen Literatur.* Bern: Francke, 1946.

Baldwin, John W. "Five Discourses on Desire: Sexuality and Gender in Northern France around 1200." *Speculum* 66 (1991): 797–819.

————. *The Language of Sex. Five Voices from Northern France around 1200.* Chicago: University of Chicago Press, 1994.

Benson, Robert L. and Giles Constable. *Renaissance and Renewal in the*

Twelfth Century. Cambridge: Harvard UP, 1982.

Bertau, Karl. *Deutsche Literatur im europäischen Mittelalter.* Munich: C.H. Beck, 1973.

Bloch, R. Howard. *Medieval Misogyny and the Invention of Romantic Love.* Chicago: University of Chicago Press, 1991.

Blumstein, Andrée Kahn. *Misogyny and Idealization in the Courtly Romance.* Bonn: Bouvier, 1977.

Boklund, Karin. "On the Spatial and Cultural Characteristics of Courtly Romance." *Semiotica* 20 (1977): 1–37.

Brall, Helmut. "Imaginationen des Fremden. Zu Formen und Dynamik kultureller Indentitätsfindung in der höfischen Dichtung." *An den Grenzen höfischer Kultur. Anfechtungen der Lebensordnung in der deutschen Erzähldichtung des hohen Mittelalters.* Ed. Gert Kaiser. Munich: Wilhelm Fink, 1991, 115–167.

Brandt, Rüdiger. *Enklaven-Exklaven. Zur literarischen Darstellung von Öffentlichkeit und Nichtöffentlichkeit im Mittelalter.* Munich: Wilhelm Fink, 1993.

Brooke, Christopher. *The Medieval Idea of Marriage.* Oxford: Oxford UP, 1989.

Brown, Peter. *The Body and Society. Men, Women, and Sexual Renunciation in Early Christianity.* New York: Columbia UP, 1988.

Brüggen, Elke. *Kleidung und Mode in der höfischen Epik des 12. und 13. Jahrhunderts.* Heidelberg: Carl Winter, 1989.

Brundage, James. *Law, Sex, and Christian Society in Medieval Europe.* Chicago: University of Chicago Press, 1987.

———. "Sexual Equality in Medieval Canon Law." *Medieval Women and the Sources of Medieval History.* Ed. Joel T. Rosenthal. Athens: University of Georgia Press, 1990, 66–79.

Bullough, Vern L. and Bonnie Bullough. *The Subordinate Sex. A History of Attitudes towards Women.* Urbana, Chicago: University of Illinois Press, 1973.

Bumke, Joachim. *Höfische Kultur. Literatur und Gesellschaft im hohen Mittelalter.* Munich: C.H. Beck, 1986.

Burns, E. Jane. "Speculum of the Courtly Lady: Women, Love, and Clothes." *Journal of Medieval and Early Modern Studies.* 29.2 (Spring 1999): 253–292

———. *Bodytalk. When Women Speak in Old French Literature.* Philadelphia: University of Pennsylvania Press, 1993.

Bynum, Caroline Walker. *Fragmentation and Redemption.* New York: Zone Books, 1991.

———. *Jesus as Mother. Studies in the Spirituality of the High Middle Ages.* Berkeley: University of California Press, 1982.

Camille, Michael. *The Medieval Art of Love. Objects and Subjects of Desire.* New York: Harry N. Abrams, 1998.

———. *Image on the Edge. The Margins of Medieval Art.* Cambridge: Harvard UP, 1992.

Clifton-Everest, John M. "Fingierte *warheit.*" *Von Aufbruch und Utopie. Perspektiven einer neuen Gesellschaftsgeschichte des Mittelalters. Für und mit Ferdinand Seibt aus Anlaß seines 65. Geburtstages.* Ed. Bea Lundt und Helma Reimöller. Köln, Weimar,Wien: Böhlau, 1992, 203–215.

Cohen, Jeffrey Jerome. "Gowther Among the Dogs: Becoming Inhuman c. 1400." *Becoming Male in the Middle Ages.* New York: Garland Publishing, 2000, 219–245.

———. *Of Giants. Sex, Monsters, and the Middle Ages.* Minneapolis: University of Minnesota Press, 1999.

Cohen, Jeffrey Jerome and Bonnie Wheeler, ed. *Becoming Male in the Middle Ages.* New York: Garland Publishing, 2000.

Cormeau, Christoph. "Artusroman und Märchen: Zur Beschreibung und Genese der Struktur des höfischen Romans." *Wolfram-Studien 5.* Ed. Werner Schröder. Berlin: Erich Schmidt, 1979, 63–78.

———. *Deutsche Literatur im Mittelalter: Kontakte und Perspektiven. Hugo Kuhn zum Gedenken.* Stuttgart: Metzler, 1979.

Curtius, Ernst Robert. *European Literature and the Latin Middle Ages.* Trans. Willard R. Trask. New York: Harper & Row, 1953.

Davis, Natalie Zemon. *Society and Culture in Early Modern France: Eight Essays.* Stanford: Stanford UP, 1975.

De Boor, Helmut. *Die höfische Literatur: Vorbereitung, Blüte, Ausklang: 1170–1250. Geschichte der deutschen Literatur.* Vol. 2. Munich: C.H. Beck, 1964.

Dick, Ernst S. "Fels und Quelle. Ein Landschaftsmodell des höfischen Epos." *Wolfram-Studien 6.* Ed. Werner Schröder. Berlin: Erich Schmidt, 1980, 167–181.

Dinzelbacher, Peter. "Gefühl und Gesellschaft im Mittelalter. Vorschläge zu einer emotionsgeschichtlichen Darstellung des hochmittelalterlichen Umbruchs." *Höfische Literatur, Hofgesellschaft, Höfische Lebensformen um 1200.* Ed. Gert Kaiser und Jan-Dirk Müller. Studia humaniora 6. Düsseldorf: Droste, 1986, 213–243.

Duby, Georges. *Love and Marriage in the Middle Ages.* Trans. Jane Dunnett. Chicago: University of Chicago Press, 1994.

———. "Introduction." *A History of Private Life.* Ed. Philippe Aries and Georges Duby. Vol. 2. Cambridge, MA: The Belknap Press of Harvard University Press, 1988, 3–31.

———. *The Knight, the Lady, and the Priest. The Making of Modern*

Marriage in Medieval France. New York: Pantheon, 1983.

———. *Medieval Marriage. Two Models From Twelfth-Century France*. Trans. Elborg Forster. Baltimore: Johns Hopkins UP, 1978.

Ehlert, Trude. "Die Frau als Arznei. Zum Bild der Frau in hochmittelalterlicher deutscher Lehrdichtung." *Zeitschrift für deutsche Philologie* 105 (1986): 42–62.

Ehrismann, Gustav. *Geschichte der deutschen Literatur bis zum Ausgang des Mittelalters. Zweiter Teil. Die mittelhochdeutsche Literatur. II. Blütezeit. Erste Hälfte*. Munich: C.H. Beck, 1927.

Ennen, Edith. *Frauen im Mittelalter*. Munich: C.H. Beck, 1985.

Farmer, Sharon. "Persuasive Voices: Clerical Images of Medieval Wives." *Speculum* 61 (1986): 517–543.

Fenster, Thelma, ed. *Arthurian Women. A Casebook*. New York: Garland Publishing, 1996.

Ferrante, Joan M. "Male Fantasy and Female Reality in Courtly Literature." *Women's Studies* 10–11 (1983/84): 67–97.

———. "Public Postures and Private Maneuvers: Roles Medieval Women Play." *Women and Power in the Middle Ages*. Ed. Mary Erler and Maryanne Kowalewski. Athens: University of Georgia Press, 1988, 213–229.

———. *Woman as Image in Medieval Literature: From the Twelfth Century to Dante*. New York: Columbia University Press, 1975.

Frakes, Jerold C. *Brides and Doom. Gender, Property, and Power in Medieval German Women's Epic*. Philadelphia: University of Pennsylvania Press, 1994.

Gerhards, Gisela. *Das Bild der Witwe in der deutschen Literatur des Mittelalters*. Ph.D. diss., Bonn, 1962.

Gilroy-Hirtz, Petra. "Begegnung mit dem Ungeheuer." *An den Grenzen höfischer Kultur. Anfechtungen der Lebensordnung in der deutschen Erzähldichtung des hohen Mittelalters*. Ed. Gert Kaiser. Munich: Wilhelm Fink, 1991, 167–209.

Gold, Penny Schine. *The Lady and the Virgin*. Chicago: University of Chicago Press, 1985.

Goody, Jack. *The Development of Family and Marriage in Europe*. New York: Cambridge UP, 1983.

Graef, Hilda. *Mary: A History of Doctrine and Devotion*. London and Westminster MD: Sheed and Ward/ Christian Classics, 1985.

Gravdal, Kathryn. *Ravishing Maidens. Writing Rape in Medieval French Literature and Law*. Philadelphia: University of Pennsylvania Press, 1991.

Green, Dennis H. *Medieval Listening and Reading. The Primary Reception of German Literature 800–1300*. Cambridge: Cambridge UP,

1994.

Grünkorn, Gertrud. *Die Fiktionalität des höfischen Romans um 1200*. Berlin: Erich Schmidt, 1994.

Gruenter, Rainer. "Zum Problem der Landschaftsdarstellung im höfischen Roman." *Euphorion* 56 (1962): 248–274.

Gumbrecht, Hans Ulrich. "Wie fiktional war der höfische Roman?" *Funktionen des Fiktiven*. Ed. Dieter Henrich and Wolfgang Iser. Munich: Wilhelm Fink, 1983, 433–440.

Haskins, Charles Homer. *The Renaissance of the Twelfth Century*. 1927. Reprint, Cambridge: Harvard UP, 1957.

Haug, Walter. *Literaturtheorie im deutschen Mittelalter. Von den Anfängen bis zum Ende des 13. Jahrhunderts. Eine Einführung*. Darmstadt: Wissenschaftliche Buchgesellschaft, 1985.

——. "Wandlungen des Fiktionalitätsbewußtseins vom hohen zum späten Mittelalter." *Entzauberung der Welt. Deutsche Literatur 1200–1500*. Ed. James F. Poag and Thomas C. Fox. Tübingen: Francke, 1989, 1–18.

Herlihy, David. "Land, Family and Women." *Women in Medieval Society*. Ed. Susan Mosher Stuard. Philadelphia, 1976, 13–45. First published in *Traditio* 18 (1962), 89–120.

——. "The Making of the Medieval Family: Symmetry, Structure, and Sentiment." *Journal of Family History* (1983): 116–131.

——. *Medieval Households*. Cambridge: Harvard UP, 1985.

——. "The Medieval Marriage Market." *Medieval and Renaissance Studies. Number 6. Proceedings of the Southeastern Institute of Medieval and Renaissance Studies. Summer 1974*. Ed. Dale B.J. Randall. Durham, NC: Duke UP, 1976, 3–28.

Honeycutt, Lois L. "Female Succession and the Language of Power in the Writings of Twelfth-Century Churchmen." *Medieval Queenship*. Ed. John Carmi Parsons. New York: St. Martin's, 1993 and 1998, 189–203.

Howell, Martha C. *Women, Production and Patriarchy in Late Medieval Cities*. Chicago: University of Chicago Press, 1986.

Hufeland, Klaus. "Das Motiv der Wildheit in mittelhochdeutscher Dichtung." *Zeitschrift für deutsche Philologie* 95 (1976): 1–19.

Jacquart, Danielle and Claude Thomasset. *Sexuality and Medicine in the Middle Ages*. Trans. Matthew Arnold. Oxford: Polity Press, 1988.

Jaeger, C. Stephan. *Ennobling Love. In Search of a lost Sensibility*. Philadelphia: University of Pennsylvania Press, 1999.

——. *The Origins of Courtliness. Civilizing Trends and the Formation of Courtly Ideals 939–1210*. Philadelphia: University of Pennsylvania Press, 1985.

Jahn, Bernhard. *Raumkonzepte in der Frühen Neuzeit. Zur Konstruktion von Wirklichkeit in Pilgerberichten, Amerikareisebeschreibungen und Prosaerzählungen.* Frankfurt: Peter Lang, 1993.

Kaiser, Gert. "Artushof und Liebe." *Höfische Literatur, Hofgesellschaft, Höfische Lebensformen um 1200.* Ed. Gert Kaiser und Jan-Dirk Müller. Studia humaniora 6. Düsseldorf: Droste, 1986, 243–253.

Kasten, Ingrid. "Häßliche Frauenfiguren in der Literatur des Mittelalters." *Auf der Suche nach der Frau im Mittelalter.* Ed. Bea Lundt. Munich: Wilhelm Fink, 1991. 255–277.

———. "Heilserwartung und Verlusterfahrung. Reisen als Motiv in der mittelalterlichen Lyrik." in: *Reisen und Welterfahrung in der deutschen Literatur des Mittelalters.* Ed. Dietrich Huschenbett and John Margetts. Würzburg: Königshausen & Neumann, 1991, 69–84.

Kellermann-Haaf, Petra. *Frau und Politik im Mittelalter.* Göppingen: Kümmerle, 1986.

Kimble, George H. T. *Geography in the Middle Ages.* New York: Russell and Russell, 1938.

Knowles, David. *The Evolution of Medieval Thought.* New York: Vintage, 1962.

Klapisch-Zuber, Christiane, ed. *Silences of the Middle Ages.* Cambridge: The Belknap Press of Harvard University Press, 1992.

Köhler, Erich. *Ideal und Wirklichkeit in der höfischen Epik.* 2nd ed. Tübingen: Max Niemeyer, 1970.

Kroj, Karina. *Die Abhängigkeit der Frau in Eherechtsnormen des Mittelalters und der Neuzeit als Ausdruck eines gesellschaftlichen Leitbilds von Ehe und Familie. Zugleich eine Untersuchung zu den Realisierungschancen des zivilrechtlichen Gleichheitsgrundsatzes.* Europäische Hochschulschriften. Frankfurt: Peter Lang, 1988.

Krueger, Roberta. *Women Readers and the Ideology of Gender in Old French Verse Romance.* Cambridge: Cambridge UP, 1993.

Le Goff, Jacques. *The Birth of Purgatory.* Trans. Arthur Goldhammer. Chicago: University of Chicago Press, 1981.

———. *The Medieval Imagination.* Chicago: University of Chicago Press, 1988.

Leisch-Kiesl, Monika. *Eva als Andere: Eine exemplarische Untersuchung zu Frühchristentum und Mittelalter.* Köln, Weimar, Wien: Böhlau, 1992.

Lewis, Gertrud Jaron. "*daz vil edel wîp.* Die Haltung zeitgenössischer Kritiker zur Frauengestalt der mittelhochdeutschen Epik." *Die Frau als Heldin und Autorin. Neue Ansätze zur deutschen Literatur.* Ed. Wolfgang Paulsen. Bern: Francke, 1979, 66–82.

Liebertz-Grün, Ursula. "Kampf, Herrschaft, Liebe. Chrétiens und Hartmanns Erec- und Iweinromane als Modelle gelungener Sozialisation im 12. Jahrhundert." *The Graph of Sex and the German Text: Gendered Culture in Early Modern Germany 1500–1700.* Ed. Lynne Tatlock. Amsterdam: Rodopi, 1994, 297–329.

———. "On the Socialization of German Noblewomen 1150–1450." *Monatshefte* 82 (1990): 17–37.

Londner, Monika. *Eheauffassung und Darstellung der Frau in der spätmittelalterlichen Märendichtung. Eine Untersuchung auf der Grundlage rechtlich-sozialer und theologischer Voraussetzungen.* Ph.D. diss. Berlin, 1973.

Makowski, Elizabeth M. "The Conjugal Debt and Medieval Canon Law." *Equally in God's Image. Women in the Middle Ages.* Ed. Julia Bolton Holloway, Joan Bechtold and Constance S. Wright. New York: Peter Lang, 1990, 129–144.

McNamara, Jo Ann. "City Air Makes Men Free and Women Bound." *Text and Territory. Geographical Imagination in the European Middle Ages.* Ed. Sylvia Tomasch and Sealy Gilles. Philadelphia: University of Pennsylvania Press, 1998, 143–159.

———. "The *Herrenfrage.* The Restructuring of the Gender System, 1050–1150." *Medieval Masculinities. Regarding Men in the Middle Ages.* Ed. Clare A. Lees. Minneapolis: University of Minnesota Press, 1994, 3–30.

———. and Suzanne Wemple. "The Power of Women through the Family in Medieval Europe: 500–1100." *Women and Power in the Middle Ages.* Ed. Mary Erler and Maryanne Kowalewski. Athens: University of Georgia Press, 1988, 83–101.

Müller, Michael. *Die Lehre des hl. Augustinus von der Paradiesehe und ihre Auswirkung in der Sexualethik des 12. und 13. Jahrhunderts bis Thomas von Aquin. Eine moralgeschichtliche Untersuchung.* Regensburg: F. Pustet, 1954.

Nagel, Bert. *Staufische Klassik. Deutsche Dichtung um 1200.* Heidelberg: Lothar Stiem, 1977.

Newman, Barbara. *Sister of Wisdom.* Berkeley: University of California Press, 1987.

Nykrog, Per. "The Rise of Literary Fiction." *Renaissance and Renewal in the Twelfth Century.* Ed. Robert L. Benson and Giles Constable. Cambridge: Harvard UP, 1982, 593–612.

Opitz, Claudia. "Vom Familienzwist zum sozialen Konflikt. Über adelige Eheschließungspraktiken im Hoch- und Spätmittelalter." *Weiblichkeit in geschichtlicher Perspektive. Fallstudien zu Grundproblemen der historischen Frauenforschung.* Ed. Ursula J. Becher und Jörn Rüsen. Frankfurt: Suhrkamp, 1988.

Ott, Norbert H. "Zur Ikonographie der Reise. Bildformeln und Struktur-prinzipien mittelalterlicher Reise-Illustrationen." *Reisen und Welter-fahrung in der deutschen Literatur des Mittelalters.* Ed. Dietrich Huschenbett and John Margetts. Würzburg: Königshausen & Neumann, 1991, 35–53.

Parsons, John Carmi, ed. *Medieval Queenship.* New York: St. Martin's, 1993 and 1998.

Pearsall, Derek and Elizabeth Salter. *Landscapes and Seasons of the Medieval World.* Toronto: University of Toronto Press, 1973.

Peters, Ursula. "Zwischen New Historicism und Gender-Forschung. Neue Wege der älteren Germanistik." *Deutsche Vierteljahresschrift für Literaturwissenschaft und Geistesgeschichte* 3 (1997): 363–397.

———. "Höfische Liebe. Ein Forschungsproblem der Mentalitäts-geschichte." *Liebe in der deutschen Literatur des Mittelalters.* Ed. Jeffrey Aschcroft. Tübingen: Max Niemeyer, 1987.

———. "Literaturgeschichte als Mentalitätsgeschichte? Überlegungen zur Problematik einer neueren Forschungsrichtung." *Germanistik— Forschungsstand und Perspektiven. Vorträge des deutschen Germanistentages 1984 I-II.* Ed. Georg Stötzel. Vol. II. Berlin: Walter de Gruyter, 1985, 179–198.

———. *Frauendienst. Untersuchungen zu Ulrich von Lichtenstein und zum Wirklichkeitsgehalt der Minnedichtung.* Ph.D. diss., Köln, 1970.

Phillips, J.R.S. *The Medieval Expansion of Europe* Oxford, New York: Oxford UP, 1988.

Régnier-Bohler, Danielle. "Imagining the Self." *A History of Private Life.* Ed. Philippe Ariès and Georges Duby. Vol. 2. Cambridge, MA: The Belknap Press of Harvard University Press, 1988, 311–394.

Ribard, Jacques. "Espace romanesque et symbolisme dans la litterature arthurienne du XIIe siecle." *Espaces romanesques.* Ed. Michel Crouzet. Université de Picardie. Centres d'Études du Roman et du Romanesque. Presses Universitaires de France: Paris, 1982, 73–82.

Rogers, Katharine. *The Troublesome Helpmate: A History of Misogyny in Literature.* Seattle: University of Washington Press, 1966.

Saunders, Corinne J. *The Forest of Medieval Romance. Avernus, Broceliande, Arden.* Cambridge: D.S. Brewer, 1993.

Schäufele, Eva. *Normabweichendes Rollenverhalten: Die kämpfende Frau in der deutschen Literatur des 12./13. Jahrhunderts.* Göppingen: Kümmerle, 1979.

Schmid-Cadalbert, Christian. "Der wilde Wald. Zur Darstellung und Funktion eines Raumes in der mittelhochdeutschen Literatur." *Gotes und der werlde hulde.* Ed. Rüdiger Schnell. Bern: Francke, 1989, 24–47.

Schulenburg, Jane Tibbetts. "Sexism and Celestial Gynaeceum, 500–1200." *Journal of Medieval History* 3 (1978), 117–133.

Schultz, James A. *The Shape of the Round Table. Structures of Middle High German Arthurian Romance.* Toronto: University of Toronto Press, 1983.

Schwietering, Julius. *Die deutsche Dichtung des Mittelalters.* Darmstadt: Hermann Gentner, 1957.

Shahar, Shulamith. *The Fourth Estate. A History of Women in the Middle Ages.* Trans. Chaya Galai. Cambridge: Cambridge UP, 1983. Reprint, London: Routledge, 1993.

Sheehan, Michael M. "Choice of Marriage Partner in the Middle Ages: Development and Mode of Application of a Theory of Marriage." *Studies in Medieval and Renaissance* N.S. 1 (1978): 1–33.

Simek, Rudolf. *Erde und Kosmos im Mittelalter. Das Weltbild vor Kolumbus.* Munich: C.H. Beck, 1992.

Southern, R.W. *The Making of the Middle Ages.* New Haven: Yale UP, 1953.

Stock, Brian. *The Implications of Literacy: Written Language and Models of Interpretation in the Eleventh and Twelfth Centuries.* Princeton: Princeton UP, 1983.

———. *Listening for the Text. On the Uses of the Past.* Philadelphia: University of Pennsylvania Press, 1990.

Stuard, Susan Mosher. "From Women to Woman: New Thinking About Gender c. 1140." *Thought* 64 (1989): 208–219.

Taylor, Irmgard C. *Das Bild der Witwe in der deutschen Literatur.* Gesellschaft Hessischer Literaturfreunde. Darmstadt: Roetherdruck, 1980.

Terkla, Daniel. *The Centrality of the Peripheral: Illuminating Borders and the Topography of Space in Medieval Narrative and Art, 1066–1400.* Ph.D. diss., University of Southern California, 1992.

Thelen, Lynn. *Beyond the Court. A Study of the wilde-Motif in Medieval German Literature.* Ph.D. diss., University of Pennsylvania, 1979.

Tomasch, Sylvia and and Sealy Gilles, ed. *Text and Territory. Geographical Imagination in the European Middle Ages.* Philadelphia: University of Pennsylvania Press, 1998.

Uebel, Michael. "On Becoming-Male." *Becoming Male in the Middle Ages.* Ed. Jeffrey Jerome Cohen and Bonnie Wheeler. New York: Garland Publishing, 2000, 367–384.

Vecchio, Silvana. "The Good Wife." *The Silences of the Middle Ages. A History of Women in the West.* Ed. Georges Duby and Michelle Perrot. Vol. 2. Cambridge, MA: The Belknap Press of Harvard UP, 1992, 105–136.

Vermette, Rosemary. "Terrae Incantatae: The Symbolic Geography of Twelfth-Century Arthurian Romance." *Geography and Literature. A Meeting of the Disciplines.* Ed. William E. Mallory and Paul Simpson-Housley. Syracuse: Syracuse University Press, 1987, 145–161.

Vinaver, Eugene. *The Rise of Romance.* Oxford: Oxford University Press, 1971.

Vitz, Evelyn Birge. *Orality and Performance in Early French Romance.* Cambridge: D.S. Brewer, 1999.

Vogt, Friedrich. *Geschichte der mittelhochdeutschen Literatur.* Vol. 1. Berlin: Walter de Gruyter, 1922.

Wais, Kurt. "Einführung in die Forschungsgeschichte des arthurischen Romans." *Der arthurische Roman.* Ed. Kurt Wais. Darmstadt: Wissenschaftliche Buchgesellschaft, 1970, 1–18.

Waldmann, Bernhard. *Natur und Kultur im höfischen Roman um 1200.* Erlangen: Palm und Enke, 1983.

Wehrli, Max. *Literatur im deutschen Mittelalter. Eine poetologische Einführung.* Stuttgart: Reclam, 1984.

———. "Strukturen des mittelalterlichen Romans—Interpretationsprobleme." *Formen mittelalterlicher Erzählung. Aufsätze.* Zürich: Atlantis, 1969, 25–50.

Wenzel, Horst. *Frauendienst und Gottesdienst. Studien zur Minneideologie.* Berlin: Erich Schmidt, 1974.

Westrem, Scott D., ed. *Discovering New Worlds: Essays on Medieval Exploration and Imagination.* New York, London: Garland, 1991.

Wetzlaff-Eggebert, F.-W. *Kreuzzugsdichtung des Mittelalters.* Berlin: Walter de Gruyter, 1960.

Wiesner, Merry. *Women and Gender in Early Modern Europe.* Cambridge: Cambridge UP, 1993.

Wolf, Gerhard. "Das Individuum auf dem Weg zu sich selbst? Frühneuzeitliches Reisen nach Osten: Hans Dernschwam, Balthasar Springer und Fortunatus." *Reisen und Welterfahrung in der deutschen Literatur des Mittelalters.* Ed. Dietrich Huschenbett and John Margetts. Würzburg: Königshausen & Neumann, 1991, 196–214.

Wunder, Heide. *"Er ist die Sonn', sie ist der Mond." Frauen in der frühen Neuzeit.* Munich: Wilhelm Fink, 1992.

Wyss, Ulrich. "Fiktionalität—heldenepisch und arthurisch." *Fiktionalität im Artusroman. Dritte Tagung der Deutschen Sektion der Internationalen Artusgesellschaft.* Ed. Volker Mertens and Friedrich Wolfzettel. Tübingen: Niemeyer, 1993, 242–256.

Secondary Literature for Hartmann, Wolfram, and Gottfried

Hartmann von Aue

Armstrong, Grace M. "Women of Power: Chretien de Troyes's Female Clerks." *Women in French Literature*. Ed. Michael Guggenheim. Saratoga, CA: ANMA Libri, 1988, 29–46.

Ashby, W. D. *The Lady of the Fountain: A Study of a Medieval Myth*. Ph.D. diss., University of Miami, 1976.

Bayer, Hans. "'bi den liuten ist so guot.' Die 'meine' des *Erec* Hartmanns von Aue." *Euphorion* 73 (1979): 272–285.

Carne, Eva-Maria. *Die Frauengestalten bei Hartmann von Aue. Ihre Bedeutung im Aufbau und Gehalt der Epen*. Marburger Beiträge zur Germanistik 31. Marburg: N.G. Elwert, 1970.

Clark, Susan. "Hartmann's *Erec*: Language, perception and transformation." *Germanic Review* 56 (1981): 81–94.

Cormeau, Christoph and Wilhelm Störmer. *Hartmann von Aue: Epoche-Werk-Wirkung*. Munich: C.H. Beck, 1985.

Cramer, Thomas. "Soziale Motivation in der Schuld-Sühne- Problematik von Hartmanns *Erec*." *Euphorion* 66 (1972): 97–112.

Ehrismann, Otfrid. "Enite. Handlungsbegründungen in Hartmanns von Aue *Erec*." *Zeitschrift für deutsche Philologie* 98 (1979): 312–344.

———. "Laudine—oder: Hartmanns *Iwein* postmodern." *Sammlung—Deutung—Wertung. Ergebnisse, Probleme, Tendenzen und Perspektiven philologischer Arbeit. Mélanges de littéature médiévale et de linguistique allemande offerts à Wolfgang Spiewok à l'occasion de son soixantiè annivsersaire par ses collègues et amis*. Amiens: Université de Picardie. Ed. Danielle Buschinger. Centre d'Études médiévales, 1988, 91–100.

Fisher, Rodney. "Erecs Schuld und Enitens Unschuld bei Hartmann." *Euphorion* 69 (1975): 160–174.

Fisher, R. W. "The Courtly Hero Comes to Germany: Hartmann's *Erec* and the Concept of Shame." *Amsterdamer Beiträge zur älteren Germanistik* 46 (1996): 119–130.

Gentry, Francis G. "Hartmann von Aue's *Erec*: The Burden of Kingship." *King Arthur Through the Ages*. Ed. Valerie M. Lagorio and Mildred Leake Day. Vol. 1. New York: Garland, 1990, 152–169.

Hahn, Ingrid. "Die Frauenrolle in Hartmanns *Erec*." *Sprache und Recht. Beiträge zur Kulturgeschichte des Mittelalters. Festschrift für Ruth Schmidt-Wiegand zum 60. Geburtstag*. Ed. Karl Hauck. Berlin: Walter de Gruyter, 1986, 172–190.

Hostetler, Margaret. "Enclosed and Invisible?: Chrétien's Spatial Discourse and the Problem of Laudine." *Romance Notes* 37.2 (1997): 119–127.

Hrubý, Antonin. "Die Problemstellung in Chretiens und Hartmanns *Erec.*" *Hartmann von Aue.* Ed. Hugo Kuhn and Christoph Cormeau. Darmstadt: Wissenschaftliche Buchgesellschaft, 1973, 342–372.

Kaiser, Gert. "'Iwein' oder 'Laudine'." *Zeitschrift für deutsche Philologie* 99 (1980): 20–28.

———. *Textauslegung und gesellschaftliche Selbstdeutung. Die Artusromane Hartmanns von Aue.* Wiesbaden: Akademische Verlagsgesellschaft Atheaion, 1978.

Kratins, Ojars. *The Dream of Chivalry: A Study of Chretien de Troyes's Yvain and Hartmann von Aue's Iwein.* Washington DC: University Press of America, 1982.

Krueger, Roberta. "Love, Honor, and the Exchange of Women in *Yvain*: Some Remarks on the Female Reader." *Romance Notes* 25 (1985): 302–317.

Kuhn, Hugo. "Erec." *Dichtung und Welt im Mittelalter.* Stuttgart: Ernst Poeschel, 1959, 133–150.

Lewis, Robert E. *Symbolism in Hartmann's Iwein.* Göppingen: Kümmerle, 1975.

McConneghy, Patrick. "Women's Speech and Silence in Hartmann von Aue's *Erec.*" *PMLA* 102 (1987): 772–783.

McMahon, James V. "Enite's Relatives: The Girl in the Garden." *Modern Language Notes* 85 (1970): 367–372.

Mertens, Volker. *Laudine. Soziale Problematik im Iwein Hartmanns von Aue.* Beihefte zur Zeitschrift für deutsche Philologie 3. Berlin: Erich Schmidt, 1978.

Pratt, Karen. "Adapting Enide: Chretien, Hartmann, and the Female Reader." *Chretien de Troyes and the German Middle Ages.* Ed. Martin H. Jones and Roy E. Wisbey. Arthurian Studies 26. Cambridge: D.S. Brewer, 1993, 67–85.

Quast, Bruno. "*getriuwiu wandelunge.* Ehe und Minne in Hartmanns *Erec.*" *Zeitschrift für deutsches Altertum und deutsche Literatur* (1993): 162–180.

Ragotzky, Hedda and Barbara Weinmayer. "Höfischer Roman und soziale Identitätsbildung. Zur soziologischen Deutung des Doppelwegs im *Iwein* Hartmanns von Aue." *Deutsche Literatur im Mittelalter: Kontakte und Perspektiven. Hugo Kuhn zum Gedenken.* Ed. Christoph Cormeau. Stuttgart: Metzler, 1979, 211–253.

Ranawake, Silvia. "Erec's *verligen* and the Sin of Sloth." *Hartmann von Aue. Changing Perspectives.* Ed. Timothy McFarland and Silvia Ranawake. Göppingen: Kümmerle, 1988, 91–115.

Ruh, Kurt. "Zur Interpretation von Hartmanns *Iwein.*" *Hartmann von Aue.* Ed. Hugo Kuhn and Christoph Cormeau. Wissenschaftliche Buchgesellschaft: Darmstadt, 1972, 408–425.

Rushing, James A. *Images of Adventure. Ywain in the Visual Arts.* Philadelphia: University of Pennsylvania Press, 1995.

Smits, Kathryn. "Einige Beobachtungen zu gemeinsamen Motiven in Hartmanns *Erec* und Wolframs *Parzival.*" *Festschrift for E.W. Herd.* Ed. August Obermayer. Otago German Studies 1. Dunedin: University of Otago Press, 1980, 251–262.

———. "Enite als christliche Ehefrau." *Interpretation und Edition deutscher Texte des Mittelalters. Festschrift für John Asher zum 60. Geburtstag.* Ed. Kathryn Smits, Werner Besch, and Victor Lange. Berlin: Erich Schmidt, 1981, 13–25.

———. "Die Schönheit der Frau in Hartmanns *Erec.*" *Zeitschrift für deutsche Philologie* 101 (1982): 1–28.

Sparnaay, Henricus. "Hartmann von Aue and his Successors." *Arthurian Literature in the Middle Ages.* Ed. R.S. Loomis. Oxford: Clarendon Press, 1959, 430–442.

Steiner, Gertrud. "'Unbeschreiblich weiblich'. Zur mythischen Rezeption von Hartmanns *Iwein.*" *Psychologie in der Mediävistik. Gesammelte Beiträge des Sternheimer Symposions.* Ed. Jürgen Kühnel. Göppingen: Kümmerle, 1985, 243–257.

Sterba, Wendy. "The Question of Enite's Transgression: Female Voice and Male Gaze as Determining Factors in Hartmann's *Erec.*" *Women as Protagonists and Poets in the German Middle Ages: An Anthology of Feminist Approaches to Middle High German Literature.* Ed. Albrecht Classen. Göppingen: Kümmerle, 1991.

Tax, Petrus. "Studien zum Symbolischen in Hartmanns *Erec.*" *Zeitschrift für deutsche Philologie* 82 (1963): 29–44.

Tobin, Frank. "Hartmann's *Erec.* The Perils of Young Love." *Seminar* 14 (1978): 1–14.

Tobler, Eva. "Ancilla Domini. Marianische Aspekte in Hartmanns *Erec.*" *Euphorion* 80 (1986): 427–438.

Wapnewski, Peter. *Hartmann von Aue.* Stuttgart: Metzler, 1962.

Wehrli, Max. "Iweins Erwachen." *Hartmann von Aue.* Ed. Hugo Kuhn and Christoph Cormeau. Wissenschaftliche Buchgesellschaft: Darmstadt, 1973, 491–510.

Wiegand, Herbert Ernst. *Studien zur Minne und Ehe in Wolframs Parzival und Hartmanns Erec.* Berlin: Walter de Gruyter, 1972.

Willson, H. Bernard. "The Heroine's Loyalty in Hartmann's and Chrétien's *Erec.*" *Chretien de Troyes and the German Middle Ages.* Ed. Martin H. Jones and Roy E. Wisbey. Arthurian Studies 26. Cambridge: D.S. Brewer, 1993, 57–67.

———. "Inordinatio in the Marriage of the Hero in *Iwein.*" *Modern Philology* 68 (1970/71): 242–253.

Wolfram von Eschenbach

Hans Bayer. *Gral. Die hochmittelalterliche Glaubenskrise im Spiegel der Literatur.* Stuttgart: A. Hiersmann, 1983.

Bindschedler, Maria B. "Der Ritter Gawan als Arzt oder Medizin und Höflichkeit." *Schweizer Monatshefte für Politik, Wirtschaft, Kultur* 69 (1984): 729–743.

Blamires, David. *Characterization and Individuality in Wolfram's Parzival.* Cambridge: Cambridge UP, 1966.

Blumstein, Andrée Kahn. "The Structure and Function of the Cundrie Episodes in Wolfram's *Parzival.*" *German Quarterly* 51 (1978): 160–169.

Brall, Helmut. "'Diz fliegende bispel.' Zur Programmatik und kommunikativer Funktion des *Parzival* Prologs." *Euphorion* 77 (1983): 1–39.

Breyer, Ralph. "Cundrî, die Gralsbotin?" *Zeitschrift für Germanistik* 6.1 (1996) 61–75.

Bumke, Joachim. "Geschlechterbeziehungen in den Gawanbüchern von Wolframs *Parzival.*" *Amsterdame Beiträge zur älteren Germanistik.* Vol 38–39 (1994): 105–121.

———. *Wolfram von Eschenbach.* 6th ed. Stuttgart: Metzler, 1991.

———. "Liebe und Ehebruch in der höfischen Gesellschaft," *Liebe als Literatur. Aufsätze zur erotischen Dichtung in Deutschland*, ed. Rüdiger Krohn. Munich: C.H. Beck, 1983, 25–45.

———. "Die Utopie des Grals. Eine Gesellschaft ohne Liebe?" *Literarische Entwürfe.* Ed. Hiltrud Gnüg. Frankfurt: Suhrkamp, 1982, 70–79.

———. *Die Wolfram von Eschenbach Forschung seit 1945. Bericht und Bibliographie.* Munich: Wilhelm Fink, 1970.

Buschinger, Danielle. "Die Minne-Idee in Wolframs *Parzival.*" *Deutung und Wertung als Grundproblem philologischer Arbeit. Festkolloquium zum 60. Geburtstag von Wolfgang Spiewok vom 28.2– 2.3. 1989 in Greifswald.* Greifswald: Ernst-Moritz-Arndt Universität, 1989, 111–115.

Christoph, Siegfried. *Wolfram von Eschenbach's Couples.* Amsterdam: Rodopi, 1981.

Dallapiazza, Michael. "Häßlichkeit und Individualität: Ansätze zur Überwindung der Idealität des Schönen in Wolframs von Eschenbach *Parzival.*" *Deutsche Vierteljahresschrift* 50 (1985): 400–421.

Delabar, Karl. *Erkantiu Sippe und Hoch Gesellschaft: Studien zur Funktion des Verwandtschaftsverbandes in Wolframs von Eschenbach Parzival.* Göppingen: Kümmerle, 1990.

Duckworth, David. "Herzeloyde and Antikonie." *German Life and Letters* 41 (1988): 322–341.

Eder, Annemarie. "Macht- und Ohnmachtstrukturen im Beziehungsgefüge von Wolframs *Parzival*: Die Herzeloydentragödie." *Der frauwen buoch. Versuch zu einer feministischen Mediävistik.* Ed. Ingrid Bennewitz. Göppingen: Kümmerle, 1989.

Ebenbauer, Alfred. "Es gibt ain mörynne vil dick susse mynne. Belakanes Landsleute in der deutschen Literatur des Mittelalters." *Zeitschrift für deutsches Altertum* 113 (1984): 16–42.

Eichholz, Birgit. *Kommentar zur Sigune- und Itherszenen im 3. Buch von Wolframs Parzival (138,9–161,8).* Stuttgart: Helfant-Eclition, 1987.

Fries, Maureen. "Gender and the Grail." *Arthuriana* 8.1 (1998): 67–79.

Gibbs, Marion E. *Wiplichez Wibes Reht: A Study of the Women Characters in the Works of Wolfram von Eschenbach.* Duquense: Duquense University Press, 1972.

Groos, Arthur. "Cundrie's Announcement." *Beiträge zur Geschichte der Deutschen Sprache und Literatur* 3 (1991): 384–414.

———. "'Sigune auf der Linde' and the Turtledove in *Parzival.*" *Journal of English and German Philology* 67 (1968): 631–646.

Hasty, Will, ed. *A Companion to Wolfram's Parzival.* Columbia, S.C.: Camden House, 1999.

Haug, Walter. "*Parzival* ohne Illusionen." *Deutsche Vierteljahresschrift* 64 (1990): 199–217.

Heise, Ursula. "Frauengestalten in *Parzival.*" *Deutschunterricht* 9 (1957): 37–62.

Jacobson, Evelyn M. "Cundrie and Sigune." *Seminar* 25 (1989): 1–11.

Karg, Ina. *...sin süeze surez ungemach . . . Erzählen von der Minne in Wolframs Parzival.* Göppingen: Kümmerle, 1993.

Kleber, Jutta Anna. *Die Frucht der Eva und die Liebe in der Zivilisation. Das Geschlechterverhältnis im Gralsroman Wolframs von Eschenbach.* Frankfurt: Peter Lang, 1992.

Kuhn, Hugo "Wolframs Frauenlob." *Liebe und Gesellschaft.* Ed. Wolfgang Walliczek. Metzler: Stuttgart, 1980, 44–51.

Kratz, Henry. *Wolfram von Eschenbach's Parzival. An Attempt at Total Evaluation.* Bern: Francke, 1973.

Krause, Burkhardt. "Wolfram von Eschenbach. Eros, Körper-Politik und Fremdenaneignung." *Kultur- und Literaturgeschichtliche Studien zum Körperthema*. Ed. Burkhardt Krause. Helfant Studien 7. Stuttgart, 1992.

Kuhn, Hugo. "Parzival: Ein Versuch über Mythos und Glaube und Dichtung im Mittelalter." *Dichtung und Welt im Mittelalter*. Stuttgart: Ernst Poeschel, 1959, 151–180.

———. "Soziale Realität und dichterische Fiktion am Beispiel der höfischen Ritterdichtung Deutschlands." *Dichtung und Welt im Mittelalter*. Stuttgart: Ernst Poeschel, 1959, 22–40.

Kunitzsch, Paul. "Erneut: Der Orient in Wolframs *Parzival*." *Zeitschrift für deutsches Altertum* 113 (1984): 79–111.

Lewis, Gertrud Jaron. "Die unheilige Herzeloyde. Ein ikonoklastischer Versuch." *Journal of English and German Philology* 74 (1975): 465–485.

Marchand, James W. "Honor and Shame in Wolfram's *Parzival*." *Spectrum Medii Aevi*. Ed. William McDonald. Göppingen: Kümmerle, 1983, 283–298.

Masser, Achim. "Gahmuret und Belakane. Bemerkungen zur Problematik von Eheschliessung und Minnebeziehungen in der höfischen Literatur." *Liebe und Aventiure im Artusroman des Mittelalters. Beiträge der Triester Tagung 1988*. Ed. Paola Schulze-Belli und Michael Dallapiazza. Göppingen: Kümmerle, 1990, 109–132.

Miklautsch, Lydia. *Studien zur Mutterrolle in den mittelhochdeutschen Großepen des zwölften und dreizehnten Jahrhunderts*. Erlangen: Verlag Palm und Enke, 1991.

Morrison, Susan Signe. "A Reader-Response to Wolfram's von Eschenbach *Parzival*: The Position of the Female Reader." *Lesarten. New Methodologies and Old Texts*. Ed. Alexander Schwarz. Bern: Peter Lang, 1990.

Noltze, Holger. *Gahmurets Orientfahrt. Kommentar zum ersten Buch von Wolframs 'Parzival' (4,27–58,26)*. Würzburg: Königshausen und Neumann, 1995.

Rahn, Bernhard. *Wolframs Sigunendichtung. Eine Interpretation der Titurelfragmente*. Zürich: Fretz & Wasmuth, 1958.

Raucheisen, Alfred. *Orient und Abendland. Ethisch-moralische Aspekte in Wolframs Epen Parzival und Willehalm*. Frankfurt: Peter Lang, 1997.

Schmid, Elisabeth. *Familiengeschichten und Heilsmythologie. Die Verwandtschaftsstrukturen in den französischen und deutschen Gralromane des 12. und 13. Jahrhunderts*. Tübingen: Max Niemeyer, 1986.

Schröder, Franz R. "Cundrîe." *Festschrift für Ingeborg Schröbler zum 65. Geburtstag*. Ed. Dietrich Schmidtke and Helga Schüppert. Beiträge zur Geschichte der deutschen Sprache und Literatur 95.

Tübingen: Max Niemeyer, 1973, 187–195.

Schröder, Wolfgang Johannes. *Die Soltane-Erzählung in Wolframs Parzival. Studien zur Darstellung und Bedeutung der Lebensstufen Parzivals.* Heidelberg: Carl Winter, 1963.

Schumacher, Marlis. *Die Auffassung der Ehe in den Wolframs von Eschenbach.* Heidelberg: Carl Winter, 1967.

Snelleman, Willem. *Das Haus Anjou und der Orient in Wolframs Parzival.* Nijkerk, Amsterdam: G.F. Callenbach, 1941.

Springer, Otto. "Wolfram's *Parzival.*" *Arthurian Literature in the Middle Ages.* Ed. R.S. Loomis. Oxford: Clarendon Press, 1959, 218–250.

Sterling-Hellenbrand, Alexandra. "Women on the Edge in *Parzival.*" *Quondam et Futurus. A Journal of Arthurian Interpretations* 3 (1993): 56–68.

Stevens, Adrian. "Heteroglossia and Clerical Narrative: On Wolfram's Adaptation of Chrétien." *Chrétien de Troyes and the German Middle Ages. Papers from an International Symposium.* Ed. Martin H. Jones and Roy Wisbey. Cambridge: D.S. Brewer, 1993, 241–257.

Szlavek, Lilo. "Der Widerspenstigen Zähmung in *Parzival.*" *Der Widerspenstigen Zähmung. Studien zur bezwungenen Weiblichkeit in der Literatur vom Mittelalter bis zur Gegenwart.* Ed. Sylvia Wallinger and Monika Jonas. Innsbrucker Beiträge zur Kulturwissenschaft. Germanistische Reihe Band 31. Innsbruck: Druckerei G. Grasl, 1986, 43–67.

Thum, Bernd. "Frühformen des Umgangs mit 'Fremdem' und 'Fremden' in der Literatur des Hochmittelalters. Der *Parzival* Wolframs von Eschenbach als Beispiel." *Das Mittelalter—unsere fremde Vergangenheit. Beiträge der Stuttgarter Tagung vom 17. bis 19. September 1987.* Ed. Joachim Kuolt, Harald Kleinschmidt, and Peter Dinzelbacher. Stuttgart: Helfant, 1990, 315–352.

Traxler, Janina P. "Dying to get to Sarras: Perceval's Sister and the Grail Quest." *The Grail. A Casebook.* Ed. Dhira Mahoney. New York and London: Garland Publishing, 1999, 261–279.

Wand, Christine. *Wolfram von Eschenbach und Hartmann von Aue. Literarische Reaktionen auf Hartmann im Parzival.* Herne: Verlag für Wissenschcaft und Kunst, 1989.

Willson, H. Bernard. "Ordo Amoris in Wolfram's *Parzival.*" *Journal of English and German Philology* 67 (1968): 183–203.

Gottfried von Strassburg

Brown, Margaret and C. Stephen Jaeger "Pageantry and Court Aesthetic

in *Tristan*: The Procession of the Hunters." *Gottfried von Strassburg and the Medieval Tristan Legend. Papers from an Anglo-
American Symposium.* Ed. Adrian Stevens and Roy Wisbey. Cambridge: D.S. Brewer, 1990, 29–44.

Cole, William D. "Purgatory vs. Eden: Béroul's Forest and Gottfried's
Cave." *The Germanic Review* 70, no. 1 (1995): 2–8.

Dayan, Joan C. "The Figure of Isolde in Gottfried's *Tristan*: Towards a
Paradigm of *Minne.*" *Tristania* VI, no. 2 (1981): 23–37.

De Boor, Helmut. "Die Grundauffassung von Gottfrieds *Tristan.*" *Gottfried von Strassburg.* Ed. Alois Wolf. Darmstadt: Wissenschaftliche
Buchgesellschaft, 1973, 25–74.

von Ertzdorff, Xenja. "Liebe, Ehe, Ehebruch und Tod in Gottfrieds *Tris-
tan.*" *Liebe—Ehe—Ehebruch in der Literatur des Mittelalters.* Ed.
Xenja von Ertzdorff und Marianne Wynn. Giessen: Wilhelm
Schmitz, 1984, 88–98.

Gillespie, George. "'Tristan- und Siegfriedliebe' A Comparative Study of
Gottfried's *Tristan* and the *Nibelungenlied.*" *Gottfried von Strass-
burg and the Medieval Tristan Legend. Papers from an Anglo-
North American Symposium.* Ed. Adrian Stevens and Roy Wisbey.
Cambridge: D. S. Brewer, 1990, 155–170.

Gruenter, Rainer. "Das *wunnecliche tal.*" *Tristan-Studien.* Ed. Wolfgang
Adam. Heidelberg: Carl Winter, 1993, 65–141.

Haag, Christine. "Das Ideal der Männlichen Frau in der Literatur des
Mittelalters und seine theoretischen Grundlagen." *Manlîchiu wîp,
wîplîch man. Zur Konstruktion der Kategorien 'Körper' und
'Geschlecht' in der deutschen Literatur des Mittelalters. Beiheft zur
Zeitschrift für deutsche Philologie.* Ed. Ingrid Bennewitz und Hel-
mut Tervooren. Berlin: Erich Schmidt, 1999, 228–248..

Hahn, Ingrid. *Raum und Landschaft in Gottfrieds Tristan. Ein Beitrag
zur Werkdeutung.* Munich: Eidos, 1963.

———. "*Daz lebende paradis.*" *Zeitschrift für deutsches Altertum* 92
(1963): 184–195.

Herzmann, Herbert. "Warum verlassen Tristan und Isolde die Minnehöhle? Zu Gottfrieds *Tristan.*" *Euphorion* 69 (1975): 219–228.

Hollandt, Gisela. *Die Hauptgestalten in Gottfrieds Tristan. Wesen-
szüge—Handlungsfunktion—Motiv der List.* Heft 30. *Philologische
Studien und Quellen.* Ed. Wolfgang Binder, Hugo Moser, Karl
Stackmann. Berlin: Erich Schmidt, 1966.

Jaeger, C. Stephen. *Ennobling Love. In Search of a Lost Sensibility.*
Philadelphia: University of Pennsylvania Press, 1999.

———. "The Barons' Intrigue in Gottfried's *Tristan*: Notes Toward a
Sociology of Fear in Court Society." *Journal of English and*

Germanic Philology LXXXIII (1984): 46–68.

———. *Medieval Humanism in Gottfried von Strassburg's* Tristan und Isolde. Carl Winter: Heidelberg, 1977.

———. "The Crown of Virtues in the Cave of Lovers Allegory of Gottfried's *Tristan*." *Euphorion* 67 (1973): 95–117.

Johnson, Laurie. "Reading the Excursus on Women as a Model of 'Modern' Temporality in Gottfried's *Tristan*." *Neophilologus* 82 (1998): 247–257.

Kaiser, Gert. "Liebe ausserhalb der Gesellschaft. Zu einer Lebensform der höfischen Liebe," *Liebe als Literatur. Aufsätze zur erotischen Dichtung in Deutschland*. Ed. Rüdiger Krohn. Munich: C.H. Beck, 1983, 79–97.

Kerth, Thomas. "Marke's Royal Decline." *Gottfried von Strassburg and the Medieval Tristan Legend. Papers from an Anglo-North American Symposium*. Ed. Adrian Stevens and Roy Wisbey. Cambridge: D. S. Brewer, 1990, 105–116.

Kucaba, Kelly. "Höfisch inszenierte Wahrheiten. Zu Isolds Gottesurteil bei Gottfried von Straßburg." *Fremdes wahrnehmen—fremdes Wahrnehmen. Studien zur Geschichte der Wahrnehmung und zur Begegnung von Kulturen in Mittelalter und früher Neuzeit*. Ed. Wolfgang Harms and C. Stephen Jaeger with Alexandra Stein. Stuttgart, Leipzig: Hirzel, 1997, 73–95.

McCracken, Peggy. *The Romance of Adultery. Queenship and Sexual Transgression in Old French Literature*. Philadelphia: University of Pennsylvania Press, 1998.

McDonald, William C. "Gottfried von Strassburg: *Tristan* and the Arthurian Tradition." *Tristan and Isolde. A Casebook*. Ed. Joan Trasker Grimbert. New York: Garland Publishing, 1995, 147–185.

Nenno, Nancy P. "Between Magic and Medicine. Medieval Images of the Woman Healer." *Women Healers and Physicians. Climbing a Long Hill*. Ed. Lilian R. Furst. Lexington KY: The University Press of Kentucky, 1997, 43–63.

Pafenberg, Stephanie B. "The Spindle and the Sword: Gender, Sex and Heroism in the Nibelungenlied and Kudrun." *The Germanic Review* 70, no. 3 (1995): 106–15.

Picozzi, Rosemary. *A History of Tristan Scholarship*. Berne and Frankfurt: Herbert Lang, 1971.

Poag, James F. "Lying Truth in Gottfried's *Tristan*," *Deutsche Vierteljahresschrift für Literaturwissenschaft und Geistesgeschichte* 61 (1987): 223–237.

Rasmussen, Ann Marie. *Mothers and Daughters in Medieval German Literature*. Syracuse: Syracuse University Press, 1997.

————. "*Ez ist ir g'artet von mir*": Queen Isolde and Princess Isolde in Gottfried von Strassburg's *Tristan und Isolde.*" *Arthurian Women. A Casebook.* Ed. Thelma Fenster. New York: Garland Publishing, 1996, 41–58.

————. "Bist du begert, so bist du wert. Magische und höfische Mitgift für die Töchter." *Mütter-Töchter-Frauen: Weiblichkeitsbilder in der Literatur.* Ed. Helga Kraft and Elke Liebs. Stuttgart, Weimar: Metzler, 1993, 7–35.

Schnell, Rüdiger. "Der Frauenexkurs in Gottfrieds *Tristan* (V. 17858– 18114)" *Zeitschrift für Philologie* 103, no. 1 (1984): 1–26.

Schröder, Werner. "Zu Aussage und Funktion des *huote*-Exkurses im *Tristan* Gottfrieds von Straßburg." *Text und Interpretation IV.* Stuttgart: Franz Steiner, 1993.

Schultz, James A. "Bodies that Don't Matter: Heterosexuality before Heterosexuality in Gottfried's *Tristan.*" Ed. Karma Lochrie, Peggy McCracken, and James Schultz. *Constructing Medieval Sexuality.* Minneapolis: University of Minnesota Press, 1997, 91–110.

Seiffert, Leslie. "Finding, Guarding, and Betraying theTruth: Isolde's Art and Skill, and the Sweet Discretion of her Lying in Gottfried's *Tristan.*" *Gottfried von Strassburg and the Medieval Tristan Legend. Papers from an Anglo-North American Symposium.* Ed. Adrian Stevens and Roy Wisbey. Cambridge: D. S. Brewer, 1990, 181–207.

Snow, Ann. "Heinrich and Mark, two medieval voyeurs." *Euphorion* 66 (1972): 113–127.

Speckenbach, Klaus. *Studien zum Begriff 'edelez herze' im Tristan Gottfrieds von Strassburg.* Munich: Eidos, 1965.

Stevens, Adrian and Roy Wisbey, ed. *Gottfried von Strassburg and the Medieval Tristan Legend. Papers from an Anglo-North American Symposium.* Cambridge: D. S. Brewer, 1990.

Thurlow, P.A. "Some Reflections on *huote* and *ere* in the 'Scheiden und Meiden' Episode of Gottfried's *Tristan.*" *German Life and Letters* XXXV (1981–1982): 329–342.

Wharton, Janet. "'*Daz lebende paradis*' A Consideration of the Love of Tristan and Isot in the Light of the '*huote* Discourse." *Gottfried von Strassburg and the Medieval Tristan Legend. Papers from an Anglo-North American Symposium.* Ed. Adrian Stevens and Roy Wisbey. Cambridge: D. S. Brewer, 1990, 143–154.

Wynn, Marianne. "Gottfried's Heroine." *Gottfried von Strassburg and the Medieval Tristan Legend. Papers from an Anglo-North American Symposium.* Ed. Adrian Stevens and Roy Wisbey. Cambridge: D. S. Brewer, 1990, 127–141.

Zak, Nancy C. *The Portrayal of the Heroine in Chrétien de Troyes's*

'Erec et Enide', Gottfried von Strassburg's 'Tristan', and 'Flamenca.'
Göppingen: Kümmerle, 1983.

General Secondary Literature: Theory

Aitken, Stuart C. and Leo E. Zonn. "*Re*-Presenting the Place Pastiche."
Place, Power, Situation, and Spectacle. A Geography of Film. Ed.
Stuart C. Aitken and Leo E. Zonn. London: Rowman and Little-
field, 1994, 3–26.

Anderson, Kay and Fay Gale, ed. *Inventing Places. Studies in Cultural
Geography*. Melbourne: Longman Cheshire, 1992.

Ardener, Shirley. "Ground Rules and Social Maps for Women: An Introduction." *Women and Space: Ground Rules and Social Maps*. Ed.
Shirley Ardener. Providence, Oxford: Berg Publishers, 1993, 1–31.

Barnes, Trevor J. and James S. Duncan. *Writing Worlds. Discourse, Text
and Metaphor in the Representation of Landscape*. New York:
Routledge, 1992.

Barthes, Roland. "From Work to Text." *Debating Texts. Readings in
20th Century Literary Theory and Method*. Ed. Rick Rylance.
Toronto: University of Toronto Press, 117–123.

Bem, Sandra Lipsitz. *The Lenses of Gender. Transforming the Debate on
Sexual Inequality*. New Haven: Yale UP, 1993.

Bennewitz, Ingrid. "Feministische Literaturwissenachaft und Mediävistik: Versuch zur Positionsbestimmung." *Mitteilungen des Deutschen
Germanistenverbandes* 3 (1992): 33–36.

Bennewitz, Ingrid and Helmut Tervooren, ed. *Manlîchiu wîp, wîplîch
man. Zur Konstruktion der Kategorien 'Körper' und 'Geschlecht' in
der deutschen Literatur des Mittelalters. Beiheft zur Zeitschrift für
deutsche Philologie*. Berlin: Erich Schmidt, 1999.

Birenbaum, Harvey. *Myth and Mind*. Lantham, MD: University Press of
America, 1988.

Bock, Gisela. "Geschichte, Frauengeschichte, Geschlechtergeschichte."
Geschichte und Gesellschaft 14 (1988): 364–391.

Bordo, Susan. "Feminism, Postmodernism, and Gender-Scepticism."
Feminism/Postmodernism. Ed. Linda J. Nicholson. New York:
Routledge, 1990, 133–156.

Butler, Judith. *Gender Trouble. Feminism and the Subversion of Identity*.
New York, London: Routledge, 1990.

Cadden, Joan. *The Meanings of Sex Difference in the Middle Ages:
Medicine, Science, and Culture*. Cambridge: Cambridge UP, 1993.

De Lauretis, Teresa. *Technologies of Gender: Essays on Theory, Film, and Fiction*. Bloomington: Indiana UP, 1987.

Foucault, Michel. "The Means of Correct Training." *The Foucault Reader*. Ed. Paul Rabinow. New York: Pantheon, 1984, 188–206.

———. "Space, Knowledge, and Power." *The Foucault Reader*. Ed. Paul Rabinow. New York: Pantheon, 1984, 239–256.

Fox-Genovese, Elizabeth. *Feminism Without Illusions. A Critique of Individualism*. University of North Carolina Press: Chapel Hill, 1991.

Göttner-Abendroth, Heide. *Die Göttin und ihr Heros. Die matriarchalen Religionen in Mythos, Märchen und Dichtung*. Munich: Frauenoffensive, 1980.

Gregory, Derek. *Geographical Imaginations*. Cambridge MA and Oxford UK: Blackwell, 1994.

Higonnet, Margaret. "New Cartographies, an Introduction." *Reconfigured Spheres. Feminist Explorations of Literary Space*. Ed. Margaret Higonnet and Joan Templeton. Amherst: University of Massachusetts Press, 1994.

Holub, Robert C. *Reception Theory. A Critical Introduction*. London: Methuen, 1984

Hubbard, Ruth. "Constructing Sex Difference." *New Literary History* 19 (1987): 129–135.

Irigaray, Luce. "Sexual Difference." *An Ethics of Sexual Difference*. Trans. Carolyn Burke and Gillian C. Gill. Ithaca: Cornell UP, 1993, 5–19.   *PMLA*

Iser, Wolfgang. "Do I Write for an Audience?" 115.3 (May 2000): 310–315.

———. "The Play of the Text." *Languages of the Unsayable*. Ed. Sanford Budick and Wolfgang Iser. New York: Columbia UP, 1989, 325–340.

———. *The Implied Reader. Patterns of Communication in Prose Fiction from Bunyan to Beckett*. Baltimore: Johns Hopkins UP, 1974.

———. "Die Appellstruktur der Texte." *Rezeptionsästhetik*. Ed. Rainer Warning. Munich: Wilhelm Fink, 1975, 228–252.

———. "Die Wirklichkeit der Fiktion. Elemente eines funktiongeschichtlichen Textmodells der Literatur." *Rezeptionsästhetik*. Ed. Rainer Warning. Munich: Wilhelm Fink, 1975, 277–321.

Jameson, Frederic. "Cognitive Mapping." *Marxism and the Interpretation of Culture*. Ed. Cary Nelson and Lawrence Grossberg. Urbana: University of Illinois, 1988, 347–360.

Kaes, Anton. "New Historicism and the Study of German Literature." *The German Quarterly* 62.2 (1989): 210–219.

Kelly, Joan. "The Doubled Vision of Feminist Theory: A Postscript to the 'Women and Power' Conference." *Feminist Studies* 5 (1979):

216–227.

Kirby, Kathleen Mary. "Indifferent Boundaries: Exploring the Space of the Subject." Ph.D. diss., University of Wisconsin-Milwaukee, 1992.

Kristeva, Julia. "Women's Time." *Feminist Theory: A Critique of Ideology.* Ed. Nannerl O. Keohane, Michelle Z. Rosaldo, and Barbara Gelpi. Chicago: University of Chicago Press, 1982, 31–53.

Kuhn, Annette. "Frauengeschichtsforschung. Zeitgemäße und unzeitgemäße Betrachtungen zum Stand einer neuen Disziplin." *Politik und Zeitgeschichte. Beilage der Wochenzeitung Das Parlament* 34/35 (1990): 3–15.

Laqueur, Thomas. *Making Sex. Body and Gender from the Greeks to Freud.* Cambridge: Harvard UP, 1990.

Lee, David R. and Mary Ellen Mazey. *Her Space, Her Place. A Geography of Women.* Washington: American Association of Geographers, 1983.

Lerner, Gerda. *The Creation of Patriarchy.* New York/Oxford: Oxford UP, 1986.

———. *The Creation of Feminist Consciousness.* New York: Oxford UP, 1993.

Lorber, Judith. *Paradoxes of Gender.* New Haven: Yale UP, 1994.

MacCormack, Carol P. and Marilyn Strathern. *Nature, Culture and Gender.* Cambridge [Eng.]: Cambridge UP, 1980.

MacKinnon, Catherine A. *Toward a Feminist Theory of the State.* Cambridge, London: Harvard UP, 1989.

Miller, Nancy K. "Representing Others: Gender and the Subjects of Autobiography." *differences: A Journal of Feminist Cultural Studies* 6 (1994): 1–27.

Mitchell, W.J.T., ed. *Landscape and Power.* Chicago: University of Chicago Press, 1994.

Moi, Toril. *Sexual/Textual Politics: Feminist Literary Theory.* New York: Methuen, 1985.

Ortner, Sherry B. and Harriet Whitehead, ed. *Sexual Meanings: The Cultural Construction of Gender and Sexuality.* Cambridge: Cambridge UP, 1981.

Pathak, Zakia. "A Pedagogy for Postcolonial Feminists." *Feminists Theorize the Political.* Ed. Judith Butler and Joan W. Scott. New York: Routledge, 1992, 426–445.

Poovey, Mary. "Recent Studies of Gender." *Modern Philology* 88 (1991): 415–420.

Rasmussen, Ann Marie. "Feminismus in der Mediävistik in Nordamerika." *Mitteilungen des Deutschen Germanistenverbandes* 3 (1992): 18–26.

Rose, Gillian. *Feminism and Geography. The Limits of Geographical Knowledge.* Minneapolis: University of Minnesota Press, 1993.

Said, Edward. *The World, the Text, and the Critic.* Cambridge: Harvard UP, 1983.

Schweickart, Patrocinio. "Reading Ourselves: Toward a Feminist Theory of Reading." *Gender and Reading. Essays on Readers, Texts, and Contexts.* Ed. Elizabeth A. Flynn and Patrocinio R. Schweickart. Baltimore: Johns Hopkins UP, 1986, 31–63.

Scott, Joan Wallach. "Gender: A Useful Category of Historical Analysis." *American Historical Review* 91 (1986): 1053–1075.

Showalter, Elaine. "Feminist Criticism in the Wilderness." *Writing and Sexual Difference.* Ed. Elizabeth Abel. Chicago: University of Chicago Press, 1982, 9–36.

———. "Introduction: The Rise of Gender." *Speaking of Gender.* New York: Routledge, 1989, 1–13.

Spain, Daphne. *Gendered Spaces.* Chapel Hill: University of North Carolina Press, 1992.

Weigel, Sigrid. "Geschlechterdifferenz und Literaturwissenschaft." *The Graph of Sex and the German Text: Gendered Culture in Early Modern Germany 1500–1700.* Ed. Lynne Tatlock. Amsterdam: Rodopi, 1994, 7–27.

———. *Topographien der Geschlechter, kulturgeschichtliche Studien zur Literatur.* Hamburg: Rowohlt, 1990.

———. "Die nahe Fremde—das Territorium des 'Weiblichen.' Zum Verhältnis von 'Wilden' und 'Frauen' im Diskurs der Aufklärung." *Die andere Welt. Studien zum Exotismus.* Ed. Thomas Koebner and Gerhart Pickerkodt. Frankfurt: Athenäum, 1987, 171–199.

———. "Der schielende Blick. Thesen zur Geschichte weiblicher Schreibpraxis." *Die verborgene Frau. Sechs Beiträge zu einer feministischen Literaturwissenschaft. Mit Beiträgen von Inge Stephan und Sigrid Weigel.* Argument-Sonderbande AS 96. Berlin: Argument-Verlag, 1983.

Young, Iris Marion. *Throwing Like a Girl and Other Essays in Feminist Philosophy and Social Theory.* Bloomington: Indiana University Press, 1990.

Index

spatialization, xiii, 10, 23, 44, 213

Thomasin von Zerklære, 12–14, 17
Tintagel, 163
Tristan, 165–166, 173

unminne, 74–76

Walter von der Vogelweide, 2, 213
Weigel, Sigrid, 2, 6, 9–10, 103–105,
    159, 208
wild, 70, 104–105
wild man, 68
wilderness, 7, 127, 166. *See also* forest
Wolfram von Eschenbach, 1, 75,
    103–105, 156–158, 181, 209
        Parzival, synopsis of, 101–102

Zazamanc, 116–123

WITHDRAWN